Charles Williams

Charles Williams

Alchemy and Integration

Gavin Ashenden

The Kent State University Press
Kent, Ohio

In loving memory of my father, Michael Ashenden (1921–2005);

Such a kind companion on the journey.

Library of Congress Catalog Card Number 2006037740
ISBN 978-0-87338-781-1
Manufactured in the United States of America

11 10 09 08 07 5 4 3 2 1

LIBRARY OF CONGRESS CATALOGING-IN-PUBLICATION DATA
Ashenden, Gavin, 1954–
Charles Williams : alchemy and integration / Gavin Ashenden.
p. cm.
Includes bibliographical references and index.
ISBN-13: 978-0-87338-781-1 (hardcover : alk. paper) ∞
ISBN-10: 0-87338-781-1 (hardcover : alk. paper) ∞
1. Williams, Charles, 1886–1945—Criticism and interpretation. 2. Fantasy literature, English—History and criticism. 3. Mysticism in literature. 4. Hermetism in literature. 5. Alchemy in literature. 6. Theology in literature. 7. Christianity in literature. I. Title.
PR6045.I5Z54 2007
828'.91209—dc22 2006037740

British Library Cataloging-in-Publication data are available.

Contents

Acknowledgments

I am very grateful to the following who spent time talking to me about Charles Williams: John Heath-Stubbs, Lois Lang Sims, R. A. Gilbert, Dr. Glen Cavaliero, Anne Ridler, and Joan Wallis.

Phyllis McDougall (née Jones) kindly lent me the letters that Charles Williams sent her toward the end of his life, invited me to use them for this project, and was very generous with her time. Stephen Medcalf and Professor Charles Huttar were as generous as they were learned.

Feliks Kwiatkowski took time from his practice at the London Bar to read the proofs.

My wife and family have as ever shown endless support and patience and made so many things possible that would otherwise not have been so.

Introduction

He was a close friend of T. S. Eliot, deeply admired by C. S. Lewis, inspirational for W. H. Auden in his journey to faith, and a literary sparring partner for J. R. R. Tolkien. Yet half a century after his death, Charles Williams's life and work remain an enigma for many. The questions that arose from his immersion in Rosicrucian and hermetic culture and ideology remain provocatively unexplored. For those who only know a little about these areas, they present something of a hindrance to reading his work; though if they are properly understood, they are an essential key to understanding Williams's thought and writing.

When T. S. Eliot described Williams as an "occult writer"[1] in his review of *The Figure of Beatrice,* he was using the word "occult" in its primary and literal sense of "hidden." Commentators with less precision than Eliot have assumed from Williams's familiarity with things occult that he was in some way over-involved with occultism, without making any of the distinctions that need to be made. The popular linguistic use of magic spans a whole variety of meanings that range from the inspirational genius of a sportsman to the fairy tales we read our children at bedtime; from myths like the Lord of the Rings to the capacity for poetic or literary enchantment. At a more technical level there are distinctions to be made among what is more generally known as the esoteric. Magic with benign intentions, known as "theurgic," is not the same as magic without them, "goetic"; and both are different from the way magic was understood in the more general esoteric or hermetic traditions, which while they might incorporate them, do not necessarily do so.

This book sets out to explore both the history that lay behind the myths and metaphysics Williams was to make his own, and the hermetic culture that influenced him. It examines and interprets its expression in his novels, poetry, and the development of his ideas. Finally, it attempts to relate these elements to the unpublished letters to his platonic lover, "Celia," written toward the end of his life.

Given that one of the foremost ideas in Williams's work is the interdependence or co-inherence of both our humanity and the creation, the extent to which he lived it or achieved this in his own life is of some importance. The correspondence is of particular interest, both for its own sake, since it is little known, and for the insight it offers. The letters to his wife, Michal, which he wrote during the Second World War, have received little attention and have only very recently been published as *To Michal From Serge*;[2] the letters to his platonic lover, Phyllis Jones, addressed as "Celia" between 1938 and 1943, were not even known to exist.[3]

Where does the magic, the esoteric influence, come from? For a decade of his early adulthood Williams participated in a form of neo-Rosicrucianism as a member of the Fellowship of the Rosy Cross, constructed by A. E. Waite. There is widespread confusion about its nature, which is to be expected, considering it was a semisecret society. Though he left this association behind, it enriched and informed his imaginative world with a hermetic myth that expressed itself in both a particular vocabulary and an underlying ideology and metaphysic. Neither was culturally fashionable or easily accessible. Those who misunderstand or know next to nothing about the nature of Waite's Rosicrucianism fear that Williams spoke from a position outside the boundaries of Christian orthodoxy. That was not the case. In fact his use of that tradition enabled him, after developing his own distinctive mythical framework and mythically charged language, to speak remedially from within Christian culture. It is not too much to claim that he prophetically confronts its contemporary conventions and prevailing ideology.

Integration and Universalization

The hermetic influence was both cultural and ideological. Central to the Rosicrucian and Q'abalistic traditions Williams learned from Waite was the hermetic approach to what was seen as the interpenetration of spirit and matter. This issue has bedeviled Christian theology since the influence of Persian dualism pervaded first-century Judaism. The Gnostic tradition saw them as being at complete odds with each. Strangely so, to some extent, does the Gospel of St. John. A pervasive dualism, so different from the integrated way they related within the Judaism that Christianity grew out of, has left its mark through Christian theology and history. This was distinguished by a split between the spiritual and the material. The spiritual was taken to be holy, while matter was corrupt. The consequences ranged from a profound suspicion of our sexuality and bodies to a contempt for the world we inhabited and carelessness about its despoliation. Both these blind spots have contributed to the secular preoccupations with sex and ecology, for very good reasons. Preoccupations with sex and anxieties about ecology have captivated the popular imagination to such an extent that the allegiance they have demanded has become virtually religious in character. If such powerful human instincts find no honored place within the prevailing religion, it is not surprising that they should produce something constituting a religion of their own.

The neo-Rosicrucian mysticism that Williams was attracted to offered something of an antidote to this dualism. Words like "magic" or "mysticism," the "esoteric" and "hermetic," have complex associations. Williams developed his own distinctive mythical framework and mythically charged language, but his use of that tradition enabled him to speak remedially from within Christian culture and prophetically confront some of its blind spots and prevailing dualism.

The Limits of Integration

Those who know a little about Charles Williams will already be familiar with his capacity to integrate both the forensically astute intellect and the compassionate heart. He believed that Christians could actually in practice "bear one another's burdens" in acts of love. One of his examples of how this might happen is found in his novel *Descent into Hell.* Two of the characters, Stanhope and Pauline, were to exchange the terrifying experience of fear, one carrying the actual experience instead of the other. He believed that the two traditions of Christian spirituality, the *Via Affirmativa* and the *Via Negativa*, which have created fault lines down Christian history, needed each other to be authentic. In particular his reading of Dante and the Psalms, along with the influence of poets like Wordsworth and Coventry Patmore, led him toward his understanding of what he called "Romantic Theology." The experience of falling in love constitutes a vision of what another person has in them to become within the love and vision of God.

The critical point in his own life came when he fell in love—twice. While remaining outwardly faithful to his wife, Florence, or "Michal," he was overwhelmed by adoration for another woman, Phyllis Jones, or "Celia," when he reached his midforties. He turned to the culture of myth to provide interpretation and safety. The mythologization of this covert relationship provided ways of managing the contradiction without being completely overwhelmed by it. Myth became a safety valve; finding an appropriate image in myth was a way of veiling, interpreting, and thus containing this relationship. The myths of Celia and of Michal, became aspects of the Dantean vision of both Beatrice and the subsequent "woman at the window" that allowed him to at least find a way of understanding what had happened to him, even if he was unable to dismiss it. It was in these myths that he looked for protection, reality, and, finally, integration. Charles Williams was not the first man or poet to have had a midlife crisis, so it is not the crisis that is distinctive—more the way in which he made his way through it. In a secular culture that is increasingly fueled by a preoccupation with sexual gratification, his own adherence to Christian moral structure made his vulnerability to unconsummated vision all the more poignant. The recent discovery of his letters to Celia (Phyllis Jones) set alongside his last letters to his wife Michal (Florence) allows the question as to his own capacity for integration to be put.

Chapter 1 will establish the facts about Williams's relationship with A. E. Waite and the details of his involvement with Waite's Fellowship of the Rosy Cross. It charts Waite's journey from being a writer fascinated by occultism and magic to the less gullible conviction that the esoteric has its proper place as an aid to mysticism within a doctrinally orthodox, if culturally heterodox, Christianity. It explores the historical background of the development of both Rosicrucianism and the Q'abalah. They were the central elements in the Fellowship of the Rosy Cross. Chapter 2 looks at the shape of modern hermeticism. It establishes the history of the relationship between the Order of the Golden Dawn and the Fellowship of the Rosy Cross, which have so often been confused with each other. It examines their different notions of magic, and draws on an original neo-Rosicrucian initiatory rite in order to substantiate my proposition that Waite provided Christian orthodoxy in a heterodox culture. Chapter 3 looks at what it was that Williams took from Waite's work on the Q'abalah, in his book *The Secret Doctrine in Israel* and how he used it in the early stages of his thinking. Chapter 4 covers what Williams developed in his more mature phase, with references to both his history of the Holy Spirit within the church, that is, *Descent of the Dove,* and his commentary on Dante in *The Figure of Beatrice* in light of the history of the *Via Affirmativa* and the *Via Negativa*, the two historic "ways" within Christianity. Chapter 5 examines what Williams gained from Waite's work on alchemy and how he used it in the earlier period of the 1930s. It charts the early development by moving through *Shadows of Ecstasy* to *War in Heaven.* Chapter 6 looks backward through the eyes of his book on the history of witchcraft, where he offers a critique of hermetic culture. Chapter 7 looks at conceptual influences from the Q'abalah that find a voice in his essays. Chapter 8 covers his more mature work in his later novels, *Descent into Hell* and *All Hallows' Eve;* it suggests that the hermetic Doctrine of Correspondence underlies the unitive ideology that they spring from, and documents a continuing development into a rich and most unusual form of Christian orthodoxy. Chapter 9 is a study of vocabulary and imagery in the later Arthurian poetry. Chapter 10 draws on unpublished poetry and original correspondence to chart the development of Williams's romantic vision as it affected his wife and platonic lover. It documents the development of his platonic relationship with Phyllis Jones found in the unpublished "A Century of Poems for Celia" and its development in her private correspondence between 1938 and 1943. In this chapter, I will compare these letters with those to his wife, Michal, between 1940 and 1945, and question how he ultimately reconciled polarities in his private life and personal vision.

CHAPTER ONE

The Encounter between Poet and Magus

A Revised History

Reactions to Charles Williams's rootedness in Rosicrucianism have ranged from the mildly suspicious to outright hostility. The Fellowship of the Rosy Cross was a secret society, and secret societies always provoke anxiety among the religious or academic orthodox, so such reactions are entirely reasonable. Nevertheless one of the main tasks for interpreters of his work is to clarify what this involvement really consisted of and what effect it had on his life and work. R. A. Gilbert, the biographer of the founder of the Fellowship of the Rosy Cross, A. E. Waite, commented that,

> Among students of Charles Williams, it has been fashionable—and indeed it still is—to play down the influence of Waite and the role of the Fellowship of the Rosy Cross in Williams' life. Such an attitude stems partly from a feeling that membership of the "Order of the Golden Dawn"—with which critics invariably confuse the "Fellowship of the Rosy Cross"—somehow brings discredit upon Williams, and partly a belief that Waite's writings are of little worth and ought not to have exercised any significant influence on the literary figure they seek to lionise. In maintaining such an attitude they perpetuate not only their own prejudices, but also errors of fact in the biography of Charles Williams.[1]

Inevitably the term "occult" covers so much ground and is used so imprecisely that its very introduction into an area of study causes as much confusion as elucidation. The study of any "occultism" generates an area of taboo that often disenfranchises any author suspected of it in the eyes of many critics. There is anxiety among people with only the most casual knowledge of the esoteric that Williams might have been some kind of occultist, and his *locus standi* as a Christian artist and writer is thereby reduced. He is, therefore, inevitably subject to a certain amount of suspicion. Commentators have, on the whole, not managed to grasp the issues that underlay Williams's experience of esoteric culture. My purpose is to explore its central significance, and also correct the consistent misleading error that Williams was a member of the Order of the Golden Dawn.

Alice Mary Hadfield, in what remains the fullest biographical work on Williams, lays down the false trail so many have followed since when she asks, "In the end what did Waite's Golden Dawn mean to him? Surely his outlook and philosophy were not generated, or indeed much affected by it? He was thirty-one when he joined and his mind was already well based, developed and directed. His following three works—*Divorce, Windows of Night,* and *Outlines of Romantic Theology*—scatter the shadows of such a suggestion."[2] This confuses a number of different issues. He was never a member of the Order of the Golden Dawn, but of the Fellowship of the Rosy Cross, which was created as an alternative to it; and the question of how much that esoteric culture influenced his mind is both fascinating and important. The answer to this question has wide-ranging implications for assessing Charles Williams's thought. There is a good deal in Williams's theology that addresses a number of important issues from a fresh angle. These include the difficulties that arise from trying to hold the relative values of matter and spirit in tension, as well as the problems of arriving at a more creative view of both marriage and sex. Other implications entail such current issues as our concerns for ecology in the face of the despoiling of our material environment, a crisis that has provoked too little criticism from the orthodox guardians of our "spiritual" traditions. From the earliest centuries of our intellectual tradition, matter—the earth—has been seen essentially as a source of resources for us to take dominion over and exploit to our benefit. This contributed to the unwillingness to acknowledge the critical degree of interdependence.

As Hadfield noted, it is certainly true that the influence of myth and ritual also have their roots in his childhood. Williams's immediate family was steeped in an atmosphere that was appreciative of romance, religion, and myth. His maternal uncle James Charles Wall was an authority on British saints and produced a celebrated work of reference, *Shrines of British Saints.*[3] His introduction to the work describes the age of the saints as "days of mystic loveliness and poetical beauty."[4] Williams was also going to be drawn to myth, legend, and romance. The nephew shared this same interest in mysticism and religiosity as his uncle. Anne Ridler describes (more accurately than Hadfield) exactly how Williams's mind was set in those early days.

> Charles Williams sometimes spoke of a fantasy which he had made with a friend in his boyhood, a world which they entered each day when they travelled to London together from St. Albans, and which remained in being for them during some years. "Hardly fantasy," Mr Robinson wrote when I asked him if he remembered it: "it was too objective for that." . . . [O]f this Gondal country nothing seems to have been recorded in writing, but the habit of fantasy making this habit remained with him.[5]

In fact, this cast of mind would find a home in Waite's order and its neo-Rosicrucianism would give it a more potent articulation and provide a milieu for its development.

To defuse the concern that association with Waite might damage Williams's reputation, one needs to establish clearly what both Waite and, through him, Williams were exploring. But first it is necessary to correct some errors in the chronology of their relationship and in the nature of the organization that Waite founded and Williams joined.

For example, in the second of her two biographies[6] Hadfield writes, "Charles's contacts with A. E. Waite had led to their meeting and thus to an invitation for Charles to join his order of the 'Order of the Golden Dawn.' . . . [O]n the 6th September 1917, Waite wrote to Charles arranging for his reception into the neophyte (lowest) Grade of the Society at the autumnal equinox (17th of September)."[7] Hadfield is correct with the date but wrong about the organization. The false trail is taken up by others. She is followed by Glen Cavaliero when he writes in his chapter "The Life," "In 1917 Williams joined for a while the hermetic order of the 'Order of the Golden Dawn.'"[8]

Surprisingly, Roma A. King Jr., who had been in direct contact with R. A. Gilbert, Waite's biographer, repeats this error by mistakenly attributing to Williams membership in the Order of the Golden Dawn in his book *The Pattern in the Web.*[9] Dennis L. Weeks makes the same mistake in *Steps toward Salvation* in 1991,[10] as does Andrea Freud-Loewenstein in *Loathsome Jews and Engulfing Women.*[11] The only two publications that accurately reflect the historical position of Williams are Huw Mordecai's chapter "Charles Williams and the Occult" in *Charles Williams: A Celebration*[12] and a chapter by Thomas Willard, entitled "Acts of the Companions: A. E. Waite's Fellowship of the Rosy Cross and the Novels of Charles Williams," in *Secret Texts: The Literature of Secret Societies.*[13] Neither traces the full implications that flow from this necessary correction.[14]

There were not only important historical distinctions between the two organizations but considerably different approaches to the central concern of the role and status of Christianity. Because the Order of the Golden Dawn had distinctive goetic (that is, involving magic that is rather more "black" than "white") elements and was involved in serious public scandal, it is essential that the two groups are distinguished from each other.[15] The Order of the Golden Dawn itself had its own schisms over the relationship between mysticism and magic, notably involving W. B. Yeats on the one hand, and Aleister Crowley on the other. But the Fellowship of the Rosy Cross came into being precisely for the reason that A. E. Waite believed a separate organization was needed in order to exclude the pursuit of the magical (black or white) and promote the experience and knowledge of mysticism.

Part of this confusion is paradoxically due to Williams himself. Anne Ridler in her introduction to *"The Image of the City"* writes, "He much admired the writings of A. E. Waite,[16] and Mr Williams tells me that it was through a letter concerning one of Waite's books that Charles made his acquaintance, and was introduced by him to the Order of the Golden Dawn."[17] Ridler is less concerned than Hadfield to distance Williams from Waite and documents the fact that Waite was influential. She does at least point out that Williams must have belonged to a "later unnamed order" that Waite referred to in his autobiography,[18] but she is not clear what it was. The matter is confused by Williams himself, as she rightly points out, writing, "Yet he always spoke of himself as having belonged to the Golden Dawn."[19]

The source of this confusion may be the fact that the Order of the Golden Dawn had attracted literary figures of the stature of W. B. Yeats and Evelyn Underhill. This may partly explain why Williams had a certain amount of anxiety about his social standing in an aesthetic culture that was only too alert to the issue of social class. The Oxford University Press, where he worked, and the literary figures with whom he rubbed shoulders as an aspiring poet were from a different social ethos. Williams seems to have been using the connection with the Order of the Golden Dawn to improve his social standing in literary circles. Hadfield is further mistaken when she writes, "His active membership was no more than four or five years. It may be that after his son was born in 1922 he had difficulty in finding a free evening besides his regular lectures and the time he needed for writing. Or he may simply have had enough."[20] In fact his active membership lasted ten years, until June 29, 1927—as significant as the error of fact is the dismissive tone of Hadfield's commentary. It is clear that in her estimation this episode in Williams's life needs to be played down. In fact, these elements play a central role in the formation of Williams's ideas.

Poet Meets Magus—Williams and Waite from 1915 to 1931

Earlier contacts led to Williams joining Waite's order in 1917. After reading *The Hidden Church of the Holy Graal,*[21] Williams sent Waite a copy of his own volume of poetry, *The Silver Stair* (1912). Although it was undated we know that the book was sent in the summer of 1915, for Waite replied on August 24 and Williams then visited him in south Ealing on September 4, signing his name in Sibyl Waite's autograph book. Waite kept the book of poetry until the occasion of their next meeting on April 22, 1916.[22] The connection between the two men was made easier by the fact that they had friends in common.

Williams had become aware of Waite's poetry by this time, since he was proofreading *The Oxford Book of English Mystical Verse,* which contained six poems by Waite. They were included because the editors, the Reverend A. H. E. Lee and D. H. S. Nicholson,[23] were friends of Waite, admired his work, and had also been members of the Independent and Rectified Rite (though neither of them continued into the Fellowship of the Rosy Cross).[24] Gilbert makes the obvious connection, "It is possible that they told Williams something of the nature of the order and they may, consciously or not, have encouraged him to seek admission into the Fellowship of the Rosy Cross."[25] Williams married Florence Conway on April 12, 1917, at St. Albans Abbey, and afterward moved to 18 Parkhill Road, London, NW3. From there he petitioned for membership in the Fellowship of the Rosy Cross.[26] In mid-1917 Williams asked for a form of profession, and signed it on July 18. He was received into the Portal Grade of the Rosy Cross under the sacramental name of Frater Qui Sitit Veniat.[27] On September 6, 1917, Waite wrote,[28]

> Sept. 6 1917.
> As intimated when I wrote on July 27th, it will be more convenient for the Fellowship to arrange for your reception at the Autumnal Equinox, which will be celebrated on Friday, Sep. 21st, beginning at 5 or 6 P.M. The temple will be opened then in the Neophyte Grade and as at subsequent meetings there is a call for other Grades, it is desirable not to have the first one for some time to come subsequently. If this is possible, you will remember that a visit to Spencer[29] is necessary, and they ought to be seen promptly, as the habit takes a little time.[30]

Williams's initiation took place on Friday, September 21 at 5:50 P.M. in hired rooms at the Imperial Hotel in Russell Square. The autumn equinox celebrations followed. He moved rapidly through the lower grades, and on August 26,

1919, he was Raised on the Cross of Tiphereth, and entered the grade of Adeptus Minor. Gilbert informs us from Waite's records of the fellowship, that from this point his progress was somewhat slower. On July 10, 1924, he attained the grade of 7=4, Adeptus Exemptus.[31] On July 27, 1925, he reached the Portal of the Fourth Order when he was integrated by dispensation on the part of the Headship into the Blessed Company. It appears that after a decade his active involvement with the organization was near an end. His last advancement was on July 29, 1927, when he was a participant in the Ceremony of Consecration on the Threshold of the Sacred Mystery, which was to be the first ritual of Waite's more exalted order, The Hidden Life of the Rosy Cross. It was Williams's last ceremony. He took part in no further rituals, but he remained an inactive member of the order. He kept in regular contact with Waite, who visited him at Amen House in September 1928, and wrote to him periodically until 1931. He retained the costume of the order until the end of his life.[32] He took his vows seriously.

Although attracted to Waite by a common preoccupation with the Holy Grail, Williams became equally interested in Waite's Q'abalistic doctrines as set out in *The Secret Doctrine in Israel.* This book informed his attempts to formulate a theology of marriage and provided a basis for his ideas about the symbolism of the body. Anne Ridler comments, "It was the *Secret Doctrine in Israel* (1913) which interested him most—and he continued to admire it, for he recommended me to read it, when I knew him in the thirties. It is a study of Jewish mystical work, the Zohar. . . . [I]n this book, I believe are the foundations of Williams' thought about the symbolism of the body, and of his lifelong attempt to develop an adequate theology of marriage."[33] The wider scope of Waite's influence will be explored in later chapters. It is found particularly in the material and ideology within his novels, within his play *The Chaste Wanton,* and in his Taliessin cycle, where he was to use Sephirotic imagery on a number of occasions, as well as in private correspondence to Phyllis Jones.[34]

The Nature of the Organization

An understanding of how Waite's fellowship differed from the Order of the Golden Dawn may best be approached through Waite's life—his journey from occultism and magic to hermetic mysticism. For the central distinction that needs to be made is that between mystical orientation and the phenomenon of practical occult inquiry. R. S. Gilbert[35] says, "Waite was after all a mystic and wished to be known as such. That his studies of the occult are remembered when his mystical writings are neglected is a tribute to the folly of an age that exalts the irrational, not a judgement upon their merits."[36] It was for his mysticism that Dean Inge, "a scourge of pseudo-mysticism," complimented him in his review of *Studies in Mysticism* in the *Saturday Review.*[37] Gilbert additionally looks to both Yeats and Masefield to establish Waite's credentials.

The turbulent waters of Victorian esotericism were redirected under Waite's influence.[38] Even the work and influence of Madame Blavatsky as well as the whole evolution of the Order of the Golden Dawn were changed by Waite's involvement. As Gilbert notes, "It is impossible to understand the development of the Hermetic Order of the 'Order of the Golden Dawn' without a detailed knowledge of Waite's role in its history and his relationship with its members."[39] Waite's own experience of faith began with formal Roman Catholicism. After the death of his sister in 1874, when he was seventeen, he moved away from Christianity, and like so many of his time and culture, he was drawn to the American imported spiritualism of late Victorian England. Waite began to immerse himself in occult journals investigating the phenomenon of séances and later he attended them in person. Whether because of the death of his sister or father, Waite found the attraction of spiritualism lay in its ability to revive his faith in the afterlife. As his biographer put it, "Undoubtedly Waite had a deep need to believe in survival and the séances seemed to reassure him."[40] By the late 1880s he was writing for *Light,* one of the leading spiritualist journals, as well as the *Occult Review.* He soon found a patron in Lord Stafford, who commissioned him to translate and produce alchemical texts, the most significant being the *Hermetic and Alchemical Works of Paracelsus.* The world of alchemical publishing proved to be as insecure as the practice and study of alchemy had always been, and before long Waite found himself working in a managerial position for Horlicks. If Horlicks's malted milk was less than the "elixir of life," Waite's job was to promote its commercial success. It was not long before *The Horlicks Magazine and Home Journal for Australia, India and the Colonies* appeared in 1904, becoming a vehicle for articles by Arthur Machen and Evelyn Underhill and promoting the values of the Order of the Golden Dawn. Gilbert's obituary gave a terse summary of the periodical: "It was a brave experiment, but it could not last."[41] It survived for fifteen issues.

If spiritualism functioned to reassure Waite of an afterlife, he swiftly moved from that platform to the better-traveled world of mysticism. In 1890 he delivered a lecture to the London Spiritualist Alliance entitled "The Interior Life from the Standpoint of the Mystics." He upset his audience by insisting on the superiority of the "transcendental," the inner experiences of the mystic, over the "phenomenal," which even included the phenomena of the séance room.

This insistence of the priority of the mystical over the phenomenal was a serious issue in the arena of esoteric London culture. It was to be the reason for the Order of the Golden Dawn's schism, and it brought the Fellowship of the Rosy Cross into being. Waite would travel still further on his orbit away from the formal and disgruntled Roman Catholicism of his youth, later returning to it; but his return would be to a heterogeneous Christianity with a different theology of the church—a secret church, and a different determining spirituality, that of the Q'abalah.

Although in his early years Waite was to embark on an assiduous exploration of the occult, he was a trenchant critic of fraud wherever he found it, and that was often. Drawn naturally to mysticism as he was, Waite's growing intellectual expertise in the field of esoteric spirituality was augmented by an accidental blow to his head that added the dimension of personal experience to intellectual knowledge. It initiated him into an apprehension of religious experience he had previously only known in theory. His deepening expertise in mystical spirituality and an encyclopedic knowledge of Q'abalistic tradition that might have taken him in any number of directions drew him back to a relatively orthodox if heterogeneous variant of Christianity. Even so, Gnosticism dies hard and he retained his devotion to a tradition of hidden knowledge practiced by adepts.

In a culture steeped in gullibility, Waite was a pungent critic. He was attracted by myth but not by charade. His encounters with Eliphas Levi, otherwise Louis Constant (1810–75), left him impressed by Levi's brilliance as an interpreter of occult philosophy, but disillusioned with the occult in general. In the face of considerable popularity, he was tersely dismissive of the whole school of Theosophy, founded in 1875 by Madame Blavatsky and Colonel H. S. Olcott, for the "Study Of Occult Science; The Formation Of A Nucleus Of Universal Brotherhood And The Revival Of Oriental Literature And Philosophy."

Alchemy was a different area altogether. It had a serious intellectual and religious pedigree, and when Waite had an opportunity to explore it he threw himself into it. The encounter came when he had found himself invited to act as editor for Lord Stafford's *Lexicon of Alchemy*. Part of his function was to provide a biographical or critical introduction to each title as it came out. With his considerable memory and talent for historical investigation, Waite became something of an expert on alchemy during this period. From alchemy to Q'abalah was a step from the West toward the East. The next stage of his education involved an encounter with medieval Jewish mysticism. Gilbert offers a succinct summary of these schools of thought:

> The Kabbalah [*sic*] is the system of Jewish mysticism and theosophy that developed in the early centuries of this era (its origins lie in the earlier Merkava [chariot] mysticism), reached its zenith in the late medieval period with the *Sepher Ha Zohar* (Book of Splendour) and fascinated Renaissance figures such as Reuchlin and Pico Della Mirandola, who believed, quite erroneously, that kabbalistic texts contained Trinitarian doctrine and would provide a means of converting Jews to Christianity. From the sixteenth century onwards the strange and complex symbolism of the Kabbalah had been utilised frequently by occultists and by the nineteenth century it had come to be associated largely, but unjustly, with magic.[42]

Like both Pico della Mirandola and Waite, Williams was to take up some of the language, symbolism, and ideology of the Q'abalah in order to find there not some proof text of the Trinity but a kind of metaphysical topography that would provide a map for the religious quest.

Waite was also much impressed by the myths of the Idra Rabba and the Idra Zutta (The Greater and Lesser Assemblies), which he found in two sections of the Zohar. His reading of the Q'abalah led him to discover and to refine his own concept of the "Holy Assembly."[43]

But his route to establishing his own Holy Assembly lay through his dealings with the hermetic Order of the Golden Dawn, and to understand those will require a survey of the early history of the Rosicrucian movement.

The History of Rosicrucianism

Modern scholars use the term "Rosicrucian" in different ways. It is as an attitude or a style of thinking that emerged in the fifteenth century and also, more particularly, the name for a seventeenth-century movement that seems to have included a secret society. Although it is swathed in secrecy, a certain amount of historical fact emerges from the myth and uncertainty.

The Rosicrucians appeared as a new sect of philosophers in the early part of the seventeenth century. Christopher McIntosh writes, "A complex of ideas known as Rosicrucianism may be seen as a loosely knit organism clustered around a central mythology whose chief symbol is the extremely simple yet suggestive image of a rose linked to a cross."[44] This organism first appeared in Germany in what were unquestionably mysterious and suspicious circumstances, and Germany remained its center for the following two centuries.

Unlike other mythologies, the origin of which can normally be traced organically, Rosicrucianism appeared to have been launched and deliberately manufactured. McIntosh offers a synopsis of what can be established historically.

In 1614 a German text with the title of *Fama Fraternitatis, dess Löblichen Ordens des Rosenkreutzes* was published in Kassel, and this work had been circulating in manuscript from as early as 1610. The *Fama* purported to reveal the existence of a fraternity founded by a Christian Rosenkreutz, who lived in the fourteenth and fifteenth centuries. It claimed that he founded the brotherhood after acquiring wisdom during a journey to the East, and that the members of his order traveled around healing the sick and gathering and spreading knowledge, but always working incognito. When Christian Rosenkreutz died, his burial place was kept secret. But recently, says the *Fama,* the burial vault has been discovered by the brotherhood and this discovery heralds the dawn of a new age.[45] Soon after the *Fama* came a second text, the *Confessio Fraternitatis,* which was also published in Kassel, but this one appeared in Latin. It reinterpreted the message of the *Fama* with even greater force, holding out the promise of a reformed world and the overthrow of papal tyranny. Like the *Fama* it boasted of the exalted and powerful knowledge possessed by the secret brotherhood.

In 1616 came the third work, the strangest of the three. It was published in Strasbourg in German under the title of *Die Chymische Hochzeit Christiani Rosenkreutz* (The Chemical Wedding of Christian Rosenkreutz). In this work, the narrator, who is, it is widely assumed, Christian Rosenkreutz himself, describes his experience as a guest at a wedding of a king and queen who inhabit a marvelous castle. At the wedding, the guests face a ritual trial of their worth in which some are killed and brought back to life again during an alchemical operation. Occult imagery predominates. Portals are guarded by lions, magical fountains feature in the work, and ships correspond to the signs of the zodiac.

The symbolism lends itself to any number of different interpretations; the connection with the other two documents is not clear, nor are the motives of the person who wrote it. It is both a romance about a husband and wife who live in a wonderful castle surrounded by marvels and images of lions (on the simple story line), but when it is interpreted symbolically as an experience of the mystical marriage of the soul, it is also more deeply and less explicitly an allegory of alchemical processes. According to this symbolic interpretation, Christian Rosenkreutz undergoes an involved alchemical experience through the visions conveyed to him in the castle, through the theatrical performances that he watches, and through the initiation into the orders of chivalry that he undergoes in the society of the court in the castle.[46]

The lure of Rosicrucianism was due in large part to the way in which it contained a rich panoply of symbolism and myth, and by means of this imagery dealt with an inner world that rational materialism cannot describe or evaluate. Those who are drawn to a more interior aspect of the human quest are attracted by a more obscure, suprarational ambience,[47] which the language of symbols provides. In this way Rosicrucianism bears striking similarities with the whole hermetic and Q'abalistic tradition, and one of its great strengths is its adaptability. Its teachings can be applied in a variety of different ways.

The phenomenon that became Rosicrucianism depended on the reemergence of a more ancient tradition less fractured by dualisms. It had sought to find a unitive way of describing or accounting for reality. The supposed rediscovery of material attributed to Hermes Trismegistus was a critical catalyst in this process. Alchemical transmutation became the "single principle" through which Rosicrucianism aimed to achieve unity with the godhead. Williams drew on this unitive tradition in his thinking that expressed itself in the ideas of co-inherence, substitution, and exchange. These ideas combined together formed a Christianized single principle, reflecting the importance he attributed to expressing in Christian terms the equivalent of the Doctrine of Correspondence, "as above, so below."

The Hermetic Tradition

Human society has always sought a certain physical and metaphysical security, attempting to control both the surrounding social environment and one's personal internal religious quest. The emergence of the hermetic and Q'abalistic traditions represented attempts by many to exercise this control at one particular end of the philosophical spectrum. Cosmology or astrology and early physics on the one hand, religion and magic on the other were fused together. Renaissance culture made no easy distinction between what would become the scientific, and what remained the magical. One example of this is presented in the history of the development of Copernican theory. Of all the people Copernicus might turn to for authoritative support for his new cosmology, he turned to an occultist, citing Hermes Trismegistus, a shadowy Egyptian occultist of dubious historicity. The explanation of why a mathematician would appeal to a magician for support proves surprisingly useful as we unravel the role magic, with its many definitions, played in the search for truth in the areas of influence that Williams was subject to.

Magic had become increasingly captivating in both popular and intellectual circles in the early Middle Ages. But the seventeenth-century mathematicians saw magic as an unwelcome rival. Common culture was addicted to it. Solutions to healing and fertility were often sought among "wise women" who had developed gifts or reputations for being able to solve common problems or ailments. After the publication of *Malleus Maleficarum,* scores of these practitioners of healing, as well as superstition, would be pursued as witches. While the numbers of so-called witches who were actually burned in Europe are often enormously exaggerated, the anxiety that their presence and influence provoked is an indication of the hold they had developed in popular culture.

Among those trying to produce a single scientific unitive theory, it was thought that mathematics was the means by which one could describe the celestial realm, but to understand the earth properly, magic was the proper tool. Consequently a serious interest in the occult of antiquity began to flourish. Ancient magic was regarded by many people as a path to true and useful knowledge of the world about them. Inevitably there were two problems that muddied the waters. The first was that many of the sources that were taken to be ancient, like Hermes Trismegistus, proved to be much more modern than was claimed; and although a natural curiosity embraced any material without careful distinction, there was still a degree of caution embodied by the church and more conventional authority. The occult arts were viewed with suspicion by those who feared their potential for evil, but the possibility that they might hold the key to "scientific" advances ensured that they were certainly not dismissed out of hand.

The battle to establish mathematically based science as the successor to Aristotelian science is one of the great sagas of Western civilization. The whole conception of nature and humanity's relationship to it was at stake. Behind this dramatic exploration lay another layer of struggle. This one was not so much an intellectual one; it was a naked power struggle. A political tussle between the old ecclesiastical order on the one hand, and the new pioneers of exploration on the other. Who was to have the epistemological power to say what was legitimate knowledge of nature and what was not? Who were the keepers of the flame of truth about the natural world?

To understand the rise of physics in the seventeenth century one has to grasp its struggle with the practitioners of magic. The physicists wanted a philosophy of nature that combined with Christianity to combat their common adversary, that is, to combat the socioreligious threat of magic. The coming break between science and religion was not as obvious at that juncture as it subsequently became. Eminent scientists turned to magic as a proper area for research. Both Roger Bacon and Albertus Magnus had been versed in it. But while Aristotelian scientists stayed cloistered in academe, the magi, the down-to-earth practitioners, went out into society, exercising what might be called their own independent "theological" praxis. They were very successful and they became even more influential as they were increasingly employed at Renaissance courts, where magic enjoyed political and popular devotion.

The birth of Renaissance magic can be traced to the Italian priest and physician Marsilio Ficino (1433–99), who worked at the court of the Grand Duke Cosimo Di Medici. Cosimo (known as "the Elder") collected ancient manuscripts. There was an enormous appetite for the wisdom of earlier cultures. It was accessed through lost and newly rediscovered Greek texts. Ficino was paid by the duke to translate the Greek texts his master bought. He was primarily a philosopher, but he was also a priest, doctor, and musician. As a scholar, apart from writing his original works, he translated into Latin the whole corpus of Plato and many of the classical writings in the same tradition. He was reputed to have worked at remarkable speed but at the same time so competently that his translations remained the standard editions until those published in national languages in the nineteenth century. One of the ingredients that made Ficino so attractive and valuable to Cosimo was a shared fascination with Plato.

At some point in the year 1460, one of the duke's scouts came home with a document discovered in Macedonia that came to be called the *Corpus Hermeticum.* Ficino immediately began to translate it. It became a key hermetic text and was referred to constantly as the interest in ancient magic grew. That was to mark the quest of occultists and hermeticists of the next four centuries. One scholar explains, "Thus a philosophy which was a kind of religious cult of nature, implying magical practices, was spread within the core of the fashionable Neoplatonism."[48] The authority of the text rested on the widespread belief that it was written by an ancient Egyptian magician, Hermes Trismegistus. Critically, this document created a supposed link between the birth of Western intellectual culture not only with Plato and Aristotle but with an even earlier civilization. In time, philological study was to wreck that link and place them considerably later, somewhere in the latter years of the Roman Empire, the second or third centuries A.D. The Pythagorean and Platonic overtones the manuscripts contained were supposed to be the product of some prescient Egyptian sage who prefigured Plato, but in fact this earlier writer simply reflected the Neoplatonic atmosphere of late antique Rome. Even St. Augustine of Hippo acknowledged Hermes as an Egyptian sage, and by the time Ficino translated the document, the myth that it contained was 1000 years old, and it was taken universally to be factually true.

Echoing Neoplatonic thought, the hermetic text espoused an organic philosophy of nature. The world was seen as a living organism with a material body and an immaterial "world-soul." Beyond the material realm was a divine intellect, the source of "ideas" (or forms) that became manifest in nature. The world-soul was the intermediary between this divine intellect and the material realm. The basic principle of hermetic magic was that the magus could manipulate the power of the world-soul by drawing down influential energy from the stars, thereby affecting events on earth and the affairs of humankind. Whereas astrologers only interpreted the stars, the magi attempted to manipulate their energy, and so break the determinism inherent in astrology. Behind this "astral magic" lay the belief that this power worked in both directions. The stars could influence the affairs of humans, and humans could influence the stars. The task of the magus was to learn how to bend the astral powers to one's command.[49]

At the same time as Ficino rediscovered the hermetic tradition, Pico della Mirandola[50] was making the Jewish mystical tradition of Q'abalah available. Ficino (who published a book for academics whose occupation brought them under the influence of Saturn and were, therefore, more likely prone to be melancholy) was convinced that he was harnessing natural, not occult, forces. This became a more easily justifiable exercise if he only applied the use of magic to health. Others were not so chary. But the distinction between occult and natural forces was of more than theoretical interest in medieval Europe.[51] Pico was convinced that Q'abalistic magic was more powerful than purely astral magic, for not only did it allow its practitioners to draw down power from the stars but it also enabled them to progress one step nearer the ultimate godhead, and thus engage the supernatural influence of the divine intellect. One scholar writes, "Where the fusion of Aristotelianism with Christianity had defined late medieval culture the Renaissance magi sought to define post-medieval culture by a fusion of Christianity and hermeticism."[52] Pico della Mirandola believed that with the discovery of both the hermetic tradition and the Q'abalah, which he brought together, a new era for man had arrived and that the powers ascribed to man by Hermes Trismegistus were reviving. In 1487, he published his oration "On the Dignity of Man." He begins with a quotation from Hermes on man, "the great miracle," and pursues the potential of this new power for new man. Yates comments, "With this oration, the Renaissance idea of man as magus is born."[53]

The Q'abalah captivated the esoteric imagination in the Renaissance, and is actually becoming popular again today.[54] But what exactly is it? It consists of a complex collection of mystical teachings the origins of which are obscure, though it seemed to emerge suddenly in the thirteenth century. Its aim is to offer access to heights of insight and illumination, using the Hebrew language and letters for contemplation and as a means of practicing what might be called "religious magic" or "practical Q'abalah." It was founded on a complex numerology and system of correspondences based on a diagram of the Tree of Life. At the turn of the twentieth century it began to exercise a wider fascination. Yeats, in *The Stirring of the Bones,* described the symbolic presentation of the Tree of Life as "a geometrical figure made up of ten circles or spheres called Sephiroth joined by straight lines. Once men must have thought of it as like some great tree covered with its fruit and its foliage, but at some period, in the thirteenth century, perhaps, touched by the mathematical genius of Arabia in all likelihood, it had lost its natural form."[55]

The Q'abalah developed in three main phases. The first phase begins with the earliest recognized Q'abalistic literature between 538 B.C. and 70 A.D. Originally this expression of Jewish spirituality was known as Merkabah mysticism, after the throne of the chariot of God, or Merkabah, a vision in Ezekiel 1:26–28. Merkabah mystics believed that by what some describe as shamanistic and others as a magical ecstatic ascent or descent, they could reach the "Throne of the Chariot of God." To assure a safe passage through the seven halls, the initiate would memorize magical names and seals pertinent to each hall. Merkabah mysticism flourished until the end of the first millennium. The surviving fragments of Merkabah mysticism were written down and edited sometime between the fifth and sixth centuries A.D. They became the scaffolding upon which practical Q'abalism developed. The magic of Merkabah mysticism became the magic of practical Q'abalism.[56] These fragments became the *Sepher Yetzirah* (Book of Formation) originating between the third and sixth centuries A.D. Practical Q'abalism was brought to Germany by way of Italy in 917 A.D. by the Kalonymus family. In Spain speculative Q'abalism flourished. The *Sepher Zohar* (Book of Splendor) appeared in the thirteenth century (1280–90) and was effective in uniting both practical and speculative strands. (The latter purports to be written by a rabbi in the second century, but was almost certainly written down by Rabbi Moses de Leon just before it was put into circulation in the thirteenth century.)

The second phase of Q'abalism is now known as the Lurianic Q'abalah, after Isaac Luria of Safed in Galilee (1534–72). He and his followers developed the Zoharic Q'abalah and introduced a number of new concepts into the structure of thought. The Q'abalah was now understood to fulfill a number of complementary purposes. It was essentially a system of cosmology and theology, attempting to explain the nature of God, the origin of the world, and the character of human destiny. It also provided a means of interpreting the scriptures by the application of certain rules that yield an "inner" meaning to the language of the Bible. Finally, it embodied certain mystical techniques whereby the individual learns to commune with "higher realities." The Q'abalah conceived of the created order emanating outward from God in a series of ten basic forces or principles called the Sephiroth, which are arranged in a pattern—the Tree of Life. These ten principles are held to run right through creation from the universe down to man—another form of the conception of macrocosm and microcosm. Part of the Q'abalistic scheme of things is the notion of four worlds descending from the godhead: Atziluth, the world of Emanation; Briah, the World of Creation; Jetzirah, the World of Formation; and Assiah, the World of Action, that is, the world of matter in which we live.[57] According to this interpretation, the Hebrew language is believed to be of divine origin, and each of the twenty-two letters is held to represent one of the elemental forces in creation.

Charles Poncé, the author of a history of the *Kabbalah,* offers a definition of the two historical divisions in Q'abalistic history, the speculative and the practical:

> The speculative branch concerns itself solely with the operations of the spiritual dimension of the universe, in an attempt to discover how it meshes with this world. Speculative Kabbalism aims also at revealing how man may find a place in both dimensions at one and the same time.[58] The practical Kabbalah is primarily concerned with winning energies of the spiritual world for the purposes of magical control. . . . Practical Kabbalism greatly influenced the magic of Western Europe during the mediaeval period.[59]

This dual approach of the speculative and practical was duplicated as part of the diverging interests of those involved in the Order of the Golden Dawn. It illustrated the difference between those pursuing magic on the one hand, and those who practiced mysticism on the other.

The esotericists of the Renaissance encountered the Q'abalah and added it to their repertoire of skills. They later adapted it to Christianity, so that out of the Jewish Q'abalah developed the Christian Q'abalah, the third phase. By the early sixteenth century a variety of different elements had been successfully amalgamated to form its own distinctive culture with its own religious language. This Christianized Q'abalah stimulated a fresh exploration of religion or spirituality. In the hands of German medieval writers, the Q'abalah flourished particularly well. When the hermetic, Q'abalistic, and Neoplatonic tradition reached Germany, the climate of thought was ready for it. Two of the more influential thinkers were Johann Reuchlin and Cornelius Agrippa.

Johann Reuchlin (1455–1522) was one of the foremost German Hebraists and Q'abalists. He had studied the Q'abalah under Pico della Mirandola and two Jewish teachers, Obadiah Sforno and Jacob Loans. He also drew heavily upon the work of Joseph Ben Abraham Gikatila, a Spanish Q'abalist who wrote at the end of the thirteenth century and taught that the divine power emanates in a series of permutations of the holy name JHWH.[60] In 1517 Reuchlin wrote his most famous and controversial book *De Arte Cabalistica.* It provoked a degree of anti-Semitic antagonism, but at the same time attracted support from adherents of the humanistic tradition. His synthesizing of the Jewish mystical tradition with Christianity, in particular the notion of the integration of spirit and matter, was taken further by Heinrich Cornelius Agrippa von Nettesheim (1486?–1535), one of the most influential figures in the whole history of occultism.

Cornelius Agrippa had been a soldier in the service of the Holy Roman Empire, and he led a peripatetic life in which he pursued wide-ranging scholarship coming into contact with leading minds in Europe. In Dole he lectured on Reuchlin, and he had a number of important European connections. He was, for instance, principal physician to Queen Louisa of Savoy. When in London, he stayed with the philosopher Dean Colet. Due to his outspokenness he was imprisoned by François I in Lyon and he died in poverty after his release. But his influence was enormous. He had been the main exponent of Ficino's Neoplatonic school of thought. This and other diverse elements went into his main work, *De Occulta Philosophia,* which was published in Cologne in 1531. It was divided into three sections. Each section examines the three realms: elemental, intellectual, and celestial. The first contains a survey of natural magic; the second, number symbolism; and the third, a treatise on the Divine Name (following Reuchlin).

He achieved both fame and notoriety by his defense of fame and magic. Once again the debate involves competing and differing definitions of what constitutes "magic." He defined it as "the wisdom of the magi." In *De Occulta Philosophia,* he wrote,

> That a Magician doth not amongst learned men signifie a sorcerer, or one that is superstitious or divelish, but a wise man, a priest or prophet; and that the Sybils were Magicianesses, and therefore prophesied most cleery [*sic*] of Christ; and that Magicians, as wise men, by the most wonderful secrets of the world, knew Christ as author of the world to be born, and came first to all to worship him; and that the name of

> Magicke was received by Philosophers commended by Divines, and not unacceptable to the Gospel.[61]

Williams, in the introduction to his history of Witchcraft, followed Cornelius Agrippa, where he wrote: "The practitioners of the high art in the Gospel narrative . . . saw a route traced in heaven. . . . [T]hey go and contemplate the adorable God; they offer sacrifice and symbolic gifts. . . . [T]he Magians were the first conquest of the Child-God."[62] Cornelius Agrippa gives a distinctive meaning in the face of a generalized and more diffuse understanding of idea of the magus. The tradition of the intellectual and artist as magus was more widespread than might have been imagined. This esoteric tradition claimed magic as an essential element in the Christian wisdom tradition.

The Influence and Later Development of Rosicrucianism

In her book *The Rosicrucian Enlightenment*[63] Frances A. Yates traces the evolution of this wisdom tradition in England. In particular, she urges historians to employ and embrace the word "Rosicrucian" despite its occultist associations. It describes, in her judgment, a certain style of thinking that is historically recognizable, whether or not a particular thinker to whom it may be applied actually belonged to a secret society. She argues, "The Rosicrucian was one fully in the stream of the Renaissance Hermetic-Cabalistic tradition, but distinguished from the earlier phases of the movement by his addition of alchemy to his interests."[64] Yates charts the influence of Rosicrucian thought through some of the major English figures of the seventeenth and eighteenth centuries. She gives evidence of traces of Rosicrucian thought in both Francis Bacon and Isaac Newton. In terms of conventional historical analysis, figures like the notorious John Dee, alchemist and adviser to Elizabeth I, are more marginal, but nonetheless he was highly regarded in intellectual and, of course, court circles at the time. Yates suggests that Dee, in particular, embodied the principles by which Rosicrucianism fertilized European thought and that under the superficial history of the Thirty Years' War one may discover a whole culture or civilization that is lost to view. She writes, "In one way of looking at it, it is the Elizabethan age, in its Rosicrucian and Dee–inspired aspects, continued abroad."[65]

Rosicrucian and hermetic culture are celebrated in Shakespeare, for example, in his last play, *The Tempest.* There he is widely seen as representing himself in Prospero, as archmagus, a figure standing in the central stream of Renaissance preoccupation with magic and secret knowledge.[66]

Poets were particularly attracted to hermetic imagery, especially, the metaphysical poets. Yates suggests that the writings of later mainstream poets like Donne and Herbert (both Anglican priests) demonstrate the extent of this movement.

> John Donne's metaphysical poetry . . . [e]xpress[ed] in a different medium a philosophical and religious outlook parallel to the imagery of Michael Maier. . . . [D]onne's Marriage Song, written for the wedding of "Lady Elizabeth and Count Paletine," uses imagery about the joining of two phoenixes, about a marriage of sun and moon, which is already in the alchemical vein which was to be so characteristic of their cult in Rosicrucian circles abroad.[67]

George Herbert drew upon the alchemical tradition in the last stanza of one of his most famous poems:

> This is the famous stone
> That turneth all to gold;
> For that which God doth touch and own
> Cannot for less be told.

Prominent though it became in English intellectual and artistic culture through Shakespeare and Donne, the future of Rosicrucianism lay in France, as it was connected with the spread of Freemasonry through a wide number of organizations and groups.

The earliest links between the two movements are opaque, but one of the earliest passages is discovered in Henry Adamson's *Muses Threnodie* (1638), in which the following lines are found,

> For what we do pressage is not grosse,
> For we be brethren of the Rosie Cross:
> We have the Mason's word and second sight,
> Things for to come we can foretell aright.[68]

In England, however, the basic ideas of Rosicrucianism expressed themselves in two different streams that often converge. The first is the utopian stream (represented by figures such as Comenius) that was driven by ideals that were social, scientific, and philosophical. The second is the hermetic-Q'abalistic-alchemical stream that was more rooted in occult aspects. Thomas Vaughan (1622–66) represents the latter, and in a later chapter we will see how he forms a link between Waite, who became one of the most important authorities on European Freemasonry, and Charles Williams.

CHAPTER TWO

Modern Hermeticism

The Creation of the Order of the Golden Dawn

Within the eclectic width of the wisdom tradition broadly referred to as magic, three currents of antiquity had been brought together—hermeticism, Gnosticism, and the practice of magic in its strictest definition, theurgy[1]—and they contributed to the development of four core beliefs:

1. The material universe reflects divine intent;
2. Divinity is defined as including a pantheon of gods and goddesses;
3. Direct access to the gods is possible by way of correct procedures and ceremonials that include the active, magical use of god-images; and
4. Secret initiation is the means of transmitting the ways by which the initiate can personally attain to the divine knowledge (or gnosis).

Practical Q'abalism employed these four concepts. An eclectic Gnosticism smuggled elements of pagan and polytheistic influence into this basic structure. Once these were removed, both Western and Jewish traditions of magic found themselves developing a new synthesis, which found expression in the late nineteenth century, and particularly in the Order of the Golden Dawn, one of the most influential of numerous cults that sprang up at the end of the nineteenth century. It influenced writers of the stature of Underhill, Machen, and Yeats, as well as Charles Williams himself (through A. E. Waite's mediation).

The origins of the Order of the Golden Dawn lie in the history of Freemasonry, which in France had become interwoven with Rosicrucianism. In 1867 R. J. Little and W. J. Hughen, two English Freemasons, were advanced through a series of grades in the Rosicrucian Society in Scotia (R.S.I.S.), so that they would be qualified to form a similar society in England, which they did on June 1, 1867. It was named the Societas Rosicruciana in Anglia (S.R.I.A.) at Aldermanbury, in the City of London. The fact that the historical links with any original historically based movement were tenuous at best did not undermine the assumed authenticity of the new Rosicrucians. R. A. Gilbert comments that

> The event was looked upon as a reconstitution rather than an inauguration, for the members maintained that they had been reviving a dormant society that had been active in the 1850s. That society in turn was thought to have preserved the ethos, if not the historical continuity, of the original Rosicrucian brotherhood of the early seventeenth century. That such a brotherhood may never have existed did not trouble the members of the S.R.I.A.: what mattered was that they should preserve its principles.[2]

During the seventeenth and eighteenth centuries, self-styled Rosicrucian bodies arose, briefly flowered, and invariably faded away again, leaving nothing behind but some greater or lesser additions to the store of esoteric wisdom accumulated among them. The S.R.I.A. was different for several reasons. It flourished in a country where neither state nor church persecuted it. It displayed great stamina (Gilbert claims that it is still alive today)[3] and it confined its membership to Freemasons who were also professed Christians.

By 1888 it was well established as a thoroughly respectable body the members of which were engaged in nothing more nefarious than the intellectual pursuit of the so-called occult sciences. But in 1880 the society was joined by a member who had the most unusual talent of imagination and invention when it came to occultist matters, a Dr. William Wynn Westcott. He was an active Freemason, Q'abalist, Theosophist, and a supporter from its inception of Anna Kingsford and Edward Maitland's hermetic society, which emphasized the Western as opposed to the Eastern tradition of occultism. He was also deeply committed to the supposed historical reality of the Rosicrucian myth.

He developed the notion of creating a secret society of men and women "for the purpose of the study of Occult Science, and the further investigation of the Mysteries of Life and Death, and our Environment." Partly influenced by the friendship of Anna Kingsford, he wanted to make the process open to women as well. Westcott claimed historical precedent for his extension of membership to include women by not requiring Masonic membership. He professed,

> On the continent many groups of Rosicrucian initiates and adepts had admitted men who were not freemasons and even learned women, to their grades and assemblies. This may have been a departure from the

> original rules of the society, as first designed by C. R. our Founder, it is a point left undecided by the early Rosicrucian published literature, but there are extant documents to show that women were admitted in the seventeenth and eighteenth centuries.[4]

This appeal to tradition apparently did not provide as robust a precedent as Westcott felt was needed, so he looked for a more contemporary, esoteric, and authoritative source. He found one, he thought, in Fräulein Anna Sprengel, or Soror Sapiens Dominabitur Astris.[5]

Westcott claimed in 1887 that he had obtained, from sources he would (unsurprisingly) not disclose, enciphered manuscripts that contained the initiatory rituals of an occult order. The manuscripts also provided the name of a German adept, Fräulein Sprengel, and her address, supposedly inviting the reader to correspond with her. Westcott claimed he immediately wrote to her, and her reply furnished him with the necessary authority and skill. He himself was appointed to the grade of Adeptus Exemptus, and thus he was authorized to found an English Order of the Golden Dawn. He was required to find and appoint two learned persons in order to make up the first three Masters, and these he found among his associates in the S.R.I.A. As secretary-general of the S.R.I.A. he choose Dr. R. W. Woodman (1828–91), a competent Q'abalist, and S. L. M. Mathers, who had already expanded the rituals for Westcott and converted them into workable forms.[6]

Once the order had been founded the fictitious Anna Sprengel became something of a liability to Westcott. The problem was solved when he conveniently received a letter announcing her death; but not before he had also supposedly received a number of occult manuscripts and letters.[7] Neither R. A. Gilbert nor Ellic Howe doubts that the manuscripts were all forged by Westcott.

The hermetic Order of the Golden Dawn was thus created to further the systematic study of the occult sciences. It was immediately welcomed by the occult establishment of its day. (Madame Blavatsky had initial reservations until she was assured that membership of the order would not offer competition for her own Theosophical society.)[8] It offered its members a sequence of initiatory rituals of a highly eclectic nature that combined Egyptian, Q'abalistic, and Rosicrucian symbolism, together with prescribed courses of study appropriate to each step in the five grades of the Outer Order, the grades comprising Neophyte, Zelator, Theoreticus, Practicus, and Philosophus. Each grade above that of Neophyte was related to one of the ten Sephiroth of the Q'abalistic Tree of Life, and these continued beyond the Outer Order into a yet more secret Second Order, the rituals of which were overtly magical.

The Order of the Golden Dawn contained a Second Order, Rosae Rubeae et Aureae Crucis. It had been set up from the beginning but had no rituals that it used. Members who wished to advance to the Second Order did so by passing examinations. In 1892 this changed, for Mathers, who had succeeded as Imperator upon Woodman's death the previous year, had developed his own highly impressive series of rituals. These were based upon the myth of Christian Rosenkreutz, for the 5=6 (each grade was numbered) grade of Adeptus Minor. Whereas the Outer Order represented theoretical occultism, the Second Order came to function for the working of specifically magical rituals.

By the time this Second Order had been developed, the Order of the Golden Dawn had some 150 members in three Temples. They were based in London, Weston-Super-Mare, and Bradford. By 1900 they claimed 300 members. Women comprised a third of the total, but as much as half of the Second Order. But Mathers had an autocratic manner unpalatable even in those circles, and it produced dissension. Rebellion broke out in 1900. The order fell into the first of its many crises when in February 1900 Florence Farr wrote to Mathers, who was living in Paris, to tell him of problems the order faced. But Mathers misread and misconstrued her letter. He assumed that she was thinking of starting a schismatic group with Westcott, so he decided to expose Westcott. Mathers's reply was illuminating and disturbing; overreacting, he attacked Westcott, making the astonishing claim that Westcott "had never been at any time in personal or written communication with the Chiefs of the Order, he having either forged or procured to be forged the previous correspondence between him and them."[9] A group of the most prominent members of the order was set up to examine these claims but failed to make any headway since Mathers refused to substantiate his claims any further and Westcott refused to deny them.[10] But clearly if they were true, then the whole order was based on a hoax. Mathers became so incensed that they had presumed to take matters into their own hands that he sent the young and soon to be notorious Aleister Crowley to enforce his demands that they hand over the Second Order vault to his charge. (Crowley made himself available because the London Chiefs had refused to allow him through to the Second Order after he had passed through the outer grades.) Farce ensued. Crowley arrived at the Blythe Road headquarters in Hammersmith, seriously overdressed in kilt, dirk, and mask. He and his accompanying bodyguard were thrown out. Mathers was suspended from his own order, and the consequence was that the Rosae Rubeae et Aureae Crucis declared its independence.

The Second Order framed a new constitution on April 21, 1900, two months after Florence Farr had sent her letter to Mathers. One of the problems the

Second Order found itself facing was the plethora of secret groups throwing themselves into a variety of different experiments with magic; in the language of the culture, "dedicated to private and unofficial working of ceremonial." One of these was Florence Farr's "Sphere" group. Annie Horniman (a respected Orientalist and an authority on Theravada Buddhism) and Yeats had deep reservations about using magic in this idiosyncratic and independent way. Above all, the influence of Yeats was critical for the development, survival, and direction of the order.

W. B. Yeats and the Interrelation of Mysticism and Magic

As one commentator describes it, "Yeats sought for some moment of intensity when the ecstasy of the lover and of the saint are alike, and desire becomes wisdom without ceasing to be desire."[11] Initially, Yeats had joined Madame Blavatsky's Theosophical society, but he was expelled from it by Blavatsky in 1890 for reasons that are obscure. Peter Washington comments on Yeats's involvement in these secret orders by writing,

> Transferring his loyalty to the Golden Dawn, . . . [Y]eats found himself better suited. He had come to understand the difference between rational scientific organisations as the Society for Psychical Research, and secret magical orders in which members constitute an exclusive mystical whole, and believed that the Theosophical Society had disastrously confused the issue by trying to be both at once.[12]

One can easily notice some clear and striking parallels between Charles Williams and William Butler Yeats. Although Yeats was twenty years older,[13] they shared a similar artistic and intellectual culture. They were both poets and they had in common a heightened awareness of the appreciation of both myth and enchantment as elements of the poet's visionary trade. They were both well aware of the overlap between magic and artistic enchantment. Yeats, too, was sensitive to the distinction between magic as an instrument of artistic creativity and its employment as a means of effecting change on one's audience, as opposed to magic as a means of pursuing occult phenomena.

They were both affected by the distinctive atmosphere that the end of the century brought, particularly among the members of the artistic community. Richard Ellmann quotes Charles Morice's observations about the phenomenon of *fin-de-siècle:* "Every true poet is instinctively an initiate, the reading of grimoires awakens secrets in him which he had always virtually known."[14] For

Yeats, poetry was magic. To be a poet was to be a magician, though not in the mold of practical, manipulative, "goetic" magic as practiced by Mathers and Crowley. His own understanding of the distinction required is well illustrated in the essay he wrote so that he might explain his position to other members of the order. In "Magic," published in *Ideas of Good and Evil* (1903), he presents magic as the credo of the romantic artist: "I believe in the practice and philosophy that we have agreed to call magic, in what I must call the evocation of spirits, though I do not know what they are, in the power of creating magical illusions, in the visions of truth in the depths of the mind when the eyes are closed."[15] Later in that same essay he explains that, for him, enchantment is simply an extension of his poetic artistry. All imaginative men cast illusions:

> Have not poetry and music arisen out of the sounds the enchanters made to help their imagination, to enchant, to charm, to bind with a spell themselves and the passers by? . . . [A]nd just as the musician or the poet enchants and charms and binds with a spell his own mind when he would enchant the mind of others, so did the enchanter create or reveal for himself as well as for others the supernatural artist or genius.[16]

Ellmann thought that Yeats's motivation in exploring occult research may have lain partly in a reaction against the skepticism of his father; but it also would have found some impetus through a wider social current that touched Yeats as well as many others. Because there was such an established movement, all over America and Europe young men like Yeats, Ellmann observed, "(and usually without his caution), were dropping into the treacherous currents of semi-mystical thought."[17] Yeats was greatly impressed, as Williams was to be later, by the central myth of the Order of the Golden Dawn, the mystical death and resurrection of the adept.[18] In the earlier grades each candidate was introduced to this concept by means of the Rosicrucian tradition. (Christian Rosenkreutz, the supposed founder in the fourteenth century, was said to have attained such a level of spiritual perfection that after his death his body remained undecayed.) In the later grades, the central figure of the myth became not Rosenkreutz, but Christ.[19]

This notion of resurrection linked with the alchemical transmutation of base metal into gold. This transmutation carried a corresponding internalized or spiritual counterpart for the evolution of the soul, the change of the dross of human matter into the pure spirit of the perfected humanity. Williams was later very concerned with transmutation, and this basic notion appears frequently throughout his work, though it has different emphases as he evolved its meaning through the phases of his thought and work. Yeats bound himself by oath to work toward this transmutation. It seems perfectly consistent that he thus progressed from personal transmutation toward thinking about a more general transmutation of society. Many of the more mature and discriminating members of the order, who were less preoccupied with what one could consider an adolescent fixation upon working magic that carried goetic attractions, felt that they had a social and religious duty to become instruments for the regeneration of the world. Across European society there was a widespread preoccupation with political revolution during this period. It had expressed itself earlier in France and would again in a cataclysmic way in Russia.[20] The spirituality of the order under discussion paralleled this political phenomenon with a spiritual variant that had both personal and universal dimensions for all concerned.

Yeats certainly had an interest in what was called the raising of spirits, but he also had a deeper concern with the need to implement the hermetic principle "as above, so below" as a template of a wider transformation:

> And surely at whatever risk, we must cry out that imagination is always seeking to remake the world according to the impulses and patterns in that Great Mind, and that great Memory.[21] Can there be anything so important as to cry out that what we call romance, poetry, intellectual beauty, is the only signal that the supreme Enchanter, or some one in His councils, is speaking of what has been, and shall be again, in the consummation of time?[22]

Between 1911 and 1913 Yeats found that the challenge of transmutation was not being met in his own personal circumstances. In particular, the tensions that lay between him and his platonic lover, Maud Gonne, caused him severe difficulties and provided the impetus for a deeper understanding of the possibilities of transformation. Maud Gonne was a militant Irish Nationalist with whom Yeats had fallen deeply in love. The love was returned, but only platonically. While she was willing to give herself entirely in the interests of Irish nationalism, she insisted on a relationship with Yeats that was free of sex. Unsurprisingly she appears frequently in some of Yeats's more tortured poetry (in particular "Leda and the Swan"). They both considered themselves to be mystics, and belonged to the Order of the Golden Dawn. Maud wanted a pure "spiritual" relationship without any physical counterpart, and so they developed the concept of spiritual marriage. It involved communication through dream correspondence and astral vision (controlled release of spiritual tension). Yeats aspired to this physical detachment, but failed to manage it successfully.

For a series of complex reasons, during this period he moved away from the inspiration derived from natural Irish myths, and the would-be alchemy of the Order of the Golden Dawn, toward a preoccupation with spiritualism. As Ellmann pithily puts it, "The Celtic gods were relegated in favour of the international dead."[23]

Yeats's own tumultuous inner struggles took him on a journey that drew him beyond the Order of the Golden Dawn. It was mainly by the means of poetic vision and verse that Yeats hoped to weave transmutation. Another critic of the experiments with magic in the Order of the Golden Dawn was A. E. Waite. Signs of his dissatisfaction with the order began to emerge. When Waite met Mathers in 1883, he was unimpressed. Mathers adopted a tone of elevated superciliousness and said, "I am a Rosicrucian and a Freemason; therefore I can speak of some things, but of others I cannot speak."[24] Waite thought it unlikely that any "real" Rosicrucians would talk in such terms and parade it as Mathers had. Waite attended a number of meetings of the hermetic society and although in 1884 Westcott wrote to welcome Waite and outline the activities of the society (according to papers found in Waite's collection),[25] their relationship soon soured. Waite infuriated Westcott when he published his book *The Real History of the Rosicrucians,* and in a chapter called "Modern Rosicrucian Societies" he published the rules and ordinances of the S.R.I.A., much against Westcott's will.

When Waite later applied for membership in the Order of the Golden Dawn he was impressed by neither the oath of secrecy nor what he found there. The oath warned what the initiate would bring upon him or herself if they should disclose the secrets: "Voluntarily submitting myself to a deadly and hostile current of will set in motion by the Chiefs of the Order, by which I should fall slain or paralysed without visible weapons, as if blasted by a lightning flash." Unimpressed by his induction, he found little else. "I met, however, with nothing worse than a confounding medley of Symbols, and was handed a brief tabulation of elementary points drawn at haphazard from familiar occult sources. . . . [They] were subjects about which it turned out that the G. D. had nothing to communicate that was other than public knowledge."[26] Waite played a leading role in preserving the emphasis on the centrality of the mystical journey at the expense of the magical experiments.

In 1903, there was a general meeting that brought to a head the identity of two factions. Waite attempted a coup that intended the abandoning of all magical work, and pursuing only the mysticism he had been advocating. There is no record of what Yeats's reaction was to this metamorphosis, although George Mills Harper documents that he was trying to mediate between the two groups.[27] He would have been sympathetic to Waite's focus on the mystical, but reluctant to abandon the experimentation in magic completely. Compromise proved impossible for Waite. The conclusion to the crisis was that Waite led a breakaway group called the Independent and Rectified Rite, which came into being on November 7, 1903. (Dr. R. W. Felkin established his own version of the Order of the Golden Dawn, called the Stella Matutina, that set out to retain as much magic as possible.)[28] Waite, a clergyman called Ayton, and Mr. Algernon Blackwood were elected as the three chiefs.

Christopher J. R. Armstrong sums up the resentment of central figures such as Mathers and Westcott:

> The great crime of Waite in the eyes of such people was that, having infiltrated their organisation, apparently in good faith, he then machinated a seizure of power and tilted the ritual in an orthodox or relatively orthodox Christian mystical direction. His "revision" of the Golden Dawn ritual apparently abandoned ritual magic and all astral workings and rewrote the texts to express "a somewhat tortuous Christian mysticism."[29]

Yeats seemed to occupy a position halfway between those of Waite and the rest of the Order of the Golden Dawn members. He had argued passionately against the setting up of small groups that practiced their own ceremonials and rituals, and in doing so he used terms that sounded remarkably like those that Williams later used to express his understanding of exchange, substitution, and co-inherence. Yeats was convinced, as Williams was, too, that individuals had the competence to enter into pacts of substitution and exchange by engaging in appropriate rituals. He warns against the danger of experimenting without understanding the wider significance of what is being done, and ensuring the proper protection. Williams would "Christianize" this process in a number of ways, particularly in depicting the relationship between Stanhope, Pauline, and her ancestor John Struther in *Descent into Hell.*[30] Yeats asked in the essay "Is the Order of R. R. & A. C. to Remain a Magical Order?":

> Was Plotinus one of a "group" organized on a "globular Sephiroth" when he was thrice united with God while still in the body? It is by sorrow and labour, by love of all living things, and by a heart that humbles itself before the Ancestral Light, and by a mind and its power and beauty and quiet flow without end, that men come to Adeptship, and not by the multiplication of petty formulae. What is this formula of the "groups," the utmost of their present practice as they say, that is to be a ladder into heaven?

> Now that the secrecy is a little faded we know enough of it to know that it is nothing new or wonderful. They use a simple meditation that has for one effect the welding those who use it into one, a little at the expense of their individual souls, which, instead of remaining each a distinct circle, become, as it were, segments of a circle that has no very great or rich life to give them in payment; and for another effect, the awakening of a sympathy, which is limited to those who use this meditation at the same hour and as part of the same sphere. A partly similar meditation is used by lovers or friends to make their union the closer, to make more intense that love that has been called "an egotism of two," and sometimes, and I know one rather terrible case, it makes the union so close that those who use it share not only emotions but sicknesses and follies. Because of this sharing of all by all, I doubt very much if these meditations should ever be used without ceremonial precautions of a rather elaborate kind.[31]

Waite was also pleased to be able to get to know and collaborate with D. H. S. Nicholson (who was also to be a close friend of Williams). Nicholson had joined the order in 1910. He and Waite worked together on the English edition of Lopukhin's *Some Characteristics of the Interior Church,* with Waite providing the introduction to Nicholson's translation. Waite's new group, the Independent and Rectified Rite, was not without its own problems. Its members were better educated than those who went with Felkin, and this had both advantages and disadvantages. On the one hand it meant that Waite was able to consult Nicholson among others; but on the other hand, when the members disagreed over anything, as the social dynamics of that kind of enterprise allowed or even dictated, they tended to argue fiercely among themselves.

The greater problem arose not over matters of detail in ritual but rather over credulity or skepticism about the original materials. Waite became increasingly skeptical about the contents of Westcott's cipher manuscripts. The members who did believe in them became restive and called upon M. W. Blackden for support. Marcus Worsley Blackden was an artist and Egyptologist who later became a journalist. He had cooperated with Waite on a venture to collect a wide range of obscure Masonic rites. He shared Waite's aims to, as Waite saw it, "return the Order to a real vitality" and conspired with Waite in his coup d'état. When he married though, he retired from the Order of the Golden Dawn.[32] But he emerged from this retirement when he was asked to by members of the order, who hoped for his support for Westcott's original manuscripts, and argued strongly for their, and therefore the order's, authenticity. Faced with opposition of this kind, and on such an essential issue by his erstwhile colleague, Waite found himself in an impossible position.[33] In 1914, after what he described as an "unprofitable debate," he withdrew his copyright rituals and dissolved the rite "as at that time constituted."

This marked the end of Waite's involvement with the Order of the Golden Dawn, and the Isis Urania Temple, but not the end of his excursions into Rosicrucianism. The question of the use of magic in the sense of phenomenal occultism was closed for Waite. He had written rather coyly, but clearly, in *The Hidden Church of the Holy Graal,*

> On the assumption that there has been a Secret Tradition perpetuated through Christian times, the place of which is in the West, it seems desirable to understand what part of it matters vitally in respect to our own subject. There are several schools of secret literature, and each of them, under its proper veil has contributed something belonging to its own particular order. There are for example the schools of magic, and it is these precisely that embody nothing for our purpose; they constitute heresies of occult practice.[34]

Waite now saw his task as taking the mystical agenda identified by Yeats and to purify it of its neo-paganism, restoring it to a Christianized though Q'abalistic community of liturgy and learning in the construction of a Rosicrucian society that was wholly Christian.

A letter by Gerald Yorke clarifies how the Order of the Golden Dawn was perceived as lacking in this respect.

> Where the G. D. called itself a Hermetic Order, Waite called his version a Rosicrucian Order, and the Rosicrucians were always more Christian than the Hermetists. In the original G. D., the Christianised Rosicrucian material did not come until the 5=6 degree in the Inner Order. Here for the first time you find the Calvary Cross, but with a rose on it instead of the figure of Christ.
>
> Now Hermetic Orders as such are only Christian in that they include some Christianity but do not stress it. Rosicrucian Orders on the other hand are primarily Christian but draw on other pre-Christian sources. In other words the Hermetists always try to become God in his anthropomorphic or in some instances theriomorphic form. They inflame themselves with prayer until they become Adonai the Lord . . . whereas the Christian approached God the Father, through Christ (Adonai) but never tried to become Christ, only to become as Christ. Thus while the

> Hermetic (or pagan) approach is as Adonai to order the averse hierarchy about, the Rosicrucian is to order them through the grace of Christ or through the power of his name . . . now the Golden Dawn used the pagan formulae, the Hermetic formulae and the pre- or non-Christian names of power, taken from the Hebrew, Greek or Coptic Egyptian and Chaldean Sources. The Rosicrucian substitutes names from the Christian systems, from the Christian Trinity. Both systems combine when it comes to the archangels Gabriel, Uriel, Michael, Seraphim etc. The G. D. way of becoming god is the dangerous one, as it leads at once to inflated ego, witness Mathers, Crowley et al. The occult orders are full of people who are for a time being in revolt against or not at home with Christianity. When they find that the occult, Hermetic, or pre-Christian way of doing things is at its best no better than the Christian way, they often find their final home back in Christianity, or Islam Buddhism or Hinduism. For the major religions are major because they have stood the test of time better. Thus my conclusion is that the Hermetic way of the Golden Dawn is primarily Hermetic and not Christian, since it is reverting to pre-Christian methods and attitudes, but some of the members will have done it in a Christian way.[35]

Accordingly on July 9, 1915, in a room at De Keyser's Hotel on Victoria Embankment, Waite consecrated the Salvator Mundi Temple of the Rosy Cross.[36]

There has been considerable difficulty in gaining access to what have otherwise been the secret rituals that Waite produced for his new order. However, the unpublished and privately printed "The Ceremony of Consecration on the Threshold of Sacred Mystery" came into the present author's possession. The frontispiece contains the declaration, "Issued for the use of serving brothers and Companions of the Order by the Keeper of the Sacred Rites." The following clauses give an indication of the tone Waite set:

> 2 The symbolism is concerned only with the quest and attainment of the human soul on its return to the Divine Centre: it is sought thereby to recall its members to the true object of research and the living method of its attainment.[37]
>
> 5 It has a message to those who are prepared in Christendom, though the lower grades of the Fellowship are not explicitly Christian Grades.
>
> 6 The tradition and symbolism of the Fellowship are a derivation from the Secret Doctrine in Israel, known as Q'abalah and embodied in the SEPHER HA ZOHAR.

7 The mode of interpretation in respect of the Kabalistic tradition is a Christian Mode.

9 The Fellowship is open to all who desire the knowledge of Divine Things and union with GOD in Christ, and its path of symbolism is a true light of understanding on the Path of Union.

In the Fellowship of the Rosy Cross the practice of magic as the engagement with some form of power to accomplish the wishes of the adept was prohibited. The divisions between the artistic, theurgic, and goetic are not clearly delineated. The Christianized concern for transmutation remained at the center of Waite's interests, and this might well be interpreted as a form of theurgy. It is no solution to take refuge in a more particular definition of the occult.[38] "Occult" simply means hidden. A good many of the elements that belonged to a gnostic or semignostic organization are, in the strictest definition, occult. The very form of change that Waite promoted, a semignostic Christianizing of the adept with a focus on Q'abalistic immanence, was very different from occult practice in its more popular sense.

The Rosicrucian Solution

What then of the anxiety of some of the more religious orthodox that Williams's interest in magic places him off-limits in terms of the practice of the Christian faith? Much depends on the definition of the terms we are using. It has become evident that the term "magic" can lend itself to anything from artistic "enchantment" by engaging the imagination, which is the practice of all poets, musicians, and storytellers, to something deeper in the realm of the occult, and encompassing both the theurgic and goetic. The latter involves the practice of magic to engage power over both matter and spirit, controlled by the adept, either for what is assumed to be beneficial purposes of others or for raw control and manipulation in the interests of the practitioner. The same range of definition accompanied its rediscovery from the beginnings of the Renaissance. In Yeats's understanding of magic as artistic enchantment, Williams was to remain a practitioner of magic only in the sense that he was a poet, and poetry was a type of artistic theurgy.

The material in this document strongly suggests that the defining creedal structure is Christian, while the interpretative commentary is Q'abalistic. Christopher McIntosh[39] follows Kathleen Raine in her book *Yeats the Initiate* in making the distinction between "Hermetic" and "Rosicrucian." The hermetic attempts identity with the godhead; but the Rosicrucian understanding of union retains the distinction between Creator and created. Raine's point is worth arguing, but hermeticism incorporated a wider culture than this definition allows; and such definitions can obscure a more complex spectrum of identification where, within the more mystical Christian tradition, the distinctions are harder to keep. The whole of the Christian mystical tradition also uses the language of identification with the godhead (as does much of St. Paul). However the hermetic approach finds its more natural theological language outside the Judeo-Christian context. It turns to language that deals in "impersonal energy" and ultimate "union." These reflect something more like Buddhist or what we would call "New Age" theology, and so the fault lines of the argument become a little clearer.

Rosicrucian Ritual in Practice: "The Ceremony of Consecration on the Threshold of Sacred Mystery"

Unlike those of the Order of the Golden Dawn, the rituals used by the Fellowship of the Rosy Cross are generally inaccessible. One exception, however, is "The Hidden Life of the Rosy Cross—The Ceremony of Consecration on the Threshold of Sacred Mystery."[40] Access to this document is very helpful. It allows us a direct examination of the language and concepts used in the rituals. An exploration of its contents offers us a clear picture of the tone and direction of the order, at least at the admission of neophytes. The ceremonies are a mixture of dramatic reading, poetic chant, scriptural injunction, and Q'abalistic reference. They may well have had a profound influence on the participants when all were clothed as the rubrics required and entering into the full liturgical drama. This rite begins with the following "stage directions":

> The MASTER OF THE RITE, officiating as HIGH PRIEST, is seated on his throne in the East between the pillars of the Temple. He wears a white robe, having a red cross emblazoned thereon and extended from neck to hem. This vestment reaches below his knees and beneath it is a white alb. He carries a wand surmounted by the Rosy Cross. All present in the sanctuary are clothed in the same manner, the High Priest only wearing an additional sacerdotal cloak or cope of thin texture. The PRIESTESS, whose wand is crowned with Lilies, and her two assistants—these bearing Rose-Wands—are on the Southern Side. Other SPOKESMEN OF THE RITE are placed in the North. Those who belong to the Sanctuary but are taking no active part may be seated on benches facing West and situated North and South of the Great Altar, which is at a certain distance forward and

> served by a Thurificans, installed at either horn. The SYMBOLUM MAGNUM of the Rose-Cross is erected upon the altar, with flowers and lights about it, in groups of seven and twelve. At the foot of the cross are four cubes of white alabaster, crystals or white wood, bearing inscriptions.

All the lights are extinguished, and a herald enters carrying a shrouded lantern. Silence is kept. The postulant enters at words of welcome from the herald. The rubric in the rite prescribes the following for the postulant:

> [The Postulant] is clothed in the weeds of a pilgrim, or in such other vesture as may be determined from time to time. A cross of rough wood is suspended about his neck, signifying his own manifest existence and all that he carries therein. It is understood that he has been prepared zealously; he has signed the form of profession: it is known that he has a certain disposition towards the inward life and the realisation of Christ in his kingdom, regarded as an attained state of inward being. He has heard also of the Soul restored in GOD.

The conjunction of traditional Christian language with esoteric definitions is to be expected in a philosophical framework that adopts the language of conventional terminology as interpreted by the Q'abalistic tradition. This allows for an interpretation with gnostic overtones and quasi-mystical categories. The goal of the ritual is said to be "the realisation of Christ in his kingdom regarded as an attained state of inward being."[41]

The high priest offers a commentary on the proceedings that has elements of homily to it. He comments from a perspective that has an antiecclesiastical and personalist tone of piety:

> How did I hear thee first? As a child at my mother's knee? As a youth in the classes? It is very well. In the Church, woe is me? What Rites, what words of the preacher? Were they not good and true? What ways of missing the message! I heard of thee only without who know Thee only within, in the one place of knowledge. The awareness becomes the Presence and Thou art That.[42]

While in conventional biblical language of metamorphosis, St. Paul is content to talk of "transformation": "Do not be conformed to this world, but be transformed by the renewal of your mind, that you may prove what is the will of God."[43]

The rite reverts to the alchemical language of transmutation, a language that Williams makes considerable use of in his early novels, and that continues to appear in his later work of *The Figure of Beatrice.*[44]

> Conversion of all conversions, change of change, stars out of dust arising, making all things new: Be ye transmuted therefore from dead stones into Living Philosophical stones, shining on everlasting hills, radiant on the mount of GOD.[45]

The stones are, of course, "philosophical stones" to be distinguished from the "living stones built into a house" of 1 Peter 2:5, and they reflect the Rosicrucian culture that venerated the traveling philosophers of the early part of their tradition. But the Rosean imagery is used to convey conventional immanent experience.

> The Tree of the Rosy Cross is Christ; the Tree is Life; the tree is the Word made flesh: IMMANUEL, GOD is with us. It is also the manifest state of our humanity; and then the Rose signifies the Immanent Divinity, which dwells within us, at once hidden and revealed. I bear my witness further that the Rose is the soul in man and then the glittering point of dew, as the jewel within the centre, is the inward and hidden Christhood.[46]

The high priest turns to the imagery of the mountain, which finally becomes Horeb and Sinai and Tabor. Mountains play a prominent part in biblical spirituality, but the mountain in the rite contains a good deal else besides the elixir as well as the true stone of the philosophers.

> The Guide is that which is said in an old traditional story to lead the seeker of the Rosy Cross up a mountain in the midst of the earth, otherwise at the middle place of the world. I say unto you that this mountain is within and that it is found at our own centre. It is a place of many treasures which the world does not value, because they do not bear its marks, or come out of its mint, as current coins accepted in its Houses of Exchange. It is said to be encompassed by cruel beasts and ravening birds, which are the evil passions within us—all the false desires. They are the lawless parts of our nature in all the ways of life, the spirit of the word within us that strives with the SPIRIT OF GOD. . . . [T]he lion and dragon, the eager birds of prey shall fly before that which is our Guard, as well as Guide in Paths. I say unto you: Believe and find. On a wind of the Spirit you shall all go up the Hidden Mountain. All that is of dead

stone in your nature shall be rent like rocks. . . . [T]here shall follow a great calm. The day and the day star shall rise on the Mount of GOD, and the place of treasure shall unveil. In the images of the old parable that Treasure is a Highest Tincture, which might turn the world to gold. But this is the Gold of God, according to another witness of the Rosy Cross and this transmutes the soul.[47]

This passage contains a number of images that are also found in Williams's novels. The houses of exchange are unlikely to be here more than what they appear to be at first sight. But the houses of exchange may well be the embryonic templates of Williams's later mature notion of his Doctrine of Exchange. The image of the mountain is also to be found in Williams. The most significant passage is in *Descent into Hell*,[48] where in the chapter "Vision of Death," Margaret Anstruther had a vision of a mountain that acts as an eschatological focal point of transfiguration and judgment that is both local to her own community and at the same time universal.[49]

Central themes in *Shadows of Ecstasy* and *Many Dimensions* appear to have embryonic images found in aspects of the rite. The former drew on the process of transmutation and the latter on the image of the mystic stone. The same images are found here:

A spokesman of the Rite:
Raised into Eternal Life, O Master, the state of the Fixed Stone, which is gold in the soul of man.
Third Spokesman:
The Divine Presence is hidden in our natural manhood and revealed when this is transmuted by the word of Divine Alchemy.
Spokesman of the Rite:
The transmutation is within in Spiritual Alchemy, unlike the work in the crucible as dreamed of old.
Second Spokesman:
The mystic stone is within us and transmutes all things. The authentic affirmation is therefore: behold I make all things new.
Third Spokesman:
But it is the soul above all things which becomes spiritual gold.[50]

In a similar pattern to that of the Order of the Golden Dawn, the concern with personal alchemical transmutation was mirrored by the desire to remake the world after the same fashion, initiated by those who had gnosis of the mysteries:

The High Priest:

Who quotes in any Houses of Exchange the everlasting values? Who deals therein? Who buys or sells?

Herald:

The everlasting values are treasured in the heart of man, when GOD has changed the heart. I open my accounts therein: I sell and buy for ever.

The High Priest:

At the back of the centuries the voice of the Rosy Cross bears witness that such an unity in spirit with Christ is possible here and now.

The Priestess of the Rite:

Not from without descending and not a soul infused, or Master Part to Servant Part attesting, I bear my faithful witness that CHRIST mystical, the Inward Christ, is a State, a Spirit of attainment.

The High Priest:

And these mysteries are hidden, for the titles of their knowledge are within.

The Priestess of the Rite:

That which is within is older than that which is without, and it has come from far away.

The High Priest:

While abiding in things without the great practical secret is to keep ourselves secretly.

The Priestess of the Rite:

Dedicated pure and naked, turn we to the soul within.

The High Priest:

Let us make the world without as the world within and thing material even as things of the Spirit.

The Priestess:

If the centre of the soul is GOD, let it be so with us, that this Centre is everywhere and the circumference nowhere.[51]

The rite ends with a rubric that promises that the gnosis is received in outline, but is to be encountered in more detail only for those who progress.

If and when those who pass on enter into plenary possession of the Rite, they will find that there is a sense in which they have received everything, as in far off summary or shadowed outline, in this Ceremony of the Threshold. On the other hand, if they go not further, in reality

> they will have received nothing, more especially if there is nothing in themselves by which they can be led onward.[52]

Where did Waite gather these images and ideas from? To understand that we need to examine his interest in the Q'abalah, and his understanding of how it might be Christianized. This he wrote about at great length in a book called *The Secret Doctrine in Israel;* and to these we turn in the next chapter.

CHAPTER THREE

The Q'abalah, *The Secret Doctrine in Israel,* and the Influence of A. E. Waite

From Waite's wider interests in the Zoharic and Q'abalistic writing on both marriage and marital sexual expressions, found particularly in *The Secret Doctrine in Israel,* Williams found a conceptual framework to explore his notion of romantic vision. It was to become "Romantic Theology." He wanted to place marriage, the romantic vision, and a proper recognition of human sexuality more restitutively at the heart of Christian theology and spirituality. Christian culture had lost something of the ease that both Hebrew culture and scriptures had with the material. The natural interrelation of sexuality and spirituality that is found in the Song of Songs, for example, finds no parallel in the Christian tradition (unless it is in the more unusual world of the allegory and metaphor of some of the medieval mystics). Heroism in spirituality became the preserve of the celibate and increasingly the monastic. Eschatological concerns in the Pauline epistles had relegated marriage as a last resort to those who could not wait. Although the church gradually accommodated itself to the delay in the Parousia, there was no return to the experience of family and married life with its accompanying sexuality as central to the religious culture as Judaism had known it.

Waite and Williams shared a common debt to and appreciation of the Victorian poet Coventry Patmore, who had inspired them both with his poetry that celebrated the spirituality of marriage. Patmore had written poetry that celebrated not just the erotic love that stood at the threshold of marriage as so many poets already had, but he continued to write about the vision his wife inspired in him as part of his Christian pilgrimage and discovery of the love of God, into the marriage. The model of marital love became for Patmore a metaphor for the spiritual love in the godhead. Waite would look into the

Q'abalah and Zohar and find there a development of the ideas that Patmore had celebrated. He found there a spirituality not only of marriage but also of marital sexuality. These ideas were so different from the more "normative" culture of the Christian tradition and the place that marriage occupied in it; and the lack of scholarly theological and critical attention to them in Williams's writing and biography leaves a large and significant gap.

During Williams's middle years, he developed the myth of romantic theophany and in doing so he wove a new strand in a Christian theology, which had been dominated by apophatic spirituality, that is, the preoccupation with what could not be said about God as opposed to what could be said. The hermetic and Q'abalistically inspired celebration of matter gave Williams the material he needed to create a synthesizing balance for the dominant *Via Negativa* (the expression of apophatic theology) of Christian tradition. The overt affirmation of sexuality and marriage in Waite's revivified Q'abalism led Williams to develop his understanding of the significance of Dante's vision of romantic love, which in turn enlarged the categories of religious experience in a form that potentially enfranchised the married and the "in-love." Mystical experience would no longer be the preserve of the contemplative monastic, but, within certain constraints, would incorporate the erotic and romantic experience in married life. The romantic and erotic metaphors employed by the mystics like St. John of the Cross and St. Teresa of Avila would become tangible practice within marriage.[1]

The categories of religious and romantic love fed each other naturally for poets. Dante and Donne were obvious examples. Before he ever became involved with A. E. Waite and his ideas about hermeticism, Williams had begun his own career as a poet, and he had published such collections of poetry as *The Silver Stair* (1912), *Poems of Conformity* (1917), and *Divorce* (1920). Williams quotes W. B. Yeats in the frontispiece of his *Silver Stair,* and it is in Yeats, who had also invested romantic love with a transcendental and mystical element, that we find hints of the greater reality lying behind erotic romanticism:[2]

Forgael: It is love that I am seeking for.
    But of a beautiful, unheard-of kind
    That is not of this world.
Aibric: And yet the world
    Has beautiful women to please every man.
Forgael: But he that gets their love after the fashion
    Loves in brief longing and deceiving hope
    And bodily tenderness . . .

Aibric: All that have ever loved
Have loved that way—there is no other way.
Forgael: Yet never have two lovers kissed but they
Believed but that some other was near at hand,
And almost wept because they could not find it.[3]

For Williams, the "some other" would become both the lover as they had it in them to become within the love of God, and, ultimately the fuller picture of the orthodox Christian God he was to give expression to in his interpretation of Dante.

Although Williams was originally attracted to Waite by a common preoccupation with the Holy Grail, he became equally interested in Waite's Q'abalistic doctrines as he explored them in *The Secret Doctrine in Israel.* This book informed his attempts to formulate a theology of marriage and provided a basis for his ideas about the symbolism of the body. Anne Ridler, who was a close friend of Williams when she was a young woman, identifies this book of Waite's as being foundational in understanding Williams's central ideas: "It was the *Secret Doctrine in Israel* (1913) which interested him most—and he continued to admire it, for he recommended me to read it, when I knew him in the thirties. It is a study of Jewish mystical work, the *Zohar.* . . . [I]n this book, I believe are the foundations of Williams' thought about the symbolism of the body, and of his lifelong attempt to develop an adequate theology of marriage, and in this last, the influence of Waite can be distinguished from that of the Golden Dawn in its original form, for the subject of sex played no part in its teachings."[4]

Sex and Marriage in The Secret Doctrine in Israel

Waite collected from the Q'abalistic literature some highly original ideas about the spirituality of sexual behavior and its theological implications within marriage. These, in particular, provided an early and critical influence on Williams. Especially important were Waite's understanding of the role that sex and marriage play within his understanding of the Doctrine of Correspondence in his book *The Secret Doctrine in Israel.* Their influence is seen clearly in Williams's early (and then unpublished work) *Outlines of Romantic Theology.* Williams's incorporation of a theology and spirituality that encompassed erotic and romantic vision has its antecedents in Waite's *Secret Doctrine in Israel.*

Williams consistently worked within a theology that contained a specific vision of the body and its constituent parts, the understanding of which is difficult unless the Q'abalistic background is explained. Q'abalistic spirituality affirmed the material as a map on which the immanence of God could be read. The human body was an important continent on the map, perhaps the most important one.

Waite begins with the body, but he moves beyond it. He thus lays the foundation for a spirituality based on a particular theology of marriage that derives from the body and its sexual expression. *The Secret Doctrine in Israel* is a large and (as is typical of Waite's works) obscure volume that sets itself the task of expounding the Q'abalistic tradition. The list of contents comprises twenty-one chapters on topics as diverse as "The Doctrine of Cosmology," "The Soul in Kabalism," and "The Alleged Christian Elements." But two chapters in particular form the central plank upon which Williams was to build his visionary and theological edifice. They focus on marriage and sex: "The Mystery of the Shekinah" and "The Mystery of Sex."

In the introduction to the book Waite explains the scope of his task:

> The question is therefore as to the fact of the Secret Doctrine and under what terms it is mentioned in the records. It is of course broadly and generally a method of interpreting Scripture. . . . [I]t is only casually that the word interpretation can be held to apply in any solid sense: the Secret Doctrine is rather the sense below the sense which is found in the literal word—as if one story were written on the obverse side of the parchment and another on the reverse side.[5]

With these words Waite prepares his reader for his exposition of a particular mystery, and one that will expound a secret doctrine that has to do with the symbolism of marriage and its associated sexual imagery:

> The last point which calls for our consideration here is whether the general references to the Secret Doctrine as a whole, apart from its various branches offer any ground of presumption concerning its radical nature. Now, it is said that the Supreme Mystery is concealed in the Law that is the secret of the Law, meaning the secret of the King—Sacramentum Regis quod abscondere bonum est—revealed only to those who fear sin, and that as to its nature, this is bodied forth by the sacred covenant concerning circumcision. In other words, it is a mystery of sex. It was on account of this that Rabbi Ben Simeon consecrated to the study of the Secret Doctrine the entire night in which the Heavenly Bride is united with her heavenly Spouse, being the night of that day when the Law was revealed to the Israelites and the covenant contracted between God and

> his people. The reason was that the mystic Knowledge constitutes the jewels of the Heavenly Bride. We can only understand this on the hypothesis that the science in question is concerned at some stage or under some aspect with a most holy mystery of sex, as if some unknown path of splendour and path to the height might open therefrom.[6]

He explores his hypothesis with particular force in the chapter entitled "The Mystery of the Shekinah."

The Mystery of the Shekinah

Waite will use the ascription of a feminine identity to an aspect of the godhead as a way of setting up polarities of male and female, which he can use to explore erotic and romantic themes in this particular aspect of Q'abalistic revelation. "There is a very true sense in which the Secret Doctrine of the Zohar must be said to centre in that mystery, whatsoever it may be, which lies behind the wonder and the glory of Shekinah—a recurring and speaking literally, incessant subject of reference in adoring honour throughout the great text."[7] Waite's argument requires him to turn to the relationship between macrocosm and microcosm and the search for a single principle of "union" between the two achieved by alchemical means, that is, one that would consist of the transmutation of one partner by the other. He writes,

> "The whole object for which the Holy One, blessed be He, sends man into this world, is to know that Jehova is Elohim." Herein is also all true joy of the heart. Now, it is in this manner that I open the high conference respecting the mystery of man and God, of man in the likeness of the Elohim, of the relation between things above and below, of intercourse for union upon earth performed in the spirit of celestial union, and the transmutation of one by the other for the work of God in the world. In this union abides the Mystery of Faith which is the synthesis of the whole Law. But union is not identity (cf. Deut, iv, 35: "Unto thee it was shewed, that thou mightest know that the Lord He is God"—or, as the Zohar quotes it, that Jehova is Elohim). It must be explained in the first place that Elohim[8] is a title of Shekinah, and so also is Adonai, in which sense she is called the Mirror of Adonai.[9]

Other phrases that are explored in this text include "Eden," the "River of Life," the "Beloved who ascends towards the Heavenly Spouse," the "Middle Pillar," and the "Divine Presence walking in the Garden in the cool of the evening." In all of these references, Waite points out, Shekinah is always and essentially female: "The Shekinah is female in its essential aspect, whether as the Bride of God in that transcendent state wherein there is no distinction between her and the Holy One, or whether as the tutelary guide of humanity."[10]

In terms of function and dynamic she occupies a similar position to that of the law in the oral Jewish tradition of the first century, where it was held that if one righteous man should keep it in its entirety, the kingdom would arrive. Waite posits that

> the wounds of the world and the Church may be wide and deep; but the Church and the world go on, for ten persons in the House of Prayer constitute the body of the Shekinah. . . . [I]n thousands and tens of thousands of cases, all the wide world over, it is true and glorious that man acknowledges the kingdom of heaven and submits thereto; that the Shekinah rests upon his head, assisting him in the quality of witness; that she testifies before the Sacred King that this man proclaims the Divine Unity—or in other words, that Jehova is Elohim—above and below, twice every day.[11]

In attempting to find a new reading of the theology of sex he explores the relationship between the concept of the Shekinah in the Zohar and some central characteristics of the Judeo-Christian tradition. Consequently the law is described as the "garment of the Shekinah,"[12] the "Mishna," and the "servant of the Shekinah." Waite ranges far and wide in drawing on a variety of images throughout the Old Testament, yet refuses to countenance what would seem to be a perfectly natural connection with Mary, the Mother of God:

> [I]t will seem at first sight that she occupies in Kabalism the same position of intercessor which is ascribed to the blessed Virgin by the devotion of the Latin Church, yet having regard to Shekinah's incorporation with the Divine Hypostases, I incline to think that the analogy is misleading. In view of all that has been done to Christianise Kabalism by every good means, and by so many that are bad intellectually, one has to be very careful of reading Christian implicits into the text of the literature.[13]

One particularly good reason for keeping a distinction between Theotokos (Mary as god-bearer) and Shekinah is simply that the former allows for no affirmative statements of marital theology, given both the orthodox understanding of her conception of her son without reference to her husband, as well as the later tradition of her perpetual virginity, and the latter does.

Having decided that that avenue of identification is not open, Waite examines the relationship between Shekinah and the Holy Spirit. He turns to the *filioque* controversy that separated Christian East and West and summarizing them briefly he concludes: "Now it cannot be said that either doctrinal position represents the mind of Kabalism." Waite adds weight to his case by pointing out that "those who are acquainted with theology will know that the Third person is not recognised as feminine,"[14] unaware apparently that his observations hold good only for the Latin West. In fact the direction in which he is heading precludes identification of the Shekinah with either the Virgin Mary or the Holy Spirit, since Waite is about to move on to what for him is the central ground of the sexual expression of heterosexual intimacy. Although there is a good deal of precedent in the language of the Western mystics for borrowing from eroticism and the imagery of sexual intercourse language that expressed the human longing for unity with the godhead, Waite is to go rather further in his treatment of the metaphor and practice of human sexuality.

After discoursing on the parallels between Shekinah and references to Spirit in the Old Testament, Waite comes to the issue of praxis. He turns to the spiritual relevance of sexual intercourse within marriage: "There have been recurring intimations there and here in these pages concerning a mystery of sex; it is imposed upon me now to affirm that this is the mystery of the Shekinah."[15] As so often in esoteric literature, there is as much obscurity as clarity. Waite continues provocatively, "The point and centre of the whole subject is the Indwelling Glory; it is declared everywhere, but everywhere it is also concealed; one aspect of its presentation—amidst great hiddenness of wording—suggests that the entrance of the High Priest into the Holy of Holies belongs to the mystery of sex."[16] He moves from principle to practice and explores the issue of the spiritual significance of marriage and the role of sexual intercourse.

> It is said further that the mystery of Shekinah comprises all women, and this—as we have seen—is why she does not abide except with him who is united to a woman. She is fixed definitely in the house of man when he marries, et quum foederis suum signum in locum ponit. . . . This is why He and the Vau follow each other in the (Hebrew) alphabet—Vau being the symbol of the male and He of the female principle. Husband and wife are one, and a ray of celestial grace covers them; it descends from Chokmah,[17] penetrates the male principle and the latter communicates it to the female.[18]

Waite is now faced with the problem that Christianity has inherited from its distinctive interpretation of the myth in the early chapters in Genesis, which lay particular blame on womankind for initiating the fall by being the first to give in to temptation. Although he is busy trying to free the feminine from some of the worst theological associations that derive from these resonances, he is unable to distance himself and the ideas in the Zohar from traditional antipathy toward the feminine. He writes, "The history of the fall of man through the intermediation of woman, acting under the virus of the serpent, is by no means the history of the Shekinah, unless under a special aspect and as a remote reflection."[19]

In a convoluted manner Waite explores the desire for union with the Shekinah, and he does this in terms of the "Mother above" and the "Mother below." He makes a distinction between vision and union, but then moves back to what he feels is firmer ground when he describes the final fate of the secret brotherhood of the Sons of the Doctrine when they die.

> So also there are some who do not die as men commonly, but are ravished by attraction which Shekinah exercises on their souls. The Mother in transcendence is, however, like the Mother below, and spiritual communion with her is so far as man has become a house or abode by attaching himself to the female: it is then that the Divine Mother pours down her blessings on both. There is—in the true sense of the term—a spiritual union below for the Sons of the Doctrine,[20] so that they are encompassed by two females—the wife who is on earth and the Unseen Helpmate.[21]

Waite attempts to make connections between the orthodox and the Q'abalistic traditions. He points out that two curious developments of the "literary vestures" of Shekinah occurred. He traces the titles and offices of the Hebrew Chokmah and suggests that they were lifted from their setting and attributed to the Virgin Mary by promoters of the Marian tradition. He suggests that although the correspondences between the two are superficially plausible, and may be deceptive because "shallow analogies still deceive many" yet "even the unusual predispositions which led up to the French translation of the Zohar have not permitted its editors to postulate that the Shekinah is the veil of Mary."[22] He does allow that a more significant correspondence exists between the "Indwelling Glory" and the Virgin Sophia than the German Theosophist Jacob Böhme accepted. He suggests that there was a borrowing of the idea and significance of Shekinah that became Gnostic *Sofia* and then developed into the Virgin Wisdom of Böhme and the later mystics of his school.

Waite maintains, having assiduously considered all possible references in the Zohar critically, that "The conclusion reached is that the Shekinah, as the President of the mystery of sex, is the direction in which we must seek if—as labourers in this strange field—we are to obtain our wages." Almost as if embarrassed at this conclusion, he makes what seems a small disclaimer: "I suppose that here, in conclusion, I have no real need to say that the Secret Doctrine in Israel is not one of sex only." He then reverts to his sweeping premise, "though intimations concerning the latter are found everywhere."[23] Having, with some attempt at delicacy, made the issue of sex central to his exploration, he pursues the way in which its importance is expressed.

The Mystery of Sex

Waite's basic premise has, from the vantage point of the shift we are experiencing away from the influence of Freud toward that of Jung, a Jungian flavor to it. While for the purpose of Jungian individuation, a reconciliation of animus and anima is required, Waite draws on the teaching of the Zohar to establish that "the union of the male and female must be a perfect union in the mystery of faith."[24] The practical expression of this lies, he believes, in marriage.

Waite begins his thesis by establishing that the tradition suggests that marriage is the union of the "Sacred Name" here below. But the "Sacred Name" is never attached to an incomplete man, and incompletion is defined as one who is either unmarried or who dies without issue. Failure to marry and beget children is so serious a defect that it requires a further incarnation in order to achieve these goals. He writes, "Such a person does not 'penetrate' after death into the vestibule of paradise, on account of his incompleteness. He is like a tree that must be rooted up, and planted anew—that is to say he must suffer rebirth in order that the sacred name may be completed in all directions."[25] From these principles it follows directly that the procreation of children effects the spreading of the radiance of the Divine Name in every direction, by collecting spirits and souls that constitute the glory of the Holy One, both above and below. Whoever fails in this goal of sacred procreation diminishes the figure of his master and prevents it from descending here below. Waite even gives some suggestion that this phenomenon parallels the second coming of Christ, and that the paucity of the descent of souls provides the reasons for the failure of the Shekinah to come down into the world, although Waite distinguishes between her manifestation—the event of the coming of the Shekina and time and space, which is affected by this, and her immanence, which is not.[26]

If one accepts these basic principles, then certain practices follow directly from them. Waite explains that the doctrine in the Zohar states that no marriage is made on earth before it is proclaimed in heaven, and that the Holy One accomplishes unions in the world above before the souls in question are born. Because the Holy One has prearranged the union of a married couple in heaven before they are born, there is a sense in which by their expressing their marriage in sexual intimacy a door is opened for their souls to image God on earth. It is from this perspective that sexual intercourse is a matter of both sanctity and necessity. "If the act of sexual intimacy is hallowed, the failure to produce children," by whatever means, is described as "an irreparable crime."[27]

There can be no lack of *mens rea* mitigating culpability. The reason does not matter. Even barrenness fails to provide escape from the criminality of failing to have children.

Waite is clear that this Doctrine of Marriage involves culpability whether or not there is the required intention. It is a mechanical issue. Not to produce offspring is to fail, or to sin. There is an automatic link, too, between the ecstasy of the body and the soul. Waite (sharing Williams's indebtedness) makes reference to Coventry Patmore in his footnotes. Claiming that salvation depends on the uninterrupted continuation of marriage, he states that

> man shall participate in the world to come because he had entered during this life into the joy of living honourably with his wife. The reason is that soul as well as body share in the *gaudium inexprimabile* by which children are engendered. This is the eroticism which characterises the Zohar, according to certain commentators: but as the Doctors of the Law beheld the supreme mystery in sex, it is obvious that whatever belongs thereto is explained thereby.

Footnote 7 in Waite's text reads: "Coventry Patmore's young lady thought the sacrament of marriage was a rather wicked sacrament, but the Zohar raises it into realms of which the Christian Churches have never dreamed, though I have met with some rare aspects of Latin theology, which seem to indicate that a Redeemer may live hidden therein."[28] Sadly, Waite does not offer references to these "rare aspects of Latin theology" and so they remain obscure, if indeed they exist. But the link between Patmore and Waite is a significant one, since it provides a common inspiration for both Waite and Williams, who found in Waite an influential interpreter of Patmore's ideas of romantic love.[29] Although Waite does not explore these rare aspects of Latin theology, Williams will uniquely attempt to incorporate back into the tradition aspects that have been lost in the post-Augustinian heritage.

Waite then looks at ritual that effectively sanctifies the act of intercourse and the consequent lives of the children. He maintains that by prayer, "whoever sanctifies himself" at the moment of intercourse will produce children who are immune to the tempter spirit.[30] But this kind of approach also has the effect of raising the relationship from the physical to a spiritual degree. Thus Waite analyzes what he understands to take place:

> The fulfilment of a particular precept is the condition attaching hereto and this is the raising of the heart and mind, on the part of the Lover and the Beloved, to the Most Holy Shekinah, the Glory which cohabits and indwells during the external act. The absconditus sponsus enters into the body of the woman and is joined with the abscondita sponsa. This is true on the reverse side of the process, so that the two spirits are melted together and are interchanged constantly between body and body. The sexes are also then interchanged in a sense, as the sex of Metatron is said to be transformed momentarily before the veil of palms and pomegranates on the threshold of the inmost shrine of the Supernals. In the indistinguishable state which arises it may be said that the male is with the female neither male nor female: at least they are both or either. So is man affirmed to be composed of the world above, which is male and the female world below. The same is true of woman.[31]

This is a long but typical piece of Waite's convoluted style of writing and thinking and aptly illustrates his polyglot (or more critically, macaronic) style. He appears to be combining a number of different ideas, including an almost Jungian conflation of both animus and anima, which, instead of being understood psychologically, is expressed somatically and pneumatically.[32] His authority for this is his reading of the Zohar, which he appears to understand uncritically. But this is part of his radical approach. He accepts the basic framework of the Judeo-Christian tradition, but reinterprets it at significant points where the hermetic tradition espouses a different hierarchy of values. At the same time, Waite looks back to the pattern of Genesis to establish that, since woman came from man's rib (as is told in one of the Genesis accounts), humanity began with an essential unity that is recovered in the act of ritually aware lovemaking between husband and wife. But he is concerned not with the unity of body but with something higher: "There is another and higher process in the fulfilment of which it is possible that they shall be one soul."[33] Waite adduces from the story of Jacob as interpreted by Rabbi Simeon that, as long as Jacob remained unmarried, God did not become manifest to him clearly. After marriage, however, Jacob arrived at the perfection that is "above," as distinguished from the perfection that is "below."

Marriage becomes the state in which the spirituality of the journey of those who have been inducted into the mystery of what Waite calls the "Secret Doctrine in Israel" is expressed. Waite claims that when the Holy One created the world, He engraved the mystery of faith in letters of sparkling light. Waite then turns to the Doctrine of Correspondence to describe how it was that God established the principle of the connection between the "above" and the "below":

> He engraved it above and below, because it is the same mystery and because the world below is the mirror of that above. By means of the mystery of faith he created the worlds. Now in another place it is asked: what worlds? The answer is matrimonial unions. These are the worlds which God does not cease from creating. It follows that creation, as the story is told, is a veil of the sex mystery; it follows also that something is understood of which physical union is the shadow as this is known here.[34]

This claim that marriages, or more accurately matrimonial unions, are microcosmic worlds of continuing creation, provides the necessary link to Williams and his exposition of "Romantic Theology," where he also makes claims for the centrality of marriage in the religious journey.

Waite's theology is steeped in obscurity and offers a highly unusual perspective that, combined with the technical Q'abalistic language, makes it relatively inaccessible to the uninitiated reader. Williams was not uninitiated. He took the essential ideas of this theology that were located in the Q'abalistic tradition and reintroduced them into the mainstream of Christian thought, thereby offering an antidote to, or a complementary strain for, the *Via Negativa.* In a way that Waite was incapable of, Williams acts as an interpreter of this secret tradition, his goal being the revivification of orthodoxy. The most obvious bridge between Williams's and Waite's thought is his early book *Outlines of Romantic Theology,* which was finished in typescript in 1924 but never published during his lifetime. It is an early and immature work, but it put his later developed thought into sharper relief. It also acts to delineate further the points of connection between both men.

Outlines of Romantic Theology

In his book *Outlines of Romantic Theology,* Williams takes up the issue of separation, which posed such a difficulty for Waite in his marital theology. One Q'abalistic principle appears to have undermined another. The separation of his wandering adepts from their wives made it difficult for them to fulfill their marital and sexual duty. Waite offers us a vignette from the Middle Ages, and describes wandering adepts as being both travelers in search of wisdom and also men of affairs, workers in the vineyards of this world as well as in the Garden of God. The Zohar is full of their little journeys, usually undertaken in the company of another adept.

> Great adventures befell them in the sense of the mysteries of doctrine, for strange people went about in those days carrying, unknown to one another, the treasures of mystic knowledge. It was after all an unincorporated fraternity, and though it looked differently there and here, initiation was by a segregating principle, and not by the communication from a common centre of knowledge.[35]

Because the union of man and wife was to have such profound spiritual implications, this wandering would cause difficulties since even temporary separation was strictly prohibited. Waite attempts to reconcile this need for the adepts' peripatetic wandering in search of knowledge with the injunction that stable marital union acts to invoke the presence of the Shekinah. He then explores wider issues of marital stability:

> Now, journeys in search of wisdom or in the prosecution of business which, it may be mentioned, was often of a humble kind, meant separation from the wife of the Doctor's household, and this would seem at first sight to involve separation from the Shekinah. To remove this difficulty it was held sufficient—as we have seen (a) that the doctor should pray to the Holy One before starting and (b) should watch over all his actions during the period of absence from home. He would not then be separated from his spiritual companion, nor would he put that stop to the union between male and female which would render him an incomplete being.[36]

Williams takes up the problematic issue of separation, and looks at it not as an issue deriving from nomadic intellectual and spiritual quest, but rather he sees it in the more normative context of the problem of divorce. He takes an absolutist position that goes even further than Jesus's exception for divorce on the grounds of adultery (known as the "Matthean Exception" in the Gospels[37]) and in doing so seems to share the overtones of Waite's particular metaphysical categories deriving from *The Secret Doctrine in Israel.*

> And to refer again to the matter of divorce, it is because marriage is a means of redemption that two lovers in whom it has begun are required to submit themselves to that work to the end. Divorce is an attempt to nullify a sacrament actually in operation; as if a man should attempt to begin the supernatural life by being re-baptised. It is not that it ought not to happen; for a Christian it cannot happen, whatever formula is pronounced or ceremonial enacted. When the work is once begun, it cannot be stopped. . . . [I]n the nature of things salvation demands an utter surrender, which is just what the known possibility of divorce prevents and forbids.[38]

The suggestion that salvation depends upon the continuity of this process seems to flow from the fusion of the spiritual and material categories that occurred in Williams's mind. He blends together the spiritual status of marriage with the idea of its physical consummation and continuation in perpetual companionship, in a way that identically reflects the categories found in Waite's writings.

In a curious addendum, Williams's absolutist stance on the impossibility of divorce is modified by his recognition that marriage may not fulfill all that is demanded of it, emotionally or theologically.

> Marriage may have been a formal matter and the religious experience of love may take place afterwards between one of the pair and some outstanding third. It is difficult to see how, in such a case, any other arrangement can be come to than that the lovers should make a formal choice between the Church and the new experience. It does not perhaps in the end matter very much which, if the choice is honestly made, but no good can come from the attempt to impose either upon the other.[39]

If the sentence that followed this were not "In the nature of things salvation demands an utter surrender, which is just what the possibility of divorce prevents and forbids," then one understands Williams as advocating a free choice between lover and wife. Further, that this choice was determined by the criteria of scrutinizing the validity of emotional experience. But the argument that he proposes in this passage appears to swing in different and conflicting directions without obvious reasons. When read without the interpolation about the "third," it is simply a principled application of Waite's position, making divorce impossible. However, the fact that *Outlines* remained in manuscript form, to which he made amendments, and was begun in 1924, just a few months after Phyllis Jones arrived at Amen House, suggests that the reference to a "third" is what it appears to be, a later addition to the original text reflecting his experience of falling in love with Phyllis Jones. Some of the tension and contradiction in the argument of this passage may well therefore reflect the pain and difficulties that Williams was to experience in the developing contradiction of his personal circumstances.[40]

Outlines contains the embryonic ideas, and sometimes even phrases, that were to be reworked more successfully in his later work. But there are a number of references that show their pedigree. He makes the essential link between the spirit and flesh that has its template in the incarnation, and extends the principle to marriage:

> Christ who is born of flesh is manifested in flesh. This is perhaps part of the sacramental grace of marriage, to which so much importance has been attributed and of which so little has been explained. Intercourse between a man and a woman is, or at least is capable of being, in a remote but real sense, a symbol of the Crucifixion.[41] There is no other human experience, except Death, which so enters into the life of a body; there is no other experience which so binds the body to another being. The central experience of sanctity is to be so bound to another, though for the saints this other is God. But what of the lover if Love is also God?[42]

Unlike Waite, Williams consistently strikes a note of realism that punctuates these early attempts at theologizing, and this continues throughout his later works. He admits, for instance, "Perhaps a happy marriage in this sense is as rare among marriages as a great saint among orthodox Christians."[43]

Williams evokes further images of union in marriage. He turns to a sacramental view of marriage that goes as far as visualizing the wife as a type of sacramental presence similar to the consecrated bread or wine. Coventry Patmore is quoted in Williams's text as saying, "The Blessed Sacrament is first of all a symbol of the beloved;[44] afterwards the beloved is a symbol of the Blessed Sacrament."[45] Williams insists that this saying contains within it the whole of "Romantic Theology," and that it needs no amplification. However potent the saying is in its compactness, however, it does need some explanation, and Williams does in fact offer it. He suggests that the Eucharistic sacrament relates to that glorious body of his beloved through which he also apprehends divinity. Just what the exact relationship is Williams chooses not to expound in detail. It is of note that this is not one of the avenues of thought that he chooses to develop in his more mature work.[46] He will however explore other connotations that lie in the perception of "the body," even if they are not confined to such a specific sacramental apprehension of the beloved.

He does not deal so explicitly as Waite does with the theology of lovemaking within the marriage; nonetheless, it has its mention. On the one hand, Williams claims that in the act of lovemaking, the presence of Christ is sacramentally imparted by each to the other, and claims it as a sacrament on the grounds that if it is not, marriage is not, and the church was mistaken to have included it in the group of rites that have the Eucharist as their crown. On the other hand, in a textual addendum, Williams complains of the phrase "consummation of marriage" to describe marital sexual intercourse: "It is of course nothing of the sort; at best it is the channel by which a deeper marriage is instituted; the consummation, however it may be in this act signified, foretold and hastened, is usually far away in the Divine Life."[47]

Waite was not alone in his divinization of romantic experience. He supplies a whole theological system derived from the Q'abalah to undergird this shift in imagination and perspective, but there were other voices to be heard. Coventry Patmore, who influenced both Waite and Williams, brought the religious and romantic sensibilities together in his poetry. He described his dead wife as "hem of God's robe, which all who touch are healed"; and "fair female twin of fullness, sucking God's glory in." She was "Queen wife who sitt'st at the right hand of the Lord of life."[48] (Williams was later to face the same difficulty in untangling the categories of romantic affirmation and spiritual association in his poems to Celia.) But it required a combination of width of vision, energy of imagination, and intellectual clarity to incorporate this spiritualized romanticism into the mainstream of Christian theology. To the extent that Williams achieved that, he did so by recovering a theology and spirituality of the *Via Affirmativa.* His task was not the imposition of the "Theology of Romantic Love"; rather it carried the hermetic influence seeking the wider resolution and incorporation of those elements of human religious experience that were set unnecessarily in opposition to one another. The integrity of the hermetic single principle required a reconciliation of the two ways. Williams set out to provide it.

CHAPTER FOUR

The "Two Ways" and the "Theology of Romantic Love"

> It will—generally speaking—be an unfortunate day for Romantic Theology if it ever gets into the hands of official ministers of the Church.[1]

The mature Williams was to draw upon Waite's work on Q'abalism and balanced the traditional *Via Negativa* with a renewed presentation of the *Via Affirmativa* in the form of "Romantic Theology." The best way to show how that happened is to present a brief overview of the historical development of the "Two Ways"; then the role that "Romantic Theology" played in Williams's synthesis becomes clearer.

The hermetic intellectual and mystical tradition provided Williams with the theological and aesthetic tools that he needed to reconstruct a theology and metaphysic that would fuse together the two ways. Other factors attracted Williams as a poet to Waite and his Rosicrucian world; the Q'abalistic tradition created a foundation on which an aesthetic, that is, an artistic or a poetic vision could find its own role as a medium of the religious quest. The deficiency of the conventional Christian tradition was its historically unbalanced reliance on the *Via Negativa,* on the one hand, and its vulnerability to a persistent substratum of Manichaeanism, on the other. Each fed the other. Waite established the hermetic priority of the unification of what one might describe as the vertical axis, of "above" and "below" within the Doctrine of Correspondence. While Williams worked from the same premise, he saw the task as remedying the imbalance of what we may call the horizontal axis, the tension between the *Via Negativa* and the *Via Affirmativa.* He clearly felt that in order to do so, the historic influence of Mani needed to be identified and countered.

> The old Gnostic view that matter was evil had no doubt affected [the Desert Fathers], and the newer Gnosticism that had begun, in the form of Manichaeanism, to sweep inward from the East. It had been forbidden by Diocletian as un-European, as a Persian import, before it was rejected by Christendom as un-Christian, as a diabolic luxury. But of all the heresies it is one of the few most generally and most subtly nourished by our common natures. There is in it always a renewed emotional energy. It is due to Manichaeanism that there has grown up in Christendom . . . [t]he vague suggestion that the body has somehow fallen farther than the soul.[2]

Williams might be misunderstood to be an advocate of the *Via Affirmativa.* This, however, would overlook the subtlety of his position. As an artist he dealt in the language of the *Via Affirmativa;* by nature, he was more drawn to the *Via Negativa.* Although his promotion of the "Theology of Romantic Love" might identify him as an exponent primarily of the *Via Affirmativa,* his ultimate purpose was their integration. However, the distinction between them can be easily overdone. Anne Ridler tells us that in the edition of Dionysius used by Williams there was a note by the editor on one of the Neoplatonist passages where the writer prays "that we may attain unto vision through the loss of sight and knowledge . . . denying or removing all things that are—like as men who carving a statue out of marble, remove all the impedimenta that hinder the clear perception of the latent image claiming that this simile shows that the *Via Negativa,* is in the truest sense, positive.[3] Although the *Via Negativa* had predominated, and Williams was to remind the church of the need to balance it with the *Via Affirmativa,* he also clearly felt that it was the business of the church to hold them together. He wrote,

> The essentials of the one way are the accidents of the other. There must be, sooner or later, even in the Way of Affirmation, some sort of seclusion of the soul to the Omnipotence. It must, in some sense, be divided from all else—for ever or for a time. I think for a time; but it will not at the moment feel this. The Rejection aims at this as a continual method; the Affirmation endures it, when it comes. As the Rejection has always to allow its debt to its parents, its teachers, its food, its shelter, perhaps its loves. These are accidents of its calling.
>
> It is true the Rejection a little tends to brag itself even in some of its nicest devotees. We have known of that for centuries; it is our Mother. The Affirmation we have not so well known; it is our Beloved.[4]

Williams insisted that the two approaches need each other. His favorite epigram, which steered him between pantheism on the one hand and Gnosticism on the other, was to say of all things, "This also is Thou, neither is this Thou";[5] from this he inferred,

> I do think that the double challenge of "This also is Thou," and "Neither is this Thou," carried into everything, probably as much as any other formula, assist the soul. They are an example of my momentarily pet obsession of asymptotes,[6] and the point at which they do meet would be the Spiritual Marriage, after which (they say), is the beatific vision.[7]

In his formal Doctrine of the Church he saw them as coexisting, almost, as he wrote in *Descent of the Dove,* co-inhering, "since each was the key to the other."

In *Descent* he comments on the dynamics of Montanism. The notion of co-inherence and its practical expression that he calls "Exchange" express the integration of all things in a similar manner to the way the hermetic single principle also links together the correspondence of things above and below. Reflecting on the history of Montanism, he examines the two ways and the nature of their interdependence: "The Rigorous view is vital to sanctity; the Relaxed view is vital to sanity. Their union is not impossible, but it is difficult; for whichever is in power begins after the first five minutes, to maintain itself from bad or unworthy motives. Harshness, pride, resentment encourage the one; indulgence, falsity, detestable good fellowship the other." Williams continues:

> Some were called to a strictness, and some to a laxity. It naturally happened that strictness, being more difficult, was regarded as superior. So far as difficulty is concerned it is. So far as vocation is concerned it is not. Relaxation is no less holy and proper than Rigour, though perhaps it can hardly be preached so. But the lovely refreshments of this world may not be without their part in the lordly rigours of others; the exchanges of Christendom are very deep; if we thrive by the force of the saints they too may feed on our felicities.[8]

This cosmic interchange with the communion of saints needed to be internalized within the individual—"as above, so below." He notes of St. John of the Cross that, "Even he, towards the end, was encouraged to remember that he liked Asparagus; Our Lord the Spirit is reluctant to allow either of the two great Ways to flourish without some courtesy to the other."[9] Williams believed more work needed to be done on the implications of incarnation: "The Doctrine of Our Lord as God with all its corollaries took centuries to work out. It is, certainly, now attacked. It is in dispute between Christendom and all that is not Christendom. . . . [T]he other Doctrine of His Manhood, with all its corollaries, has still to be worked out and put into action."[10] However continuously the cycles of rejection and affirmation act as correctives the one to the other, the centrality of incarnation is undermined if affirmation is not given a central role. The "Theology of Romantic Love" is not only an authentic expression of Christian spirituality and metaphysic; it is also a means by which the Way of Affirmation finds its proper and remedial place in the intellectual and aesthetic traditions of Christendom.

The Historical Development of the "Two Ways" in the Christian Tradition

The roots of this issue lie in patristic debate. Dionysius the Areopagite, from whom the conceptual categories of the two ways are derived, was well aware of their interdependence. The history of the culture of Christendom has taken a different direction. The emphasis and the status has all lain with the path of renunciation. This seismic shift raises the question: "why did the body, why did sexuality and why, therefore, did finally marriage suffer such devaluation?"

Elaine Pagels, an authority on Gnosticism, explores the reasons for apophatic theology becoming dominant by the fifth and sixth centuries in her book *Adam, Eve and the Serpent.*[11] A vigorous debate raged involving first Jerome against Jovinian, and followed by Augustine in opposition to St. John Chrysostom and Julian of Eclanum. Jerome took a fierce view on chastity, sexuality, and the body, and laid the energetic charge against Jovinian: "He puts marriage on a level with virginity, while I make it inferior; he declared that there is little or no difference between the two states; I claim that there is a great deal. Finally . . . [h]e has dared to place marriage on an equal level with perpetual chastity."[12]

The future belonged to Jerome. But mainly because in the next generation, where Augustine and St. John Chrysostom developed the controversy, and Julian of Eclanum joined them and broadened the debate, the issue had evolved to become one of human self-determination. Augustine had spent ten influential years as a Manichaean, learning to despise the body and all that was not overtly spiritual. His contribution was distinctly hampered by the burden of his carrying the suppressed baggage of the ghost of Mani after his long period as a disciple. Not only that, but when it came to confronting the North African Donatists' victory of the Doctrine of Grace over the more muscular Pelagians, the Donatists carried with them a secondary effect. Augustine joins together the thesis that human will had suffered badly post-Eden, with a reading of Romans 5:12[13] that justified his idiosyncratic understanding of original sin[14] and of course its transmission in the sexual act.[15]

Williams's judgment is that Augustine's genius has always represented a danger to the devout. "Without his genius they lose his scope."[16] *The Confessions*[17] stress redemption, as the church had always done, but they lacked *anima naturaliter Christiana.* Williams makes the ironic point that the expulsion of Augustine's paramour was a price almost too high to pay for Augustine's presence and theology. Almost, but not entirely. It was utterly destructive of co-inherence. The delicate interrelationship of human love, human longing, and human sexuality with the godhead became only and wholly a problem. The solution that expulsion represented became an example of a situation where the medicine for an illness threatened the patient's health as much as the disease.

> [*The Confessions*] divide, in an agony, the natural body from the spiritual body, and their readers and followers have divided even more fervently. When St. Monica drove St. Augustine's eighteen-years paramour, the mother of his son, back from Milan to Africa, something went with her which perhaps Christendom and Augustine needed almost as much as they needed St. Monica, though not as much as Christendom needs St. Augustine.[18]

Augustine's sayings, once dislocated only a little from the center of his major concerns of the moment, have the capacity to obscure a wholesome spirituality and, instead, to threaten a latent damnation. He may personally have kept his eyes on Christ as a matter of devotion, but his theology, even a little decontextualized, had the effect of directing the eyes of later Christendom toward humanity in the hopeless shadow Adam rather than the more optimistic light of the risen Son of God.

And yet Williams has a fond weakness for Augustine's insistence on our early incorporation into Adam, and our later incorporation into Christ, since it affirms the nature of the web of co-inherence, unlike the rejection of Augustine's paramour.

> Whatever ages of time lay between us and Adam, yet we were in him and we were he. . . . [A]nd indeed if all mankind is held together by its web of existence, then ages cannot separate us from one another. Exchange, substitution, co-inherence are a natural fact as well as super-

> natural truth . . . [c]o-inherence did not begin with Christianity; all that happened then was that co-inherence itself was redeemed and revealed by that very redemption as a supernatural principle as well as a natural. We were made sin in Adam, but Christ was made sin for us and we were taken out of sin.

Augustine's theological opponents, the Nestorians, insisted that Christ had a dual personality; one side incorporating his humanity and the other his divinity. On the other flank of the theological divide, the monk Pelagius argued that salvation was a matter of improving our moral performance and that perfectionism was something humanity was capable of if only it tried hard enough. In the face of Nestorian dualism and Pelagian independence, Williams insisted with Augustine (and with the later Q'abalists),

> The mystery was in the flesh and blood. It was this profundity of exchange and substitution, natural and supernatural, that the zeal of Augustine profoundly declared through Christendom. Christendom never quite committed itself to Augustine, but it has spent centuries escaping from the phrases of Augustine. But without Augustine it might have ceased to be Christendom.[19]

Williams recognizes the Augustinian theology of co-inherence, but his wariness of sexuality and the traditional chariness that the church had about the full implications of Christ's humanity have meant that Augustinian thought has been responsible for the theological and psychological demeaning of humanity. Human love, human bodies, the full interchange of our maculate intercourse were distasteful to the followers of the *Via Negativa.* The spirit of Mani needed to be countered by the redemptive somatism of Hebrew spirituality, which had always preferred Abraham to Adam.

Williams naturally turned to pre-Augustinian ecclesial culture, and found there the authority that endowed his view with an orthodox imprimatur.

> Counter checking the asceticism it admired, the formal Doctrine of Christendom concerning matter remained constant. . . . (An) ancient canon, said to date from the second or third century, illuminates(s) the official view: "If any bishop or priest or deacon, or any cleric whatsoever, shall refrain from marriage and from meat and from wine, not for the sake of discipline but with contempt, and forgetful that all things are very good and that God made man male and female, blasphemously

> inveighs against the creation *(blasphemans accusaverit creationem)*, let him be either corrected or deposed and turned out of the Church *(atque ex Ecclesia ejiciatur)*. And so with a layman."[20]

It has always been difficult to avoid overreaction to the negativity of ascetic self-denial. Affirming can as soon become condoning as rejection can slip into repression and denial.

> Rejection was to be rejection but not denial, as reception was to be reception, but not subservience. Both methods, the affirmative way and the negative way, were to co-exist; one might almost say to coinhere, since each was to be the key to the other. . . . [T]he Communion of the Eucharist, at once an image and a Presence was common and necessary to both. The Way of Affirmation was to develop great art and romantic love and marriage and philosophy and social justice; the way of rejection was to break out continually in the profound mystical documents of the soul, the records of the great psychological masters of Christendom.[21]

Williams makes a plea for the church to find some way of healing the antagonistic polarities of these two positions. They are not to be alternatives to each other, but complementary. They need each other as antidotes to their own excesses. But opposing denominations and competing spiritualities have turned these balancing mutualities into competing polarities that deny or denigrate each other's validity.

The "Theology of Romantic Love"

The word "romantic" can carry several different meanings. And so the way in which Williams uses the word is very different from the associations that some readers might assume that it carries. To clarify this, the poet and critic John Heath-Stubbs observed that "Williams's use of the term romanticism must be distinguished from the use of the word by some other modern writers. It does not for him mean an affirmation of emotional values to the exclusion of formal and intellectual ones."[22] Romanticism for Williams comprised essentially the value of vision. He was romantic about theology, but theological about romantic vision. He believed that seeing clearly was the means by which one made progress on the human journey. The way in which one looks at other people is often controlled by superficial prejudice, desire, or fear. But when one fell in love with another human being, looking or seeing could become a visionary experience. It was as one fell in love that a moment of visionary lucidity took place.

> But however in those states of "falling in love"
> the vision of a patterned universe is revealed to us, the revelation vanishes, and we are left to study it slowly, heavily and painfully.[23]

It was not only that one saw the beloved in the light of radiant insight. Williams went further than that. He saw beyond the beloved a pattern that gave the beholder in question an insight into the macrocosmic reality. With these ideas, he drew on both Waitean culture and his own experiences. The theology of the Zohar met with his own personal experience to provide a synthesis that would become his "Theology of Romantic Love." It is no accident that he also found inspiration in Wordsworth, for whom nature was also a means of illumination and revelation of the divine. Williams's theology fuses Wordsworth's agnosticism and Dante's orthodoxy:

> "This unknown mode," which is in Wordsworth "nature," is in Dante "Romantic Love." I keep the word romantic for three reasons. The first is that there is no other word so convenient for describing that particular kind of sexual love. The second is that it includes other love beside the sexual. The third is that in following the Dantean record of his love, it may be possible to understand something more of Romanticism itself, and of its true and false modes of being. The word should not be too narrowly confined to a literary manner. It defines an attitude, a manner of receiving experience.[24]

It was Wordsworth who had early on influenced him so as to interpret the inner significance of the natural and material order. He quoted lines from Wordsworth's *Prelude,* book 8:

> The human form
> To me became an index of delight,
> Of grace and honour, power and worthiness.[25]

But Williams went much further than Wordsworth when, in some of his early poetry, Williams set out to integrate the material and the romantic vision with the divine and sacramental, in a daring leap of imagination. He drew together both his wife and the Eucharist sacrament. In a poem for his wife, quoting the first line of a hymn in which the blessed sacrament is carried from the altar of reposition to the main altar on Good Friday, he develops an idea found in Coventry Patmore but that originated in Dante's works.[26] Williams connects the consecrated host with the beloved herself as sacrament:

> *Vexilla* regis prodeunt,
> The double banners move
> Before one altar to confront,—
> Twice manifested love!
> Your face, your soul, a double veil
> Are closely wrapped round him
> Who now, in yon material grail,
> Is nearer, yet more dim![27]

Williams constructs as an important missing link in a theological chain that unites the twin traditions of affirmation and negation. He would take this idea further still when he wrote in "To Michal: After a Vigil":

> That body's beauty,
> Where your dreams coast,
> Knew I and neared I
> Hid in the Host,—
> O, else was beauty but dream![28]

All doctrines have their perversions, and most religious insights suffer perversion at some stage or, if not that, succumb to dilution into superstition. Williams claimed,

> Like many other religious ideas [romantic love] became a superstition: on the other hand, it was to be naturally, but regrettably, cold shouldered by the ecclesiastical authorities. It was to be an indulgence to the populace and a stumbling block to the Puritans—using both words of an intellectual state of mind. It was to save and endanger souls. . . . [I]n fact, and in itself, it is a thing not of superstition and indulgence, but of doctrine and duty, and not of achievement, but of promise.[29]

The promise that he speaks of is one of a renewed vision, a way of seeing, and is thus a way of acting that essentially has the entire redemptive process behind it: "It flashes for a moment into the lover the life he was meant to possess instead of his own by the exposition in her of the life she was meant to possess instead of her own. They are 'in love.'"[30]

C. S. Lewis more succinctly defines the phenomenon with, "It is the recovery (in respect of one human being) of that vision of reality which would have been common to all men in respect of all things if man had never fallen."[31] Both men are invoking the revisioning of the beloved by her lover as an antidote to the myopia that more normally affects the way we look at, see, and judge each other. Williams is no sentimentalist: he is promoting vision, rather than illusion, so warns against the folly of claiming for the beloved, "a purity as non existent as the purity of the Church militant here on earth. Hers, or his, is an extremely maculate humanity, and all the worship under heaven ought not to prevent her lover from knowing (with reasonable accuracy and unreasonable love) when she is lazy, shrewd or malicious. She has a double nature, and he can have double sight."[32] Being in love does not usher one into a new utopian world where the beloved is experienced as impossibly perfect. Instead there is this duality of vision as Williams sees it, which takes in both the mundane reality of our humanity, but splints alongside it, a vision of what the beloved can become, or already is in the eyes of God. Clearly this double vision is not an easy balance for lovers to maintain. Where might it go wrong?

Heresies

The development of this "double sight" can lead to a distortion of reality as well as a renewed vision. Williams identifies three distortions of romantic love and the heresies that accompany it, all of which are indigenous to the condition: first, that the vision is going to last; second, that it belongs to the lover, producing the possessiveness and jealousy so common, and involving a desire to retain the glory for oneself, and this in turn means that one is not adoring the glory but one's own relation to the glory; and third, that it is simply enough to be in love. In fact lovers exist for the function of love; hence, they live not only for but from each other. However, at the heart of this re-visioning insight lies the idea that when two people are in love, the partner is glimpsed for a moment, in a moment of visionary lucidity, rather as God sees them, in the fullest maturation of their created potential.

Williams was profoundly frustrated by the way in which the church and its theology of love and marriage allowed no place for the physical body and an accompanying spirituality of romantic vision and even sexuality. He took the church and its traditions to task in making moral demands without providing the visionary fuel to meet them. In a piece of pungent criticism he complained that "the hungry sheep look up for metaphysics, the profound metaphysics of the awful and redeeming body, and are given morals." He felt that the church had in effect put the cart before the horse: "Speaking generally we have up to the present time insisted on the morals of marriage but we have not based them on any Doctrine of Love. We have rejected the idea of divorce but we have done so without any clear idea of the reason."[33]

Williams set out to provide that Doctrine of Love and new vision in a number of works, but particularly in his exposition of Dante's *Divine Comedy* in *The Figure of Beatrice* (1943). His commentary on Dante's famous poem fuses together a double perspective in the eyes of the lover; it is both a sense of what the potential of the beloved may be when transformed by love, and also a sense that this potential is already real and realized for and by God who loves us as a lover. If this almost universal experience of falling in love is reclaimed by the Christian tradition, where Williams claims it properly belongs, the experience and gift of romantic love may be rescued and revitalized. In the hands of the secularized idolatry of what might be called a Hollywood culture, romantic experience becomes a perpetual tale of repetitive fantasy. Falling in love is treated like a drug or panacea that has no sequel, but that simply has to be repeated. The second and subsequent stages of relationship are usually ignored. Marriage becomes the graveyard of romantic vision, not the environment of its flowering. But for Williams, the original romantic vision is the fuel that provides an initial burst of energy and commitment, driven by this new envisioning of the beloved, and marriage becomes the studio in which this new enterprise of human love becomes sculpted. Marriage may become more than a category of social stability and respectability, but also a visionary enterprise of practical spirituality, a workshop of the realization of human potential. It may then be seen as an enterprise with a goal of realizing the original vision for and of each other, rather than just surviving the strains of commitment and holding consequent escapist immorality and adultery at bay.

Williams was well aware of the danger of being overly sentimental. Anne Ridler summarizes his views in a public lecture he delivered:

> The experience of romantic love, then, he conceived to be capable of infinite good, and he defined that love (in the lecture I have mentioned) as "a sub-species of love between the sexes": "that kind in which the lover, generally by a process utterly beyond his own will finds himself in a state of adoration." His definition would have included love between members of the same sex, though he would have held that this was subject to

> the same law as that which should govern the vision of the "Second Image," quoted above. He disliked the cautious approach of some clergy and older people, which ignores the nature of romantic love, as much as he disliked the sentimentalizing which the experience endures in 1000 films and novels. He proposed, in this lecture, four Evangelical Counsels of Romantic Theology which I paraphrase: (1) Reality—it's true: the Incarnation is our proof. (2) Eternity: no later defections can alter the original moment of the vision. (3) Divinity: "The vision is a grace bestowed, not a natural right or a natural capacity; it is true of the beloved person in his or her heavenly nature, but we must not confuse this with the beloved person in her fallen state, or deny that the vision could be seen in every human creature if we had eyes for it, or try to take possession of it for ourselves." (4) Charity: "The beatitude of Love being seen, it briefly exists in us towards others." So Dante describes in The New Life how, when he saw Beatrice, if anyone had done him an injury, he could not but have forgiven it. "This is perhaps the cardinal point. It does not mean a vague goodwill towards Chinamen, but a definite humility towards one's neighbour. Humility is bestowed in that state of adoration."[34]

As Williams interprets it, the Way of Affirmation begins with the experience of stupor that the young undergo at their vision of the latent possibilities of the world around them as a so-called astonishment of the mind focuses on some particular image.[35] The assumption is made that "the vision must derive from something greater than itself, and must represent in itself that greatness from which it derives."[36]

So, for Dante, "Beatrice was in her degree, an image of nobility, of virtue, of the redeemed life, and in some sense of Almighty God himself."[37] But none of this is realized automatically. It has to be studied and sought. "The way to this knowledge is in the practice of charity and humility and all virtues."[38] Williams suggests that the pattern of this experience, which he finds also in Wordsworth, has four stages and Dorothy L. Sayers points out that the same pattern is found in both Traherne and Blake.[39] The steps are:

1. The first vision—or image of glory;
2. The loss of the vision and abandonment of the quest;
3. A second and lesser vision on a more intellectual level;
4. And finally the return of the first image, when the glory is found diffused over all experience.[40]

Perhaps the most traumatic aspect of this process is not the loss but the recurrence of the vision: for Dante—the lady at the window—who many of his commentators decided was merely a representation of philosophy, was in all likelihood a real woman. She was not one, however, whom he continued to relate to.

For Williams, the second vision came in the form of a real woman, not at a window but at the press: it came in the form of Phyllis Jones, who while she was without doubt a platonic lover,[41] evoked all the guilt, angst, and confusion that such a triangle inevitably produces. The experience of falling in love with a woman he was not married to resulted in an agony of contradiction. However common an experience this was, the poignancy and difficulty of the process itself was overwhelming. He wrote autobiographically about the pain of the contradiction when commenting both on Shakespeare's play *Troilus and Cressida* and also Wordsworth's outrage at the political response of his own government to the idealism of the French Revolution.

> The crisis which Troilus endured is one common to all men; it is in a sense the only interior crisis worth talking about. It is that in which every nerve of the body, every consciousness of the mind, shrieks that something cannot be. Only it is. Cressida *cannot* be playing with Diomed. But she is. The Queen cannot have married Claudius. But she has. Desdemona cannot love Cassio. But she does. Daughters *cannot* hate their father and benefactor. But they do. The British Government *cannot* have declared war on the Revolution. But it has. The whole being of the victim denies the fact; the fact outrages his whole being. This is indeed change.[42]

He turns beyond Shakespeare and Wordsworth to Dante in his book *The English Poetic Mind.* Dante's own solution may well have influenced Williams's. The reality can't be suppressed or denied, but it can be entertained without a desire to possess utterly and sexually.

> Having thriven in one manner, we are offered the opportunity of thriving in another; we are offered the opportunity of being free in the glory. The second image is not to be denied; we are not to pretend it is not there, or indeed to diminish its worth; we are only asked to free ourselves from concupiscence in regard of it.[43]

However commendable this may be as a statement of moral intent, it is more easily said, or written, than achieved. In fact, when in chapter 13 his early poetry to Phyllis is examined, it becomes clear that concupiscence was not so easily avoided by Williams himself. It also becomes clear that the situation was aided by the fact that Phyllis Jones was unwilling to develop the erotic opportunities the vision may have provoked in Williams.[44]

Williams's own trauma of contradiction did not blind him to the awful necessity of choice. When he comes to comment on the *Commedia* we find him presenting the Beatrician moment as a moment of judgment:

> It is a choice between action and no action, intellect and no intellect, energy and no energy, romanticism and pseudo-romanticism. There is a brief time when the Imagination—the power of grasping images and exploring distances of meaning—remains suspended in contemplation. . . . [T]hat imagination in action becomes faith, the quality by which the truths within the images are actualised within us. But the temptation to turn aside is immediate, swift, subtle and very sweet. It is only to linger in the moment, to desire to be lost passionately and permanently in the moment, to live for the recurrence of the moment.[45]

The agonies of the moral dilemmas he faced may well have played their part in moving him from what might otherwise have been too easily labeled an overidealized romanticism to something more authentically grounded. The evidence of his letters and poetry in chapter 13 suggests that his concern for clarity of choice may have arisen out of his own experience of compromised imagination.

In his analysis of the *Inferno* he expands upon the implications of making the lesser choice, of fully indulging the adulterous second love. The soul is "incontinent to its function; it treats its function as created for it."[46] And so it embarks on the perverted Way of Affirmation down the ever-narrowing funnel through greed, anger, and obstinacy. "Hell is a funnel, Heaven a rose. The narrowing inorganic rock of the one is the chosen antitype of the intensifying organic heart of the other."[47] At the mount of Purgation one is faced with another choice:

> It was said of God that "his necessity is in Himself," and this is the only necessity. Hell is the place of those spirits who wish to have their necessity in themselves. But Purgatory is the growing realisation that there is no necessity in us, except indeed that of being united with the primal and only Necessity. . . . [T]he only illusion is that there is in us a necessity to demand something other than He; the only disillusion is to find it is not so, and that our only necessity is love.[48]

He might have added for the sake of clarity, "love functioning from authentic imaginative vision freed from the desire for either concupiscence or possession." Love must be defined by its direction and the evacuation of elements of illusion, control, power, or possession.

Williams does address this in his charting of the only escape from the purgatory that lies in the growing apprehension of our place in the web of coinherence. He describes it as "the 'I' for the 'We' and the 'We' for the 'I.'"[49] The purgatorial process is the transforming of contradiction, the change from Hell, "where grace is not known but as punishment," to purgatory, where "grace and punishment are two manners of one fact."[50] In the paradisal knowledge, the image is seen in its fulfillment, at one with the primal truth from which all the images derive. It is a state where love is necessity, where "existence is equal, function hierarchical,"[51] where everything may be recalled as a cause of joy. The *Paradiso* is "an image of the whole act of knowing which is the great 'Romantic Way' . . . [i]n which Dante is the Knower, and God the Known, and Beatrice the Knowing."[52]

The way may be regarded as a technique of living that springs from an attitude of mind. It is no straightforward process from well-mapped stage to well-mapped stage; rather, to use the image that Williams himself valued, it is an interior movement from the circumference to the center of a circle, of which the Way of Affirmation and the Way of Negation are complementary aspects. At the end of *The Figure of Beatrice* Williams sets the task for the church and the individual.

> It is a way not confined to poets. That way is not only what the poem is "about"; it is what love is "about." It is what Love is "up to," and the only question is whether lovers are "up to" love. Were they, the *Vita* and the *Paradiso* would be the only way. The complex art of this knowledge is not confined to the romantic love of the male-female kind. Wherever the "stupor" is, there is the beginning of the art. Wherever any love is—and some kind of love in every man and woman there must be—there is either affirmation or rejection of the image, in one or other form. If there is rejection, of that Way there are many records. Of the affirmation, for all its greater commonness, there are fewer records. "*Riguarda qual son io*"—we have hardly yet begun to be looked at or to look.[53]

His own experience suggests that it is not enough to grasp the affirmation of the image instead of its rejection. Perhaps the difficulty in handling images of the Way of Affirmation well accounts for the church's chariness in recommending such an approach. The dangers of succumbing to the image are in proportion to the depth of reality the image is understood to represent.

CHAPTER FIVE

Alchemy as Metanarrative

The aim of "Romantic vision" was not a detached intellectual or aesthetic voyeurism. Rather it was intended to begin a process of human transformation. The idea of transformation was, of course, central to the alchemical tradition. Waite, as we have seen, believed that a lack of understanding of alchemy's aims constituted a serious deficiency in the Christian tradition. Williams's work introduces perspectives from the alchemical tradition in much the way Waite envisaged. But what then did Williams draw from Waite's own understanding of alchemy, and how did he use it? This alchemical culture, so far from undermining theological credibility, provided Williams with the remedial means of holding together the disjunction between the two "Ways" and between the material and spiritual. It was the language and means of integration.

Although the alchemical tradition that Williams made use of had begun in pre-Christian syncretism, the form in which he encountered it had been deliberately Christianized by Waite. Waite was an authority on the history and place of alchemy in the esoteric tradition, and used alchemical concepts freely in his own rites. Williams follows Waite in using alchemical language to describe the journey of the believer toward union with the godhead. Such language and the worldview it carried was to provide a rich cultural and conceptual milieu for his developing theological outlook.

One of the striking features of Williams's intellectual style is the extent to which he encloses himself in a literary and conceptual world the metaphysics of which have little to do with his own immediate historical context. He does not overtly engage with the intellectual cultural climate of his own era, although he does react against it. In his essay "The Athanasian Principle in Williams's Use of Images," Stephen Medcalf observes that, "The attack on reductionism is perhaps above all what united [C. S.] Lewis and Williams."[1] Both

Williams and Lewis adopted a metaphysic that was rooted outside the normative presuppositions of modernist culture. Williams moved into the metanarrative of alchemical transmutation, adopting and adapting the medieval myth of alchemical development. Running throughout Williams's novels and poetry is the consistent reference to the language and concepts of alchemy and transmutation, embedded in the wider tradition of related magic. The early novels contain the most explicit hermetic culture. In the later novels there emerges a developing and more refined notion of transformation that merges with the more traditional language of the Christian dynamic that is explored below. *Witchcraft* explores the practice of the culture. The intellectual and cultural structure for his Taliessin cycle is set within it, and to some extent, it also informs the language he uses for his theology.[2] There is a clear distinction between the way in which Waite and Williams engage with the ideology. Waite simply adopts it wholesale and uncritically incorporates it within the Christian tradition, but Williams sets out to significantly modify and evolve it.

In his early writing, however, Williams followed Waite's uncritical immersion in the alchemical culture. But Williams's thought moves from this relatively uncritical use of the genre to an evolved form that he makes his own. His clear intention is to exercise a metaphysical critique that has become increasingly rooted in Christian orthodoxy. The world of alchemy and transmutation offered just the antidote that Williams was looking for as part of his rejection of an all-encompassing rational empiricism. It was this shared concern that also bound him so closely to Lewis.

The Evolution of the Alchemical Tradition

The alchemical tradition begins as pre-Christian syncretism. In their quest for metallic transmutation, the European alchemists drew on theory and practice that had its roots in Greek and Egyptian intellectual and religious culture of the period several centuries before Christ. The alchemists of the Middle Ages were indebted to the Arabs in Spain and southern Italy. They had adopted it from the Greeks, who had discovered the principles of alchemy in Egypt during the fourth century B.C. Alchemical interests expanded into the tombs and labyrinths of Egyptian religion, and the Hellenistic figure of Hermes Trismegistus, who is the model for the medieval Mercurius, derives ultimately from the ancient Egyptian Thoth, god of mathematics and science.[3]

During the twelfth and thirteenth centuries alchemy had filtered into western Europe through Sicily and Spain. Christian students were welcomed at the universities of Palermo, Toledo, Barcelona, Segovia, and Pamplona, and they began to provide translations of the early texts that had been rediscovered. The most significant of these translators were Robert of Chester, Adelard of Bath, and Gerard of Cremona, all working in the first half of the twelfth century. During the next 100 years there emerged European "adepts" who moved beyond merely adapting the Arabian texts and created their own original work. The names that have come down to us among medieval alchemists include Albertus Magnus (1193–1280), Roger Bacon (1214?–1294), Arnold of Villanova (1235–1311), and Raymond Lully (1232–1315). They all believed in the basic theory of alchemy, namely the possibility of metallic transmutation, the sulfur-mercury theory of metallic constitution, and the Aristotelian tenets of "prime matter" and the four elements. Still more important, they arrived at a broader view of nature by combining alchemical experiment with ancient natural philosophy and Christian theology.

The first scientists of the West practiced alchemy as part of a single comprehensive philosophical system. Their ideas rested on the hermetic doctrines formulated by Alexandrian science and Greek alchemy and disseminated throughout the Roman Empire on the wings of syncretism. During this development, the hermetic doctrines became saturated with a number of mystical teachings and myths. They included a broad variety of early religious or quasi-philosophical movements: astrology and Gnosticism; Orphic speculation and Eleusinian mystery religion; the worship of Isis and Osiris; the worship of Serapis and Sol Invictus; and the teachings preserved by the Nestorians, Monophysites, and Manichees in Persia, Syria, and Iraq. With that interruption of cultural and intellectual continuity that we know as the "Dark Ages" in European history, this heritage could not pass directly to the Western alchemists but, as with much of ancient classical culture, it was mediated through the scholarship of Islam.

It became the function of the Arabian philosophers to re-create the hermetic doctrines of antiquity when large parts of the empire succumbed to the Arabs during the Islamic conquests of the seventh and eighth centuries A.D. The Arabs retained the hermetic doctrines with their intention of both attempting to refine gold and also revealing a way that would bring enlightenment to the soul. In drawing from the Arabian alchemical tradition, the European alchemists resuscitated the Hellenistic syncretism of the ancient world that the Christian church thought it had overcome.

It was a legitimate concern that the introduction of an alternative worldview should ride on the back of the rediscovery of Neoplatonism:

> The potentialities open to human integrity were greatly enhanced by the tide of Neoplatonism which swept through Renaissance Europe. The revival of this, the last school of ancient pagan philosophy, fostered a disposition to blur the difference between matter and spirit. Instead of being regarded as an inanimate mass, the earth was deemed to be alive. The cosmos was an organic unity in which every part bore a sympathetic relationship to the rest. Even colours, letters, and numbers were endowed with magical properties.
>
> The investigation of such phenomena was the business of the philosopher, and their employment that of the magician.[4]

Both Waite and Williams, particularly in their later works, believed this religious and intellectual milieu provided the orthodox Christian with insights into an authentic semimystical tradition that served the Christian quest for both truth and transformation. We have noted that critics of Williams respond to this reintroduction of pre-Christian syncretism with anxiety. The issue that divides those who follow the interests of Williams and Waite on the one side and those who are concerned to maintain a *cordon sanitaire* on the other is the question of whether metaphysical authenticity can be found outside the Christian tradition as it developed in European intellectual culture. The understanding of the cosmos as an "organic unity" in which matter and spirit were not divided is part of the distinctive Hebrew culture that is maintained throughout the Old Testament. Gnosticism and its many variants introduced the unhelpful division of spirit and matter onto the religious agenda, one from which Christianity never fully freed itself. Waite and Williams may well have the more orthodox revelatory tradition on their side as they take back into the Christian tradition elements that could only be restored through exploration of the heterodox.

The intellectual study of magic and associated arts emerged in the Florentine Renaissance with the Platonism of Ficino and Pico della Mirandola. Paracelsus and Cornelius Agrippa spread the movement to northern Europe. Both the nature and definitions of magic were a matter of wide and energetic debate. But magic had not always been seen as antipathetic to the intellectual quest. From the middle of the seventeenth century most serious scientists were moving from an animistic view of the universe to a mechanical one. But for much of the previous period magical inquiry possessed at least a degree of intellectual respectability. The boundaries between religious and academic integrity were at that time blurred. William Vaughan wrote in 1600: "Nowadays among the common people, he is not adjudged any scholar at all, unless he can tell men's horoscopes, cast out devils or hath some skill at sooth-saying."[5]

The link of alchemy and the magic that it entailed with sanctity was originally a close one. Whatever the doctrinal fissures between established faith and the more hidden scientific arts, alchemy was seen as requiring a degree of spiritual discipline and purity:

> [A]t this level the practice of magic became a holy quest; the search for knowledge, not by study and research, but by revelation. The notion that purity of life was an essential preliminary to scientific discovery ran through the long history of alchemy and shaped the Rosicrucianism of the seventeenth century. It remains uncertain whether the Fraternity of the Rosy Cross ever had more than a symbolic existence, but its values were familiar: they went back to the ancient tradition of *gnosis:* the seeking of knowledge by revelation, through prayer fasting and communion with God. From this point of view, religion and magic were not rivals, but travelling companions along the path to one identical and comprehensive truth. Religious perfection would bring magical power.[6]

Waite had been influenced in similar ways by this school of spirituality. He wrote in his work *The Hidden Church of the Holy Graal:*

> [W]e have to lay down one irrevocable law—that he who has resolved setting all other things aside—to enter the path of the Quest must look for his progress in proportion as he pursues holiness for his own sake. He who in the Secret Orders dreams of the adeptship, which they claim *ex hypothesi,* to impart to those who can receive, and who does not sanctify his heart till his lips are cleansed, and then does not say it with his lips, is not so much far from the goal as without having conceived regarding it.[7]

Charles Williams's poetry and prose demonstrate this view, as will be shown.

The Decline of Alchemy in the Seventeenth Century

Alchemical preoccupations were common among certain members of the Anglican clergy of the seventeenth century. Notable among them were the Bishop of Worcester, John Thornborough (who was also Robert Fludd's patron), and William Oughtred, also known as a mathematician. Two prominent hermeticists in the mid-seventeenth century, Thomas Vaughan and John Everard, had both been Anglican clergymen, though Everard became a Familist.[8] Evidently it was among the more mystically minded sects that alchemy proved most popular.

Anglican culture on the whole associated alchemy and magic with pre-Reformation spirituality, but in this was partly mistaken. The adherents of Anglicism were of course the product, and were deeply influenced by the Renaissance discovery of the classical tradition. However, the overlap between magic and pre-Reformation religious issues can be discerned in the way that the medieval church had tried to counter the popular use of magic by developing a rival system of ecclesiastical magic to take its place. The ecclesiastical magic that it used was fundamentally undermined by the Protestant solution, which was to replace ritual with rationalism. This exercise was of only limited success since magic constantly crept back into the popular religious perception. The Protestant emphasis on self-help and prayer helped change that direction. Seventeenth-century rationalism effectively drove magic and alchemy from the sphere of intellectual concern. The dominance of the mechanical philosophy that underlay scientific rationalism effectively displaced scholastic Aristotelianism and Neoplatonic theory, both of which were its rivals. With the collapse of the microcosmic theory went the entire intellectual basis of astrology, chiromancy, alchemy, and all their associates. If the universe was subject to immutable mechanistic laws, two fundamental changes were bound to follow. There would be less or, for some, no room for any belief in the process of prayer and the notion of divine intervention.[9] The Cartesian concept of matter dismissed the concept of spirits to an imaginary world. Conjuration ceased to be either meaningful or intellectually respectable.

However swift the decline of hermetic science, it was to provide a way forward for science if not for religion. It gave rise to some remarkable discoveries, including the circulation of the blood. The mystical insistence that numbers were the key to everything also played its part in the revival of mathematics; astrology, in kind, nurtured astronomy in being concerned with the observation of the planets, their movements, and the consequent measurement of time. Alchemy was to later develop into chemistry, though it was not until the twentieth century and the development of atomic theory that transmutation in the form of the transformation of elements took place.[10]

The Resurgence of the Alchemical in A. E. Waite

> There is no labyrinth which it is quite so difficult to thread as the Theatrum Chemicum. It is beset on every side with pitfalls, and its clues, though not destroyed have been buried beneath the ground.[11]

Alchemy became chemistry as the manipulation of the elements was separated from the human quest for personal transformation and change. But Waite wanted to bring the skills for material change back in touch with the deeper human quest, and alchemy provided the language with which to achieve that. His engagement with these ideas of alchemical transmutation is found in two substantial works.

The Hidden Church of the Holy Graal set out the history of the Grail legends and Waite's own distinctive interpretation of quasi-Gnostic strands that inform his whole approach to spirituality. This inspiration lies behind his founding of a neo-Rosicrucian secret society for the transmission of these and similar ideas that so influenced Williams.[12] Waite's second book in this area, *The Secret Tradition of Alchemy,*[13] is a long and dense historical approach to the subject. In the chapter "The Mystic Side of Alchemy" he details the link between the Fellowship of the Rosy Cross and its alchemical antecedents. In 1784 the alchemical quest was being pursued along the two paths that were both contrasted as well as harmonized by Heinrich Khunrath, Jacob Böhme, and, to some extent, Robert Fludd.

> The great work in its proper and plenary understanding is spiritual, and it is this only which matters for those who are on the quest of reality—transmutation performed in the spirit rather than that of physics.[14] It is affirmed categorically that the transmutation of human nature is Alchemy and that man must therefore be iron so that he may become gold.[15]

In his book *The Hidden Church of the Holy Graal* Waite returns to a number of these central themes. He makes the straightforward connection between the mystery of the Eucharist and the transformation that alchemy concerns itself with.

> The same exalted mystery which lies behind the symbols of Bread and Wine lies behind the undeclared priesthood which is according to the Order of Melchisedech, was expressed by the alchemists under the guise of transmutation; but it is understood that I refer here to the secret school of adeptship which had taken over in another transcendent interest the terminology and processes of occult metallurgy.[16]

Waite chides the traditional church for not understanding that the Grail indicates there is more to the Eucharist than just the provision of grace. But that is the message of the Grail to those who can read it. Waite asserts,

> Now it is indubitably the message of the Graal that there is more in the Eucharist than is indicated by the sufficing graces imparted to the

> ordinary communicant, and if it is possible to show that behind this undeclared excess there lies that which has at all times been sought by the Wise, that *est in sacramento quicquid quod quaerunt sapientes,* then the Graal literature will enter after a new manner into our heritage from the past, and another corner will be lifted on the path of knowledge.[17]

If the connection between alchemy and the Eucharist is not obvious, Waite sets out to establish it. He realizes that it may appear almost "fantastic" that he should attempt to use the old and dubious science of metallic transmutation to shed light on the Eucharistic element of the Grail mystery. The thrust of his research would be to establish that the great Eucharistic experiment had its "analogy" in the rationale that lies behind alchemy. He also suggests that the Grail tradition provided a means of properly Christianizing both the Q'abalistic and Masonic traditions. He theorized that the loss or diminution of the Grail tradition acted as a vehicle of Eucharistic and transformative theology and thus it contributed to what he described as the "loss of the word in Q'abalism and in the symbolic science of masonry."[18]

Waite criticized the church's failure to incorporate the insights of the Grail tradition. This omission undermined its ability to recognize that transmutation was central to the mystery of the Christian's journey toward unity with the godhead. Waite felt that a further exploration of the implications of the Grail for Eucharistic theology would provide a means to that unity.

> The Graal at its highest is the simulacrum or efficacy of the Divine mystery within the church. If she as an institution, has failed so far—and as to the failure within limits there is no question—in the transmutation of humanity, the explanation is merely that she has been at work upon gross and refractory elements—though this is true assuredly—but that in the great mystery of her development she has still to enter into the fruition of her higher consciousness. Hereof are the wounds of the Church and for this reason she has been in sorrow throughout the ages.[19]

Williams followed up Waite's critique and concern. He was to adopt the Grail legend as his means of constructing a cycle of poetry that he could use as a vehicle for his own treatment of transmutation. The genre was not to be set within the strict alchemical tradition. Instead, he would construct a hermetic culture that would serve to introduce the richness of alchemical insights to traditional Christian orthodoxy. The quest for the Grail and the emphasis on transformation and integration would be expressed in hermetic imagery.

In Waite's view, and to some extent in Williams's also, Western theological culture lacked the conceptual means to describe the fuller vision of what Williams was to call co-inherent transformation.

The Language of Alchemical Transmutation in Williams

Although Williams's early preoccupations are often framed in alchemical language, his thought develops considerably thereafter. Later transmutation grows into the wider metaphysic of universal interdependent exchange. The clearest example of the early tensions is found and explored in his first novel, *Shadows of Ecstasy.* Throughout Williams's writings he uses not only occult symbolism in his poetry, and devises plots that depend upon the occult for their framework and substance, but also employs notions of transformation as well. Williams consistently uses the alchemical term "transmutation" (as Waite did also) and repeatedly demonstrates his dependence on alchemical ideology.

Williams's thought progresses from "transformation" being expressed in the individualistic language of alchemical transmutation to his more fully developed concept of "exchange" that occupies a central place in his overall scheme of co-inherence. Among his most prominent stylistic mannerisms is the way in which he continues to use the alchemical term "transmutation" where more conventional Christian language has been content with "transformation." St. Paul writes, for example, "Do not be conformed to this world but be transformed by the renewal of your mind."[20]

While Williams intends the same meaning as St. Paul, he frequently uses the hermetic "transmutation" instead. As he matures he develops its meaning into a wider concept of a change toward interdependence and integration. He took the language of alchemical transmutation he inherited from Waite, and developed it into a richer concept that moved from the isolationism of personal transformation into the mutuality of co-inherent universal exchange. The language that had been the preserve of the agnostic adept thus developed into the universal language of Christendom.

Three pieces of writing reflect his intermittent dependence on the alchemical vocabulary of transmutation. In his early work *A Myth of Shakespeare* (1928), Williams hints at his own poetic ambitions. Shakespeare, "the poet," justifies his work to Beaumont as follows:

> You wrong yourself too much. No . . . no . . .
> I am stifled with it. See you, when at first
> The sun we call Apollo strikes on us,

Forth peep the primroses and gillyflowers . . .
. . . What's beyond?
What's in the sun's self, the vastidity
And circumambulation of the world
Which lights the rest? I don't misjudge my play.
There's freshness in it, youth and decent age;
But the last secret—but age touched with youth,
Ripeness of being, ripeness of poetry;
No longer life transmuted into words,
But words transmuted into life and veined
From the blood at the centre, having one beat with that;
Immortal not with poor everlastingness
But out of starry knowledge into . . . stuff—
That's not there.[21]

The italicized words well describe his role as a poet using the "magic" of the poetic imagination to transform existence from the mundane into the visionary.

In his play *The Chaste Wanton* (1930), the Duchess is presented to the alchemist Vincenzo, who is described as "a master of Philosophy in the Sorbonne of a large repute in alchemy."[22] As they discuss the virtues of alchemy, she says that she knows little of it, but that they appear to share the same overall views, and he explains its significance.

Vincenzo: All is significant that undergoes
process and transmutation; all that flies,
obedient or rebellious, into change,
whether in the unknowledgeable salt of earth
or the knowledgeable spirit of a man.
The Duchess: Messer Vincenzo, do your studies teach
that change hath meaning?
Vincenzo: Not to the idle dust
flying in clouds from where men quarry stone,
nor to the wolf-cub fleshing his young claws,
but to the will that knows each change a depth
enlarged within it, from the abyss whereof
arise auguster giants of consciousness,
more antique genii, more original truth,
swallowing the earlier. Highness, if you doubt,
your studies miss the root of all.

In the discussion later in the play as to what love exactly may be, Vincenzo is given an authoritative tone as he describes it as alchemy:

> Vincenzo: Love laughing to itself, Love mightily
> prevailing in its work alchemical
> to change our souls and sinews; yea that art
> whereof the theory and experiment
> brings forth the black stone to the white and red,
> with its uncouthness civilized in heaven.
> We are the stone; the art, the chemists we.[23]

The Duchess, who seems to be rehearsing the *Via Negativa,* argues that it is for nuns and saints, not for her. Vincenzo replies in a passionate defense of love alchemical:

> Do not believe it; 'tis for all or none.
> We have lost the adepts formula—'tis no more
> vocally uttered; 'tis discoverable
> but in the operation: which you know
> in the excitements and loose transmutations
> of the first stages—ask the thrilling blood—
> but to become God, but to be God—nay,
> elswise to think were to turn infidel,
> Islamite.

Williams is of course aware of the debate he extends in *Shadows of Ecstasy* over the nuances of union with the godhead, and has the Bishop rebuke Vincenzo for his language, "Take heed sir; you talk rashly. To be God—I sniff the heretic." Vincenzo's riposte is in the classical Johannine language of union:[24]

> O my good lord, what saith the Testament?
> I, Love, will come and make my abode in him.
> What saith the Canon? This is my body and blood;
> shall this be more than we who live by it?
> No gift, no benediction, but my blood.

Toward the end of the play, when rejected by the Duchess, Vincenzo is chided by the Bishop:

Now my deep alchemist, cannot your fires
burn prosperously for the bridal day?
cannot her chemist to her bridals bring
the philosophical tincture for a gift
making her plate gold as the Prince her days?

Vincenzo: O my lord,
the Red Dragon is too volatile; he flies
zenith to nadir—the infixed mercury
looses the colour, then the seventh house
fades—all's amerced with liquid. If it
stood in the Rosicrucian fire—your lordship knows
how the black shifts: there's the first calculation
spraying the salt right: but the pallor's red.
The Red—there's no help but at the Red.[25]

The last lines in the play speak of a deeper alchemy that takes place in the form of a transformation of vision:

Duchess: Can there be any miracles but this,
that I was blind: you touched me, and I saw?
Vincenzo: And now you touch me also, and I see.[26]

The Taliessin cycle contains a wide range of images drawn from pagan and Christian and astrological and literary forms of myth. Although Williams's range of imagery has widened, alchemy is still to be found, as we are told of the journey of Galahad, Guinevere's son:

Fierce in the prow the alchemical Infant burned,
red by celerity now conceiving the White;
behind him the folded silver column of Percivale,
hands on the royal shoulders, closed wings of flight,
inhaled the fine air of philosophical amazement;
Bors, mailed in black, completing the trine. . . .
By three ways of exchange the City sped to the City;
against the off-shore wind that blew from Sarras
the ship and the song flew.[27]

A few verses later Galahad leans against the wind and is described as glowing white, in a phrase reminiscent of the transfiguration of Christ. While the ship is propelled by wind that is driven by doves' wings (with all the biblical imagery that is thus evoked) both Galahad and the wind sing "*Judica, te, Deus.*"[28] In much the same way as Pauline's change is depicted in *Descent into Hell*, here transmutation has become transfiguration.

When Williams writes on Milton, he castigates academic critics who, opposed to high speculations on the great nature of chastity, had been unable to appreciate the great miracle of the "transmutation of flesh" proposed in *Comus*.[29] When commenting upon that seminal phrase in Wordsworth, the "feeling intellect," Williams describes the *Prelude* as a work of "transmutation and union."[30]

In his later work, he uses much the same concepts. When Williams describes the changed eyes of the Virgin Mary in *The Figure of Beatrice*, he writes, "Virgil could hardly, without (in spite of the Fourth Eclogue) ceasing to be Virgil, have addressed himself with passion to the glory of the Virgin-Mother. But this is necessary; it is she into whose eyes the eyes of Beatrice are transmuted."[31] Furthermore, when he deals with the *Inferno*, robbers are bitten and they are not changed, but transmuted; "Robbers, stung by serpents and transmuted into serpents."[32] But more significant, when gazing upon the double nature of adored womanhood that he will refer to as the reality of romantic love, he once more looks into eyes, and sees,

> These then are the eyes of the Florentine girl; this is the origin of Amor. He looks; he sees her "shining eyes" gazing into the eyes of the Griffin; he sees the double nature mirrored in hers.
>
> "*Come in lo specchio il sol, non altrimenti*
> *la doppia fiera dentro vi raggiava,*
> *or con uni, or con altri reggimenti*—

Williams translates this into his own and the reader's vision:

> As the sun in a mirror, not otherwise shone the twofold beast within them, now with the one, now with the other nature. Think, reader, if I wondered in myself when I saw the thing motionless in itself and transmuting in its image.

He then comments, "It is this fact which not then understood or expressed, underlay the whole *Vita*. . . . Love, that then 'unknown mode of being' has shown him in Beatrice a reflection of the exchanged Two Natures . . . this uncovenanted mercy, . . . stupor rides in our very nature—within and without the Church: say rather, this is that ancient covenant which reveals what all others support. 'My covenant will be in your flesh.'"[33] The process of transmutation reveals the essential nature of our gifted divinity and shows our unity with the divine, and it also changes us internally.

But Williams's development can be most clearly traced over the span of his many novels.[34] *Shadows of Ecstasy,* his first novel, has as its central theme, as we shall see, the lure of transmutation, and the possibilities and potentialities inherent in it. By his penultimate novel, *Descent into Hell,* he has developed a very different attitude to change. Here again, the metaphysical authenticity of a life is dependent on the existence of a capacity for change; and those who do not change are faced with the prospect of ultimate decay. Simon the Clerk in *All Hallows' Eve,* his last novel, will also practice the same energies that inspired Considine in *Shadows.* But Williams's diagnosis of them is more discriminating. The energies are now either devoted to the sustenance of the web of co-inherence, or else they are perverse, or inverted. He has refined his metaphysical agnosticism.

The Development from Alchemy to Co-inherence in the Novels

Williams wrote his novels between 1926 and 1945. They offer an opportunity to chart the ideological evolution of the development of Williams's schema from the Rosicrucian world-order of Waite, with its notions of gnostic adeptship and alchemical aspiration, to a wider and more mature Doctrine of Correspondence that Williams names co-inherence. Sadly it is outside the scope of this book to work through each novel in close detail, but a study of the first two novels and the last two novels demonstrates a distinctive movement in his presentation of adeptship, transmutation, energy, power, and love. His first two novels display a certain ambiguity about the use of power by an adept. Readers have always been concerned about the degree of sympathy and affirmation that he confers on Considine. Williams seems almost too familiar and at ease with the goetic. His apparent sympathetic treatment of the dark arts casts something of a shadow over his treatment and interpretation of energy and its transmutation. His treatment of magic seems to lie awkwardly across the boundary that separates the realm of Christianized culture from the occult in his two earliest novels. But by his last two novels, power, energy, and adeptship have themselves evolved and been transmuted and redefined by the broader and more subtle concepts of exchange and substitution within the co-inherence.

Exploration of the progression from the earlier to the later novels will illustrate the development in Williams's thought between 1926; that is, from when the outlines of *The Black Bastard* were laid down, and 1945, just before his death, when *All Hallows' Eve* was published. *The Black Bastard* was not published until 1933, and even then it appeared in a slightly reworked form and with a new title as *Shadows of Ecstasy.* Two other novels are *War in Heaven* (1931) and *Descent into Hell* (1937).

In the earliest of the novels, *Shadows of Ecstasy,* Williams demonstrates his interest in the notion of an energy that may act as a means of expressing power in some metaphysical or magical sense. This preoccupation has its roots in the conceptual framework of magic and the language of the occult. The novel is littered with references to alchemical concerns with transmutation of the individual and the way in which this transformation might be achieved. The central theme of *War in Heaven* is the "Graal" and the energies that it evokes and that surround it. By taking these two early novels, we can tease out the way in which the ideas of alchemy, change, and exchange develop in Williams's work in the early 1930s.

Alchemy and Transmutation in Shadows of Ecstasy

Shadows of Ecstasy, like the other novels that Williams wrote, contains a range of voices and personalities that display and reflect the width of Williams's own ideas and the complexity of his personality. Williams's fiction, and its portrayal of his own range of personas within it, allows us to chart the development of his own outlook and values. Considine, a master of adepts, is a heroic figure who demands a degree of admiration and even awe. Williams's own immersion in the culture of alchemy provides the spring for the plot. The lectureship that Considine has endowed is "Ritual Transmutations of Energy."[35] From the very beginning of the book it is clear that the setting is Rosicrucian, alchemical, and, at a lower level of significance, magical.

The plot of the book serves as a vehicle for the different voices that argue the case between two parallel ideologies: orthodox Christianity, and a particular form of alchemical experiment—which is understood as poetry—having at its heart the old quest of the adepts, the prolongation or the controlled resurrection of life, and the celebration of ecstasy, driven by a sublimated flow of energy. The way in which the arguments develop in competition throughout the book is particularly striking. Orthodoxy prevails in the end, but only barely. Two particular questions are left at the conclusion of the book; the second is whether Considine really has failed in his attempts at auto-resurrection. The first and the more subtle, however, is posed by the presentation of the figure of Considine within the novel and within the hierarchy of metaphysical ethics that Williams is adopting and endorsing thereby. This is the question that I call "The Ambiguity of Considine."[36]

The enigma posed by the last pages of the novel is teasingly provocative. Here Williams pens such passages as the following:

> Roger tried to order his thoughts, but they only repeated themselves: "Considine is dead; is he dead?" Was he dead? or would he, first again in the great experiment, achieve the work he had desired? The question beat at his brain as he ran.[37]
>
> Nigel Considine was dead; the treachery he had despised had taken him; the final dereliction had swallowed him. If he returned—but Roger fled from that return. His nerve broke.[38]

On the final page, Williams toys with the reader through the uncertain musings of Roger, driven by his dream of Considine's survival:

> If he returned. If he carried out the experiment of his vision, the purpose of his labours. If he, first among his peers, when all believed him lost, thrust himself out of the place of shades back into immortal and transmuted life, if he held death at his disposal, if he knew how the vivid ecstasy of experience dominated all shapes and forms, all accidents of time and place. If he came now humming those last songs which the greatest of poets had made his own from his vision of Ariel flying free, smiling at the blindness of extreme pain and the paralysis of extreme possession, guardian of myths and expositor of power . . . if he returned. . . . [I]f—Ah beyond, beyond belief !—but if he returned.[39]

The question left hanging in the air at the end of the novel acts as a crossroads on the metaphysical map that Williams has traced. On the one hand, on the road that assumes the impossibility of Considine's return lies Christian orthodoxy. On the other hand, the road that envisages the possibility of the triumph of esoteric adeptship allows for the existence of a different metaphysical ordering of things. The reader is left to guess which road on this map Williams endorses.

If orthodoxy has after all triumphed through the apparent death of the master adept, it is a triumph that Williams undermines through his attempt to tantalize the reader. This may simply be a strategy to sustain the level of drama on the final page. But it also offers a certain level of authorial endorsement to Considine's experiment. Williams endows his antiheroes in the first two works with a degree of dramatic and personal sympathy that is entirely lacking in the case of Wentworth and Simon the Clerk in the last two novels, who represent damnation of an unambiguous kind.

The sympathy we find for Considine is created by the deliberate ambiguity of all that Considine represents. As the novel progresses, an energetic debate between the values of what we can loosely call Rosicrucianism, which Considine embodies, and those of more orthodox religious metaphysics takes place. There is a third worldview that Williams sets out to expose and then criticize through ridicule, that of the decaying English secular post-Christian culture. It was rooted in the Enlightenment, but in his estimation failed to act as a channel of spiritual and ethical enlightenment. On the contrary, he felt that it led to a fear of death and an abandonment of love. The plot of the novel contains a moment when the High Executive of African Sovereigns breaks into a radio broadcast with a warning that contains elements of Williams's own critique of his culture:

> It urges the English to consider carefully what they are fighting, and if any among them believe that in love and art and death rather than in logic and science the kingdom of man lies, it entreats them not to any transfer of allegiance, for it recognises in the folly of patriotism a means of obedience to the same passionate imagination, but to a demonstration on behalf of peace. In the name of their own loyalties it appeals to the children of passion and imagination; in the name of a vaster strength than their own, it threatens the children of pedantry and reason.[40]

Williams uses Considine's opinions to ridicule the apathy of the decayed culture of the Enlightenment, using a critique rooted in the alternative values of the hermetic worldview. In this detachment from the basic values of his own culture lies the strength and potency of Williams's hermetic critique:

> I have let the English feel panic, panic such as they have not felt since the Vikings raided their coasts and burned their towns a thousand years ago. They have been afraid of their feelings, of ecstasy and riot and savage glee; they have frozen love and hated death.[41]

The debate that Williams sets up between the two opposing "ways" in the novel is founded on an enigmatic presentation of Considine as a magus, but he is also magisterial and attractive, both for his potency and also for his multifaceted role as prophet, magus, and explorer. He is set against rationalistic modernity and secularism.[42]

From the moment of his formal reply at the university dinner, Considine sets an agenda that provides an alternative to the contemporary intellectual European culture, which is seen as being trapped in the process of decay. He challenges it with a revivified hermeticism:

> [For] the children are growing and the old man is dying. . . . [I] have wondered whether there may not be colleges and faculties of other experiences than yours . . . [a] more intense passion for discovery, new raptures, unknown paths of glorious knowledge . . . [w]hether the fakirs, the herdsmen, the witch-doctors may not enter the kingdom of man before you.[43]

This deliberate echoing of the challenge to the Pharisees in Matthew 21:31 acts to invoke messianic status for Considine himself. Outside the confines of the novel, such colleges and faculties were to be found in the arenas of hermetic exploration represented by both the Order of the Golden Dawn and the Fellowship of the Rosy Cross.

Even if this messianic gauntlet thrown down before a faintly sterile image of academe did not expose the interest the author was investing in Considine as a character, the imprimatur for "poet-adept" is bestowed on him. There can scarcely be a higher accolade from the author. Sir Bernard quizzes Roger as to his developing interest:

> On the other side Roger also moved. "It's true" he said. "He's right."
>
> Sir Bernard, a little startled, looked at him. Was Roger becoming a convert to this new Gospel? He said, "You believe in him?"
>
> "No," Roger said, "but I believe he knows what poetry is, and I never met a man before who did."[44]

In the words of the High Executive, Williams presents an alternative religious and personal agenda—a type of alchemical, aesthetic existentialism—that embodies many of the elements that he himself promoted through his own writing:

> To those among the peoples of Europe who know that their lives have origin and nourishment in the great moments of the exalted imagination,[45] the High Executive offers salute and recognition. To all who owe their devotion to music, to poetry, to painting and sculpture, to the servants of every more than rational energy; greater than those and more

> numerous, to all who at this present moment exist in the exchanged or un-exchanged adoration of love, it calls more especially.[46]

Not only is this a call to all those who live in the Way of Affirmation but the particular call to those who know about exchange and the imagination is the purest Williams.[47] As the novel progresses, the path of exploration Considine urges upon his listeners continues to parallel at best, and mimic at worst, the conventional Christian voice. When Ian Caithness determines to offer a mass for the rescued King Inkamasi to attempt to free him from his hypnotic trance, Sir Bernard replies, "My dear Ian, you've no idea of how like Mr. Considine's conversation yours is."[48]

During the mass, the power of the magus-adept is matched by the power of the priest-adept in the person of the Celebrant; and the parallelism continues as the Archbishop effects his work of "cutting and binding." A primitive form of competition takes place between the forms of adeptship. The Archbishop confronts power with power: "By the power of Immanuel who only is perfect man, by his power committed unto us, we recall all powers in thee to their natural obedience."[49] The two ways vie with each other in a contest of potency. Considine offers Roger the possibility of the consummation of his artistic instinct in a presentation of a quest that, apart from its context, could sound thoroughly Christian. The opening exchange with Sir Bernard evokes a degree of ambiguity sympathetic to Rosicrucianism:

> Sir Bernard said: "It's a little cheap, isn't it? The conquest of death?"
>
> "There are two things it might mean," Considine said, "living for ever or dying and living again. And will you tell me, Mr Ingram, that you haven't felt one or both of these when you deal with great verse?" . . . [P]hilip saw Roger's face change. He was looking steadily at Considine and continued to look for over a minute before he answered. In that time the sardonic and almost bitter humour which often showed in him, as if he were weary of fighting that stupidity against which "the gods themselves contend in vain," and as if he despised himself both for the strife and weariness—that half angry mockery vanished, and it was with a sudden passionate sincerity that he said , "No, no; you're right. One dies and lives in it, but I can't tell how."[50]

We hear the undiluted accent of Williams himself in the mouth of Considine as he replies in language that bridges both the Affirmative Ways of poetic spirituality and "Romantic Theology":

> "Only because you haven't looked that way," Considine said with an illuminating smile."[51] You handle the stuff of the experiment, the stuff which the poets made, but they made it out of what is common to us all, and there are things which they, even they never knew. And as for love, is there any one of us, since we are men and have loved, who doesn't know that there is within the first moments of that divine delight some actuality of the conquest of death?[52]

Perhaps only the term "experiment" betrays the esoteric roots of Considine's philosophy in this fusion of the conventional and the exotic.

Whatever ambiguity there may be in Considine's robust presentation of the lure of adeptship that was in Williams's mind at this point, Williams makes it clear he is only too aware of the alternative mode of interpretation that is presented in the character of Isabel. It will be her accent and not Considine's that will provide the more evolved metaphysics of the later novels.

The Re-presentation of Rosenkreutz and His Experiment

When *Die Chymische Hochzeit Christiani Rosenkreutz* was published in Strasbourg in 1616, with its great experiment of trial and resurrection of the guests at Rosenkreutz's wedding, the text acted as a template for the experiments of the Renaissance adepts and the quest for a further evolution. Waite sums up the preoccupations of this tradition with its themes of transmutation, experiment, adeptship, and union.

> There is another school of occult students who believe themselves to have discovered in alchemy a philosophical experiment which far transcends any physical achievement. . . .
>
> The hermetic experience was a spiritual experiment, and the achievement a spiritual achievement.
>
> The exaltation of the base nature in man, by the development of his latent powers; the purification, conversion and transmutation of man; the achievement of a hypostatic union of man with God.
>
> Not only was all this the concealed aim of alchemy but the process by which this union was effected, veiled under the symbolism of chemistry, is the process with which the literature is concerned, which process also is described by all veritable adepts.
>
> From the standpoint of this criticism the power which operates in the transmutation of metals alchemically, is in the main, a psychic power.

> That is to say, a man who has passed a certain point in his spiritual development, after the mode of the mystics, has a knowledge and control of physical forces which are not in the possession of ordinary humanity
>
> As to this point, there is nothing inherently unreasonable in the conception that an advancing evolution, whether in the individual or in the race, will give a far larger familiarity with the mysteries and laws of the universe.[53]

Considine's reply to Roger is identical to Waite's description, except that the means of the experiment is now the notion or experience of ecstasy evoked by poetry, art, or love:

> The Middle Ages wondered at visions of the truth—alchemy, sorcery, fountains of youth, these are part of the dream. The Renascence knew the splendour but lost the meaning, and it was tempted by learning and scholarship, and ravaged by Calvin and Ignatius with their systems, and it withered into the eighteenth century.
>
> "But the time is very near now."
>
> Roger said, "But how, but how."
>
> Considine answered, "By the transmutations of your energies, evoked by poetry or love, or any manner of ecstasy, into the power of a greater ecstasy."[54]

The catechetical examination of Nielsen by Considine, who is described as "the ardent postulant of transmuted energy,"[55] sets the agenda for the great experiment in the evolution of adeptship. Williams, when describing the spiritual heights to be mastered, does so in the language of love. Once again, the notion of love that Considine describes has an ambiguity about it. Considine presents his energies as being founded on what Williams would present as an attractive but false resolution of opposites, the fusion of love and hate.[56] Considine's journey began in an experience of frustrated and rejected love, but develops into a quest for ecstasy, founded on sublimated sex and the fusion of love and hate. Williams will come to describe the practice of love more accurately in his later novels. Considine offers his apologia:

> I have endured love and transmuted it. I have found, when I was young, that the sensual desire of man can be changed into strength of imagination, and a physical burden become the bearer of the burden. I have transmuted masculine sex into human life. I am one of the masters of

> love. And I've done this with all things—whatever I have loved or hated, I have poured the strength of every love and hate into my own life and what is behind my life, and now I need love and hate no more . . . [b]ut now I long to go further.[57]

The nature of this further step is referred to in the classical terms of orthodox alchemy as evolution; the second communication of the High Executive runs, "The second evolution of man has begun."[58] Williams anticipates the quest for development of human potential that New Age spirituality will embody and Jungian language will describe as individuatation. The old dogmas will be set against a hunger for a new and different kind of experience.

Dogma, Dichotomy, and Death in Shadows of Ecstasy

In the next juxtaposition of two ways, the issues crystallize into one that is old dogma opposing revisited experience. Roger's complaint is that orthodoxy fails to deliver the necessary experience and offers no real protection against the debilitating fear of death. A dialogue takes place between Sir Bernard and Roger. While presenting the voice of rational skepticism, Sir Bernard acts a foil to Roger's increasing, despairing hunger for some deeper form of aesthetic actuality. King Inkamasi strikes a note of wisdom that will represent part of the final synthesis in the final ontological outcome: "I do not think mankind can be saved without the intellect and without God." To which Sir Bernard soberly replies, "It must be the first time in the history of the world that those powers have been united."[59] Williams appears to present each of these different voices in the debate that follows as representing some aspect of his own views. Sir Bernard and Roger enter the debate as antagonists, one the voice of European intellectual and aesthetic culture, the other the questing artistic existentialist with gnostic appetites.

> "Sir Bernard and I don't believe the same things," Roger said. "I can't stop him but I won't have anything to do with it."
>
> Philip got up—for him violently. "Roger," he cried out, "what are you talking about? Are you on this man's side?"
>
> "Yes I am," Roger said. "At least I can't go against him. He knows there's something in it, and which of you does that?"

King Inkamasi answers that he knows it very well, and declares he will kill Considine as a consequence.

> "You've a right to do as you please," Roger answered, "but I haven't. I've no right except to follow what I know when I find it."
>
> "Roger," Sir Bernard said dulcetly, "is it Mr Considine's feeling about poetry that affects you so much? Because the unfortunate white race has not been entirely silent. Was Dante a Bantu, or Shakespeare a Hottentot? A few of us read it still."
>
> "O read it!" Roger said contemptuously. "God knows I don't want to live for ever, but I tell you this fellow knows. So do I—a little bit, and I believe it's important. More important than anything else on earth. And I won't help you shut it up in a refrigerator when I ought to be helping keep it alive." "Can't you leave that to God?" Caithness flung out.
>
> "No," said Roger, "I damn well can't, when he's left it to me. I know your argument—it's all been done, death has been conquered, and so as nothing ever dies somewhere else, we needn't worry about its dying here. Well thank you very much, but I do."[60]

Sir Bernard's response is one that Williams was to develop with greater clarity in *The Figure of Beatrice.* One of his most consistent concerns, and one that underlies the whole structure of his vision of the unitive holding together of all things in the co-inherence, is the rejection of "dichotomy."[61] Whereas until now Sir Bernard has pronounced with the tones of laconic skepticism, Williams gives him a speech that provides an antidote for Roger's self-centeredness.

> "Really Roger must you dichotomize in this appalling way? It's so barbarian. It went out with the Victorians. If you insist that you are betraying an 'Ode to a Nightingale' or something by agreeing to call on the Prime Minister, must you insist that your emotions are so universal?"

Roger's response evokes the perennially present harnessing of power and energy, and raises the bidding from Keats to Milton and Shakespeare, effectively trumping with Williams's favorite suit.

> "O you're charming, you're lovely all of you, but how much do you care what the great ones are doing? And in the centuries you've nearly killed it, with your appreciations and your fastidious judgements, and your lives of this man and your studies in that. What do you know about 'huge and mighty forms' that do not live like living men? Power, power, it's dying in you, and you don't hunger or feel it live. What's Milton, what's Shakespeare, to you?"[62]

As Caithness dismisses Roger's rhetoric, in the name of the church—entirely missing the point of the argument, and assuming it to be a "literary discussion"—Roger explodes with heterodox fury, "Can't you understand any other gospel than your own damned dogmas?"

It is clear from the route the argument has been constructed to follow that Roger's frustration was one that Williams himself had some significant sympathy with. Caithness is not the magnetic central figure that his ecclesiastical orthodoxy might bestow on him. Roger is demanding exactly the element that is missing from the spiritual and intellectual quest taking place within the status quo. The critique he is pursuing may frame itself in terms of power and energy, but its final purpose is transmutation with union as its goal. The last word is given to Sir Bernard, who is also conscious of the need for union, and so the parallelism is continued:

> He saw the intellect and logical reason of man no longer as a sedate and necessary thing, but rather a narrow silver bridge passing over an immense depth, around the high guarded entrance of which thronged clouds of angry and malign presences. Often mistaking the causes and often misjudging the effects of all mortal sequences, this capacity of knowing cause and effect presented itself nevertheless as the last stability of man. Always approaching truth, it could never, he knew, be truth, for nothing can be truth until it has become one with its object and such union it was not given to the intellect to achieve, without losing its own nature. But in its divine and abstract reflection of the world, its passionless mirror of the holy law that governed the world, not in experiments or ecstasies or guesses, the supreme perfection of mortality moved.[63]

When Caithness falls short in his presentation of the authentic voice of the Christian tradition, it is left to King Inkamasi to provide the final refutation of Considine. The parallelism will continue symbolically as the novel draws to a close since Inkamasi's death will involve Christlike elements of voluntary submission and his self-sacrifice: "And now a child of unknowing things, he set his face to go up to Jerusalem, that the king's crown might be properly received by the unvestmenting hands of Death."[64] It is Inkamasi who is now given messianic associations. His death is mirrored by Considine's own death, which takes place simultaneously. Both of them have parallels with Christ—Inkamasi in the voluntary nature of his sacrifice and Considine, who is shot but who then shares the pattern of Christ's end at the hand of a traitor.

The Ambiguity of Considine

Given that all Williams's novels have the struggle between good and evil running through them—a series of studies in the enigmas of metaphysical morality—*Shadows of Ecstasy* presents something of a difficulty. Most moral tales allow the reader to identify the ethical fault lines of the drama. In the more sophisticated, these fault lines are hidden until the actions or unfolding of the drama reveal what had otherwise been obscured. But in this novel it remains unclear until the end where those fault lines lie. We are presented with a myriad of voices, all of which contain an identifiable tone belonging to the author. Intellectually he bestows the authentic messianic mantle upon King Inkamasi. But the color, the drama, the excitement, and the magnetism are all with Considine. Charles Huttar concludes that there is about Considine, as with Milton's Satan, "A genuine greatness and a breath-taking attractiveness,"[65] and he poses the question why, though he was deeply committed to the Christian tradition throughout his other works, Williams presents Considine so sympathetically.

> What are we to make of the fact that . . . [W]illiam arouses the readers' sympathy for a hero, Nigel Considine, who repudiates that tradition, while of the three avowedly Christian characters in the story, one is a would-be murderer and then a suicide, and another, a priest, connives at murder and has a disagreeable aggressive streak which contrasts unfavourably with the hero's serene self-assurance?[66]

He argues that *Shadows of Ecstasy* belongs to the same stage in the development of Williams's thought as "The Hero in English Verse," in which Williams had not yet broken away from the prevailing critical attitude to *Paradise Lost,* which viewed Satan as a "heroic, even august figure," and God as a "capricious tyran[t]."[67]

The figure of Considine stands at the cusp of the change. It is possible that Considine's charisma reflects the allure that Williams felt at that stage, in the heroic and indomitable adeptship of Satan's self-styled independence against a form of divine oppression. But if Williams felt such an allure, that feeling must reflect the magnetism he experienced in the Rosicrucian culture of adeptship. Waite may have sought to Christianize Rosicrucianism, Q'abalism, and the role of magic, but he did not carry his esoteric culture fully beyond the rich heterodoxy that defined it.

That was Williams's task, but in *Shadows of Ecstasy* he was not yet ready to accomplish it: that would remain to be done in the later novels. There we find his developing treatment of good and evil, transmutation and transfiguration, energy and perversion, power and love. The heroism of the adept and his preoccupation with the change wrought by alchemical practice will give place to the practitioner of substitution. The Doctrine of Correspondence will be extended into the co-inherence of the Web of Exchange. Considine will be represented by Wentworth, or Lily Sammile—Lilith, or Simon the Clerk. Williams was destined to become more discerning and more "accurate."

We may conclude that the ambiguity we find portrayed in Considine reflects something of Williams's own ambiguity. It was as yet unresolved in the face of the competing attractions provided by the esoteric agenda of the Fellowship of the Rosy Cross and conventional orthodoxy.[68] There was not only the lure of aesthetically colored transmutations but also whatever other more heterodox connections provided for their adepts willing to delve further.[69] Williams was clearly familiar with these goetic explorations, as is evident from the rituals in the novels and his grasp of the issues underlying his historical study of witchcraft. He is quite clear about the role of magic: "My father was a surgeon (Considine) answered . . . (a)nd knew something of the old magical traditions; such as are of value, are natural properties of the developing and unstunted nature of man, and the rest are of no value."[70] He is less clear about the heroic status of the adept. Williams may have felt some identification himself with the role of the adept, particularly in the 1920s. The later novels however are characterized by a distancing from this form of heroic adeptship and a clearer ethical boundary that Williams draws between the central roles of love and power, interdependence and independence.

It will become clear that the central issue for Williams is that the danger lies in the perverse more than the profane. Perversion in *Shadows of Ecstasy* is of a milder kind than that which Williams will present us with in his later novels.[71] It has been camouflaged here by an ambiguity that is finally exposed as a perversion of idolatry. But, unlike that of Simon in *All Hallows' Eve,* where the perversion will be the more serious blasphemy, the perversion of idolatry that Considine exposes derives from the confused notion of "self" that lies relatively undisturbed in our popular culture. The Achilles' heel of existentialism is exactly the invitation to displace the One God with the lesser gods of a variety of notions of our "selves." This, finally, despite all talk of union, is what Considine offers, though not without laying down the challenge of the impoverished record of Christianity at enabling the process of transformation into the unity of the godhead.[72]

> I have always, so far as I could, done according to the gospel which moves in me and my friends, the Doctrine of Transmutation of Energy,

> the conscious turning of joy and anguish alike into strength and will, and of that passionate strength and will into all the capacities of man. Such men as the priest who was with you just now will tell you to endure or enjoy because this and that is the will of God—at best but a few of them will tell you to use the experience as a way of uniting yourself with God. In all the generations of Christendom how many have done that?

Inkamasi replies with a statement of christological affirmation that cuts across the arguments and the experiential seduction. "I am a Christian. . . . [I] believe that love and death are at the feet of Jesus who is called Christ."[73]

He also issues his own challenge: "(Death) has been opened once and it is enough. And you—are you sure that man can conquer till he has wholly been defeated? Are you sure that he can know plenitude till he has known utter despair? You will not let him despair of himself, but it may be that only in such a complete despair he finds that which cannot despair and is something other than man." Considine responded, "Despair if you will, and hope that despair may save you. Entreat the gods; I do not refuse you your prayer."[74]

There is no metaphysical argument adduced to recommend one way or the other to the reader. In fact, on the contrary, Williams deliberately introduces an element of doubt for the reader as well as that which consumes Roger on the final pages: "The body of Inkamasi lay on its royal couch, but the body of the master of adepts had disappeared."[75]

The final synthesis is found in the experience of Roger's wife, Isabel, who has come to know both the secret of exchange and the union that derives from the love that enables exchange.

> He had perhaps never entirely trusted her before, for all their sweet friendship. But his defences were down, and he lay exposed, terribly sensitive to her looks and words. She neither sympathized nor condoled; in the deep practice of her love her heart was struck equally with his. She suffered his desolation as she had his desire; the trust of spiritual necessity with which she had charged herself knew this union also. He realised at that moment the vast experience of love which she had undergone, and accepted it.[76]

Williams teases his reader with the possibility of ultimate success for the transmutation of energy and the recapitulation of life that Considine promised and represents. Whatever ambiguities remain, Roger is allowed to meet the union he craved in the experience of exchange within what Williams was to call the "Theology of Romantic Love." So far from the conclusion of the novel celebrating this, the expectations of Roger and Isabel hang equivocally in the air of the narrative, as Williams concludes: "But she wondered whether in his heart he—and she also—secretly awaited a return."[77] The ambiguities of this novel will give way to an increasingly explicit Christian orthodoxy in the next and subsequent novels.

The Decline of the Antihero in War in Heaven

Shadows of Ecstasy uses the material of Rosicrucian alchemy for its dramatic framework. In his second novel, *War in Heaven* (1931), Williams turns to another significant preoccupation of Waite, the Grail legend. The narrative plot concerns the Holy Grail. In terms of the development of Williams's theological ethic, his understanding and presentation of power and ecstasy are refined. So indeed is their relationship with the focus of metaphysical struggle, "the one integrating Good." At this stage there remains the ambiguous parallelism between occult and holy quest. In *Shadows of Ecstasy* the ambiguity is heightened by the symmetry of metaphysical language used by the antagonists. Good and evil, in terms of simplistic drama at least, are here more clearly identifiable. Those who venerate the Grail within the tradition that gave birth to it are literally on the side of the angels, while those who attempt to capture it have about them something of the appeal of the pantomime villain; they are mainly repugnant, but endearing in their obvious villainy.

A different strand in the novel deals with the question of motivation that drives the narrative. In this novel Williams develops a paradox between the external and internal ethic. The internal ethic returns to the same celebration of values of the antihero that exalted Considine. The descriptions of the spirituality of Gregory Persimmons are no longer of the skilled hero-adept, but more those of the mystic *manqué*, the natural man of prayer; i.e., the man who knows what adoration and delight mean in practice; the determined pilgrim who searches assiduously for "The Way" as he understands it; the man who finally is saved by what appears to be a mixture of disillusion incorporating penitence. In the external narrative of the drama the adept is a pantomime villain who hovers between the child snatcher and the repressed pedophile; the sadistic father who enjoys tormenting his son and anyone else he can bully; the thief for whom the ends always justify the means. Williams has yet to resolve this dichotomy, but it has evolved into an integrated ethic by the time he writes his last two novels. In the meantime, there remains something of the early confusion inherent in Considine, his earlier antihero.

The Integration of Spirit and Matter and the Quest for Monotheism

There are two ways in which Williams pursues his concern for the co-inherent reintegration of spirit and matter in this novel. One is through his presentation of the material as holding some kind of memory of energy or power, a form of initially low grade background "arch-natural" radiation, until it is invoked or provoked and so released. The other is through his theological exploration of the ethical consequences of monotheism, which brings him face-to-face with the ancient ethical question that confronts all monotheists: "If God is both good and in control, how may evil be permitted?" In response to this Williams turns (as he does frequently elsewhere) to the theology and metaphysics of Mother Julian and her *Showings,* as we will see. This essential dichotomy, at least, he is determined to resolve.

The worldview espoused by the author depends on how the reader understands the interrelation between spirit and matter embodied in the Graal. Williams sets out to make it very clear, through first the Archdeacon:

> "It interests me very deeply" the Archdeacon agrees. "In one sense of course the Graal is unimportant—it is a symbol far less near reality now than any chalice of consecrated wine. But it is conceivable that the Graal absorbed, as material will, something of the high intensity of the moment when it was used and of its adventures through the centuries."[78]

Gregory Persimmons displays a similar understanding:

> "Say it's what we think, it's been as near the other centre as anything in the world can get," Gregory went on. "And it's been kept pretty deep down in that world all the time. It's close to the place where all things meet and all souls—anyhow their souls."[79]

The Archdeacon takes this holistic view a step further as he finds himself resenting the abuse of his furniture by the apathetic contamination of the incompetent Mr. Batesby:

> The Archdeacon felt a pang, slight but definite, at the idea that this tall, lean, harassed, talkative and inefficient priest would sit in his chair and sleep in his bed; not so much that they were his chair and his bed, as that it seemed a shame that such ready and pleasant things should be subjected to the invasion of human futility: . . ."I am becoming sentimental," he

> thought to himself, "How do I know that a chair is full of goodwill, or a bed anxious to please?"[80]

This pragmatic approach to the integration of spirit and matter must of course be reflected in a unitive approach to good and evil; and Williams sets himself the task of expressing the integration of matter and spirit with a unitive, metaphysical ethic. Whereas the genre of supernatural thriller will usually involve a philosophy of dualism as its foundational tenet, Williams is scathing about attributing status to both evil and evil acts. As he demonstrates with his later views of Satan in Milton, they are accorded the status of the futile rather than the heroic.

The Archdeacon fulfills his function, which is to redraw conventional religious lines of dualism, in a variety of exchanges. Typical of them is one in which he is used to demote the status of blasphemy and so reduce the danger of dualism. Williams is sardonically scathing about the provocative blasphemies with which Gregory Persimmons needled Mornington:

> "Sorry?" the Duke cried. "After that vile blasphemy? I wish I could have got near enough to have torn his throat out."
>
> "Oh, really, really," the Archdeacon protested. "Let us leave that kind of thing to Mr Persimmons."
>
> "To insult God—" the Duke began.
>
> "How can you insult God?" the Archdeacon asked. "About as much as you can pull His nose."[81]

The moral is that evil has no being in itself, no separate and opposite status. Whereas in his later work Williams will be explicit about the different forms of magic and their metaphysical implications, here he draws in the whole of magic into the economy of the monist metaphysic. This may be an effective if clumsy way of resolving a Considinian ambiguity. How does Williams express this in the narrative? One way in which he does is the figure of Prester John, who acts as an agent of the inclusive and unitive theology. His role shares something with a figure who appears at the beginning of the Book of Revelation at the end of the New Testament. There the author sees someone "like a Son of Man," clearly some sort of experience of Christ, who claims, "I am the First and the Last. I am the Living One; I was dead, and behold I am alive for ever and ever."[82] Prester John makes no direct messianic claims for himself in that way, but he almost does. He is both only a messenger and yet the effective conduit of all magic and holiness. He identifies himself by stating, "I am the messenger only, . . . [b]ut I am the precursor of things that are to be. I am John,

I am Galahad, and I am Mary; I am the Bearer of the Holy One, the Graal, and the keeper of the Graal. . . . [A]ll magic and holiness is through me."[83]

Glen Cavaliero criticizes the characterization of Prester John, an ambiguous type of Christ, as appearing in terms of the narrative more like an "intruding rescuer that a controlling providence."[84] It is in fact precisely this dramatic presentation of the simplistic rescuer that is in keeping with the conventional myth of heroic adeptship, in this case one that has messianic overtones. Aside from the implicit affirmation of magic as a concomitant of sanctity (which Williams has slipped in), the obvious consequence of this unitive theology is that Williams confronts the fact of evil and God's supposed permission of it. This classical moral dilemma requires careful attention. Williams provides it as he raises the issue in a discussion between the three protectors of the Graal.

He begins with a statement that hovers between the faithful and the fatalistic. The inevitability of accepting God's will through circumstances has an almost Islamic slant:

> "There is no use in thinking of it and weighing one thing against the other. When the time comes, He shall dispose as He will, or rather He shall be as He will, as He is."
>
> "Does He will Gregory Persimmons?" Kenneth asked wryly.
>
> "Certainly He wills him," the Archdeacon said. "Since He wills that Persimmons shall be whatever he seems to choose. That is not technically correct perhaps, but it is that which I believe and feel and know."
>
> "He wills evil, then?" Kenneth said.
>
> "Shall there be evil in the city and I the Lord have not done it?" the Archdeacon quoted.[85]
>
> Neither Kenneth nor the Duke accused the priest of evading the issue, for both of them he was speaking from a world of experience into which they hardly entered. They fell back on the simpler idea that agony and evil were displeasing to God, but that He permitted them, and indeed Kenneth . . . [f]ound it necessary . . . [t]o keep this firmly in his mind as a counterbalance to the anxiety he felt. For never before had he been confronted with the fact that certain strong and effective minds were ready and willing to inflict pain with or without a cause. He was becoming frightened of Gregory and he naturally and inevitably decided that Gregory was displeasing to God. It was his only defence; in such a crisis "if God did not exist, it would be necessary to invent Him."[86]

Williams faces the same difficulty over the existence and nature of evil as that with which the Old Testament wrestles. There, theodicy is developed by establishing the sovereignty of God as of such prime theological importance that the emergence of Satan, as adversary with dualistic implications, is only embryonic. But there, as here, the price paid for such a single-minded affirmation of God's sovereignty is that it increases the difficulty of integrating the widespread human experience of evil into a balanced worldview. Though this dualism is theologically unacceptable to the orthodox, it has always had the merit of reflecting a natural theology of human experience. Williams's dismissal of the permissive explanation for evil provokes the question as to what theological rationale lies behind his understanding, and how he integrates the problem of evil into his metaphysic.

He begins the process in the way in which he introduces the mystical theology of Mother Julian of Norwich through the Archdeacon's devotional reading. Williams was familiar with the *Revelations of Divine Love*, or *Showings* of Mother Julian, and refers to them (among other references) in an essay entitled "Sensuality and Substance," written for the journal *Theology*.[87] There he reflects on the uproar caused by D. H. Lawrence's writing among the conventionally religious. Williams's reconciliation of ethical dualism will emerge as a concomitant of the integration of body and soul. Lawrence is commended for taking up the need for the integration of the body and spirit in the face of popular ignorance and disapproval. But Williams insists, "It is the vast union of visible and invisible, tangible and intangible, which is the real business of exploration—anyhow for Christians."[88]

Mother Julian embarked on just such an exploration:

> For I saw full assuredly that our Substance is in God, and also I saw that in our sensualite God is; for in the self point that our Soul is made sensual, in the self point is the City of God ordained to Him from without beginning; into which seat He cometh and never shall remove it . . . [a]nd as anent [*sic*] our substance and sensuality it may rightly be cleped [*sic*] our soul: and that is because of the oneing [*sic*] that they have in God. The worshipful City that our Lord Jesus sitteth in is our sensuality in which He is enclosed: and our kindly Substance is enclosed in Jesus with the blessed Soul of Christ sitting in rest in the Godhead.[89]

Williams comments:

> Whatever the Lady Julian meant by "sensualite" she certainly meant nothing less material or less vital than the whole physical nature; she was not weakening or refining it away. She followed the Church, which,

> ever since it had rejected the Nestorian idea of a merely moral union of the two natures in Christ, had been committed to a realistic sense of the importance of matter: "our soul with our body, and our body with our soul, either of them taking help of other," which is not Browning but the Lady Julian again. The operations of matter are a means of the operation of Christ, and the body has not, in fact, as some pious people suggest, fallen a good deal farther than the soul.[90]

If there is an integration between body and soul, then there may also be some integration between what we understand as good and evil. This integration is one of the more powerful aspects of Julian's visions. Williams would have had this in mind as he created a clear link between the Archdeacon and Mother Julian. He has him turn to her mystical visions as he prepares for his own death: "The Archdeacon had left off looking out of his window and was reading the Revelation of Lady Julian close by it."[91] The descent into darkness that threatens to overwhelm and destroy him is similar to the experience of utter darkness and paralysis that preceded Julian's visions.

As Williams found in Mother Julian both inspiration for his Archdeacon's trial by occult fire (she experienced the stench and flames of the fiend) and an endorsement for the conjunction of sensuality and substance, so he also drew from her *Showings* an eschatological determinism by which evil and good are reconciled. She asks in her *Showings* the same question that Mornington and the Duke ask of the Archdeacon: "And so in my folly I often wondered why, through the great prescient wisdom of God, the beginning of sin was not prevented. For then it seemed to me all would have been well. . . . [J]esus answered in these words and said: 'Sin is necessary but all will be well, and all will be well, and every kind of thing will be well.'"[92]

Julian persists in trying to understand by what mechanism all shall become well, and is answered:

> There is a deed which the blessed Trinity will perform on the last day, as I see it, and what the deed will be and how it will be performed is unknown to every creature who is inferior to Christ, and it will be until the deed is done. . . . [A]nd the cause why he wants us to know it like this is because he wants us to be at ease in our souls and at peace in love, disregarding every disturbance which could hinder our true rejoicing in him. . . . [T]his is the great deed ordained by our Lord God from the beginning. . . . [F]or just as the blessed Trinity created all things from nothing, just so will the same blessed Trinity make everything well which is not well.[93]

While the nature of the deed itself is not made clear, its effect will be that, in direct proportion to sin and failure, God will bring about honor and reconciliation.

> And God showed that sin will be no shame, but honour to man for just as there is indeed a corresponding pain for every sin, just so love gives to the same soul a bliss for every sin . . . [a]nd then God brought joyfully to my mind first Magdalene, Peter and Paul, Thomas of India, St. John of Beverly and others to without number; how they and their sins are known to the Church on earth, and this is no shame to them, but everything is turned to their honour. And therefore our courteous Lord gives a partial revelation about them here of what is there in fullness, for there the mark of sin is turned to honour.[94]

It would be entirely fanciful to assume that the fall of St. John of Beverly from grace and his subsequent restitution were identified with by Williams in his own struggle with the impossibility of his adoration of Phyllis Jones. But it is not fanciful to allow Williams to draw by implication on the solution Mother Julian presents. Her goal to resolve the dilemma posed by freedom and evil in the face of benign monotheism is Williams's goal also. They share a joint preoccupation with treating evil seriously while eschewing any form of dualism.[95]

Persimmons, the Occult Pilgrim: Power and Penitence

The ambiguity in the first novel, *Shadows,* is continued in the second, *War in Heaven.* In this second novel there is a developing ethic when compared to *Shadows.* Considine heroically pursues union; but we are shown, finally, and almost reluctantly, that it is a union founded on an incoherent notion of "self," not a union with the revealed God of the Judeo-Christian tradition.[96] Persimmons, however, as I have suggested above, is cast in the role of villain in terms of the narrative, but he is also treated as something of a hero. The heroism is presented in terms of the values that Williams operates from, which derive from the authenticity of spiritual exploration. He is both an adept and at the same time a pilgrim of sorts. The parallelism of the first novel between the terms of the esoteric pilgrimage and the conventional Christian one continues in much the same way, as his experiences of rapture and his desire for union mirror those of the conventional pilgrim who has discovered the language of mystery, prayer, and union. There are two narratives at work in this novel: (1) a narrative of plot, and (2) one that contains spirituality, ethics, and a hierarchy of values. There is, moreover, a certain incoherence between the two at times. The second does not run evenly with the exterior dramatic narrative. At the same time as Persimmons is planning villainous acts toward the child Adrian, for example, he is described as achieving heights of spiritual awareness and achievement.

The discontinuity between the two narratives derives from Williams's lack of clarity over the attractiveness and metaphysical status of power. As the novels progress, there is a developing awareness of the danger and lure of power as the main source of the perversion of love. While Williams is clearly aware of the principle at this stage, nonetheless "power" is closely woven into his natural language of spirituality that he uses to describe the baseline of his universal metaphysic. In this he is not overtly at odds with parts of the Christian tradition, which has often enough lacked a robust critique of power and its exercising. If we look at the roots of the Christian drama, there is a complementarity between the potency of attraction that Jesus exercises and the power of his actions. But at the level of sheer drama, the Gospels are a celebration of power over nature, evil, and sickness. A simpler reading of the way the drama of power is acted out reduces the operation of power as one in which evil is simply ejected or driven away. The drama of the exorcism has caught the imagination in a way that is out of proportion to its importance in the scheme of the New Testament. In fact a more subtle approach to power runs alongside the overt dramatic action. Jesus has a potency that connects with humanity's ultimate belonging to God and being in the image of God. Coercion is not his language. The real "victory" is achieved by some mechanism that is opaque to us on the cross of dereliction; the clash of power between Christ and both the Sanhedrin and Pilate is also a deeply subtle one. Even St. Anselm in his culturally attuned ransom theologies of the atonement tried to inject some element of subtlety into a primitive, dramatic narration. To read the struggle in terms of raw power, whatever terms power is conceived in, would be far too simplistic.

Similarly, the historic church has been obtuse in its insensitivity to the lure of the exercise of power. It has constantly been corrupted by mistaking its agency on God's behalf as one that required or enabled an exercise of control of some kind. Stretching from St. Augustine of Hippo's attraction to the Gospel phrase "compel them to come in" or the willingness of the Inquisition to torture so that St. Paul's admonition that it was better to waste the body in order to save the soul, the history of the church's mishandling of power has been a tragic one. The nature of God seems, in terms of the incarnation at least, to be a more winsome potency of ultimate attraction rather than the less subtle actions of coercion. But, as Williams will tease out more clearly in his later work, the use and abuse of power in spiritual categories needs careful analysis. In this novel, power acts only as a neutral energy. In *Shadows of Ecstasy* two symmetrical kinds of power were ranged dualistically against each other (as in the mass at Lambeth). Here power has been demoted from its place on the metaphysical scale, and now finds its role as a catalyst in whatever process is being pursued.

At the final moment of judgment, for example, when Gregory "renewed his effort to offer up both the captives in sacrifice to the tremendous power he adored . . . [s]omething further was needed and something further came. . . . [T]he Graal blazed with fiery tumult before them; and its essence, as at last it was touched, awoke in its own triumphant and blinding power."[97]

The Graal personified, Prester John appears in theophany and declares,

> "I am John," a voice sounded, "and I am the prophecy of the things that are to be and are. You who have sought the centre of the Graal, behold through me that which you seek, receive from me that which you are. He that is righteous, let him be righteous still; he that is filthy, let him be filthy still. I am rejection to him that has sought rejection; I am destruction to him that has wrought destruction; I am sacrifice to him that has offered sacrifice. Friend to my friends and lover to my lovers, I will quit all things, for I am myself and I am He that has sent me. This war is ended and another follows quickly. Do that which you must while the time is with you."[98]

Here lies the ambiguity that the novel rests on. Were both Gregory and the Archdeacon seeking the center of the Graal? It seems that they were since Gregory will respond obediently to the ultimatum that is about to be placed before him by John. But the conclusion obscures the confusion of the two narratives. Gregory was seeking the Graal by chasing it. At the level of the second or inner narrative, he was not seeking it for what it was, only for what it might do, or what he might do with it. His main objective and intention was control. Within this narrative, then, he cannot be said to have been seeking the Graal for what it truly embodied; and yet John says that he was. The Archdeacon was not seeking the Graal itself, but was seeking what it led to or was connected with. Here the Graal shares something of the ambiguity that magic has had for Williams; it is a tool or device for exploration. But it is also clear that Gregory, as the mystic and occult pilgrim, was searching for power to adore, and has now found it, albeit personified in Prester John. What Williams does not make clear is the distinction between the power that the Graal contains latently within it, the power of the godhead released, and the power that Gregory seeks union with. This may partly be because of his unwillingness to make a distinction between a material object and the spirituality it literally embodies. Whatever the reason, the nature of the adored power remains opaque.[99]

The contrast between Persimmons and the Archdeacon serves to demonstrate the subtleties in both the similarities and the differences between the two spiritualities they represent. The Archdeacon had by long practice

> [a]ccustomed himself in any circumstances—in company or alone, at work, or at rest, in speech or in silence—to withdraw into that place where action is created. The cause of all action there disposed itself according to that Will which was its nature, and, so disposing itself moved him easily as a part of its own accommodation to the changing wills of men, so that at any time and at all times its own perfection was maintained, now known in endurance, now in beauty, now in wisdom, now in joy. There was no smallest hesitation which it would not solve, nor greatest anxiety which it did not make lucid. In that light other things took on a new aspect. . . . [N]othing but Destiny could defy destiny.[100]

The attractiveness or otherwise of the characters in the novels is a matter of personal taste but, if one compares the spiritual experiences and journeys of the Archdeacon and Persimmons, it is that of the latter which contains the color, the passion, and the sense of exploratory adventure that embodied the values Williams was drawn to.[101] God for Persimmons is presented as "Destiny." Williams will differentiate Persimmons as being the only character in the book with "a natural religious spirit." God for him was "hierarchical presence of power." This heroic antihero is part of the ambiguity that the gravitational pull of his immersion in the Fellowship of the Rosy Cross may have accentuated in those earlier years. Persimmons has become less overtly attractive than Considine, and there are a number of pungent criticisms of his addiction to power, but he is nonetheless a dramatic and magnetic adept. Williams credits him with the practice of adoration, ardent faith, and self-sacrifice:[102]

> Of all those who lay awake under the midnight stars he was the only one who had a naturally religious spirit; to him only the unknown beyond man's life presented itself as alive with hierarchical presences arrayed in rising orders to the central throne. *To him alone sacraments were living*

> *realities;*[103] the ointment and the Black Mass, the ritual and the order of worship. He beyond any of them demanded a response from the darkness; *a rush of ardent faith believed that it came;* and in full dependence on that faith acted and influenced his circumstances. Prayer was natural to him as it was not to Sir Giles or Lionel, or, indeed, Barbara, and to the mind of the devotee the god graciously assented. Conversion was natural to him and propaganda, and the sacrifice both of himself and of others, if that god [Satan] demanded it. He adored as he lay in vigil, and from that *adoration issued the calm strength of a supernatural union.* As the morning broke he smiled happily on the serene world around him.[104]

The descriptions of Persimmons's quest have about them many of the marks of co-inherence. Devoted to the union with a source he identifies with mastery, he declares his desire to search out the abandoned spirits that are scattered over the face of the earth and draw them together.

There are limits to Persimmons's apprehension of cosmic malignance. Williams sculpts a paradox of dark humor, in a delightful passage full of black irony where Persimmons attempts to taunt Lionel Rackstraw—a figure intended to represent an aspect of the author himself—with despair.[105] It transpires that Persimmons is a complete amateur in the contemplation of despair and nihilism that Williams puts into Rackstraw's mouth; it is a despair that Williams had no doubt lived with himself. He is forced from his taunting to move on to the defensive, and to the language of personal disclosure, to defend "rapture" even though it be found in iniquity. Rackstraw responds to the taunting,

> What did people like Gregory know of adverse fate? "Not much of an ambush, I think. It's pretty obvious once one had had a glimpse of the world."
>
> Religion normally has a stupefying effect on the minds of its disciples and this Gregory had not altogether escaped. He had thought it would give him half an hour's pleasant relaxation to worry Lionel, and had not realised that Lionel was, even in his usual state, beyond this.
>
> "No hitch surely," Lionel said. "The whole scheme of things is malign and impotent. That is the way they work. 'There is none that doeth good—no not one.'"
>
> "It depends on one's definition of good," Gregory answered. "There is at least satisfaction and delight."
>
> "There is no satisfaction and delight that does not have treachery

> within it," Lionel said, "There is always Judas; the name of the world that none has dared to speak is Judas."
>
> Gregory . . . [h]ad expected a door and found an iron barrier.
>
> "But," he said doubtfully, "had Judas himself no delight? There is an old story that there is rapture in the worship of treachery and malice and cruelty and sin."
>
> "Pooh," said Lionel contemptuously; "it is the ordinary religion disguised; it is the church-going clerk's religion. Satanism is the clerk at the brothel. Audacious little middle class cock-sparrow!"
>
> "You are talking wildly," Gregory said a little angrily. "I have met people who have made me sure there is rapture in iniquity."
>
> "There is a rapture of anything if you come to that . . . [b]ut all is horrible in the end."
>
> "There is a way to delight in horror," Gregory said.
>
> "There is no way to delight in the horrible," Lionel answered. "Let us pray only that immortality is a dream. But I don't suppose it is," he answered coldly.
>
> A silence fell upon them, and Gregory was suddenly conscious that he felt a trifle sick.[106]

This reductionist nihilism finds Gregory's Achilles' heel and prepares the way for his disillusionment with the capacity of raw power to effect ecstasy. Williams makes it clear that Persimmons is on a passionate religious quest of adoration, even though it is the adoration of raw power. "Power was the purpose of spiritual things, and Satan was the Lord of power."[107]

While Williams has engaged our sympathy for both Lionel and Persimmons in this moment of stark irony, the plot of this novel falls between two stools. The first is the influence of the lure of what one might call "trial by energy," that is, that contest of power in which, rather like Elijah and the prophets of Baal, the hero-adept will win. Williams's dilemma in *Shadows of Ecstasy* was that while Considine was the hero-adept, Williams was unable to allow him to triumph overtly. It competed with but could not contradict his Christian perspective. Here the Archdeacon must win, but Williams appears unable to decide what the currency of victory is. At the level of external narrative of plot, he looks backward to *Shadows,* and the currency is the greater power of the Graal and its keeper. At the level of his inner narrative of spirituality and developing theology he introduces, albeit without explanation, the concept of exchange, the second stool. The emphasis on alchemical change evolves into the idea of Christian exchange. This progression evolves still further in his novels. It is introduced with the Archdeacon offering himself for Persimmons:

> This anger was the effluence of a similar centre, a centre which as known on that earth they had left as Gregory Persimmons, and trembled still with all the desires natural to man. So far as in him lay, the Archdeacon presented to himself that spirit and profession as a means whereby the satisfaction of all desire might meet it; not by such passions was hell finally peopled and the last rejection found.[108]

The idea of alchemical change in Rosicrucian ideology becomes in Williams's hands substitutionary exchange in the Christian sense. It is Williams's own Christianizing of the dynamic. Here is the beginning of a convergence between two allied systems of thought that Williams is bridging and moving between. He places the Christian theology of substitutionary personal exchange within the mechanics of hermetic magic culture. It will not be until his final novel that he moves this experience fully into a Christian dynamic and explains how it might actually be resourced, rather than, as he does here, assume that this is the kind of thing that adepts, whatever their allegiance or metaphysical flavor, can perform.[109]

Williams appears not to have quite made up his mind about the experience of redemption and damnation for Gregory. He writes earlier, on the one hand, that in his moment of ecstasy beyond his dreams Gregory existed supernaturally, and in hell; but Gregory shows no sign of any kind of experiencing anything like hell at the time.[110] But in a later passage that is similar in its imagery to Wentworth in *Descent into Hell,* climbing to the void of damnation down his rope, Gregory too will find at the moment of ultimate judgment that he experiences a threatening proximity to hell: "The sudden action had precipitated him down a thousand spirals of slow descent, and he hung above an everlasting void."[111]

On the other hand, the Archdeacon is able to offer himself by the means of exchange of what is described above as "natural desire." We are to excuse Gregory the exercise of his natural religious and human passions directed toward the encounter with power and exercise of power, for they can be redirected. We are to accept that the wave of aggressive despair will not overcome the Archdeacon as he encounters it, for it is also a perversion, which for Williams is the definition of sin. Describing the third wave of energy, the Archdeacon has to contend with "rejection absolute." We are given a theology of damnation that is based on rejection, not the rejection by God of the damned, but the rejection that flows from refusing to know all things as ultimately good:

> No mortal mind could conceive a desire that was not based on a natural and right desire. Even the hunger for death was but a perversion of the death which precedes all holy birth. But of every conceivable and inconceivable desire, this was the negation. This was desire itself, sick but not unto death.[112]

If there had been an ambiguity about the nature and role that power plays between the two competing systems of thought and behavior, Williams offers an analysis at the *dénouement.* The arbitrating voice is given to Dmitri, who warns his occult co-adepts that the end of all things, including power and destruction, is the ceasing of all desire in a sickness and weariness.

Williams has taken a line similar to C. G. Jung's theory of the shadow, where there is no distinction between the desire of good and bad, only between the desire that can be recognized and the desire that has become attached to objects that carry a degree of shame. They are consequently unable to be recognized, and so are consigned to the "shadow" until some form of reintegration can take place. Gregory Persimmons is saved by his capacity for ecstasy, in its more sedate expression, "delight," and his horror at discovering that power is not the key to delight. He begins to become quizzical about the occult company he is keeping when he realizes that what was lacking among his *confrères* was delight.[113] The process of Persimmons's repentance is blurred. It appears to be based on the Archdeacon's self-offering in the process of exchange, and the sobering experience of the evacuation of delight. There is no articulated repentance in the manner assumed by the Accuser in *Judgement at Chelmsford.*

Williams further refines his concept of union. Considine's was expressed in terms of the self, and gods who are an extension of self. Williams has two notions in this novel that will both appear in more developed forms in later work. One is a perversion of the Communion of Saints, the unity of lost souls that Persimmons has experience of; and the other is something quite unique once it is perceived through Williams's particular perspective. This involves a visionary awareness of the material dimension and its flowing movement. The very matter of creation enjoys what theologians describe as *Heilsgeschichte.* One of the distinctive elements of the Judaic revelation was the linear and progressive conviction that history was teleological, moving toward a goal. Williams's unusual achievement is to incorporate into that sense of the historical flow a vision of the accompanying movement of all matter into what he understands to be the co-inherence. The effect will be heightened in both of the last novels, which contain passages involving the vivid flow of matter (or space) through time, toward a synthesizing *eschaton.* This too derives from Williams's vivid sense of the interpenetration of spirit and matter.

The parallel to the unity of the Communion of Saints is found in the manipulation of lost souls where Gregory, who combines both these concepts, talks of a recognition of the current of desire in which all things move, which he has guided, a little: "There is the circle of souls and I will gather them together and marry them as I please. I will bring them from this world and from another and I will bind the lost with the living till the living itself be lost."[114] These lines contain echoes of the Dantean circles of Hell, and Persimmons is driven in recognition of the current of desire to unify them in himself, a perversion of Christ's actions.

It is through Williams's perception of his theology of the Grail that the notion of a flow of matter toward ultimate union with God is incorporated. He is well aware of the rich diversity of the Grail tradition (the hermetic elements that Waite documented so fully), and Williams allows his three virtuous characters to represent three different strands of the tradition. As they hold vigil over the recaptured Grail, the Duke reflects on the romantic medieval sacramental tradition. Its universality was fractured on the rocks of European Eucharistic theological dispute. Kenneth also embodies a romantic tradition, but his is an awareness of the entire "Grail Quest" that comes down through "Hawker and Tennyson, John and Malory and the mediaevals." This is Williams's own concern as he came to it through Waite's approach. He offers the conventional reading of the quest, incorporating union, companions devoted to the cause, and the unbroken tradition: "He saw a grave young God communicating to the rapt companionship. They took oaths beyond human consciousness. Liturgical and romantic names melted into one cycle."[115]

Then comes the idiosyncratic touch, as Williams takes this conventional reading and develops it into his own unitive vision of the Grail acting as an eschatological focus and catalyst for spirit and matter:

> The Archdeacon found no such help in the remembrances of kings or poets. He looked at the rapt faces of the young men; he looked at the vessel before him. "Neither is this Thou," he breathed; and answered, "Yet this also is Thou." He considered, in this, the chalice offered at every altar, and was aware again of a general movement of all things towards

> a narrow channel. . . . [S]ky, sea and land were moving, not toward that vessel, but towards all it symbolised and had held.[116]

Williams provides an extraordinary Eucharistic theology that transcends the conventional lines of argument that fall into categories of symbolism, real presence, or transubstantiation.[117] Instead we are moved into an altogether wider dimension that incorporates time and space, spirit and matter, in a sense of the drawing together of all things into union with the godhead through, in this case, the Grail.[118]

> The consecration of the Mysteries was for him no miraculous change; he had never dreamed of the heavenly courts attending Christ upon the altar. But in accord with the desire of the Church expressed in the ritual of the Church the Sacred Elements seemed to him to open upon the Divine Nature, upon Bethlehem, and Calvary and Oliphet, as that itself opened upon the Centre of all. And through that gate, upon those tides of retirement, creation moved. Never so clearly as now had he felt that movement proceeding, but in his mind nevertheless knew no other vision than that of a thousand dutifully celebrated Mysteries in his priestly life; so and not otherwise all things return to God.[119]

Williams has moved from *Shadows of Ecstasy* and its alchemical agenda of auto-resurrection to one that more clearly involves the notions of salvation and damnation. But his soteriology is undeveloped. Gregory as a murderer, would-be child snatcher, manipulator, and sadist experiences a kind of repentance, but one that is not clearly articulated. His penitence and salvation are brought about by the priority given to delight rather than power. Whatever love there is presumably is expressed through the Archdeacon's act of exchange. Whatever the motives for repentance, it needs to be expressed in action. The voice of judgment, Prester John, requires a further sacrifice, which will have to be Persimmons's own, and then, as he says, "Die then, as this other has died and there shall be agreement with you also in the end, for you have sought me and no other."[120]

Magic and the Grail have managed to lure Gregory as a pilgrim and adept because they incited his appetite for union with the source of all delight. It was the desire for union that would add a redemptive coloring to the use of the occult knowledge in his quest, and so allow his salvation. Williams continues to make a special plea for a redefining of magic and the appetites that take up the pursuit of the esoteric. Where they are the tools for a quest for ultimate union with the godhead, they are capable of being used for an end that is wholesome. But the ambiguity flowed from Williams's association of the omnipotence with ill-defined power. This association is one that he will refine. The metaphysics used here lack the quality of astute theological discernment that is the hallmark of the later Williams. He continues to use epithets for the godhead that he has drawn from the Q'abalistic tradition which in keeping with its Judaic roots would be very chary of naming God.[121] While "omnipotence" remains one of his favorites, nonetheless in the later novels there is a greater awareness of the danger of power and the need to define it. His metaphysical structure will involve a clarification of power and its lure as a perversion of ultimate reality. He will articulate the deeper values of the incarnation by identifying a vulnerable interdependency within the Web of Exchange as the clearest focus of the nature of God.

In his last two novels, Williams will move to a Christ-centered substitution both as the means of salvation and as the means to enable the mechanism of exchange. At this stage of his theological development, he appears to be working from a sub-Christian language of sacrifice colored by hermetic culture. Indeed if one looks back to the period in which Williams wrote *Shadows of Ecstasy*, it is a matter of some fine judgment as to what extent Williams personally identified with Considinian aspirations of alchemical adeptship. What is clear is that by his last two novels a simplistic notion of transmutation was replaced by a more developed concept of change and exchange; it is the dynamic of the co-inherent life that moves those involved continually closer to Christ, the godhead, and one another. Williams's diagnosis of energies will become more discriminating.[122]

CHAPTER SIX

The Goetic, Theurgic, and Wisdom Traditions

Later in this text, we will observe a distinct development in the way that Williams uses the esoteric and alchemical culture as his thought develops during the course of his writing. But some of the more explicit work on esotericism of the mature Williams is to be found in his one book on the history of magic, *Witchcraft.* Here Williams explicitly considers the hermetic and magic traditions. It becomes immediately clear that one of the central influences on both Waite and Williams is Thomas Vaughan.

Within the hermetic orders of the Order of the Golden Dawn and the Fellowship of the Rosy Cross, we see at least four elements: (a) neo-gnosticism, (b) the role of the skilled adept, (c) a preoccupation with the history of alchemy and the central role of transmutation, and (d) disputes over the nature of magic. There had been a movement from neo-paganism in the Order of the Golden Dawn to a Christianized Q'abalism in Waite's Rosicrucian order. There was then a further development in Williams to a particular but distinctive form of orthodoxy that is shaded by the Q'abalistic overtones derived from Waite. All these elements appear in Williams's book *Witchcraft,* written in the last few years of his life.[1] He shows in this book an alert awareness of the need to make the necessary distinctions between the goetic, the theurgic, and the alchemical.

In case the reader is tempted to assume the book was written to show special pleading for Williams's position, the fact is that he was commissioned to write it. He clearly used the book to represent his interests and his analyses of the issues; but he wrote it to order, as he did a number of his works, particularly the historical biographies.[2] Nevertheless, written as a piece of history as it was, he chooses to emphasize, as part of that history, what seems fitting by his own immersion in the culture of hermetic exploration. In various places his distinctive worldview leaps out of the text, particularly in the chapters that cover the period when alchemy and Rosicrucian ventures flourished.

The remarks that Williams makes in the preface clearly indicate that he valued as a top priority a keen sense of the definitions of words and ideas that he used. While he explains that the book will deal mostly with the perverted way of the soul and the lower level of the cosmic order, Williams does note in passing the two other areas where magic has had some involvement throughout history, that is, science and secret societies. The nobler idea of virtue energized and enabled by power worked its way out in experimental science. Alchemy was a particular stage on the route to the development of chemistry. The second route was "secluded in its own rites," and Williams had direct experience of that option, which, by implication, he clearly distinguishes from the occultism of the lower kind. This he describes as either the perverted way or else the goetic.[3]

His approach to the culture of hidden knowledge is an unusual one. Interpreters of magic or Christian theology usually fall into either one of the two camps of proponents or opponents. Williams occupies a position that straddles both traditions; he assesses the actions of his subjects partly according to their intentions and motivation, and partly according to his particular understanding of orthodox metaphysics. He aims to provide a new synthesis between the wisdom traditions and the edifice of orthodox "catholic" Christianity by establishing the credentials of a secret but acceptable group of practitioners of "pure learning."

In his introduction he makes the essential distinction that the early Christian community established between its own outlook and that of the surrounding Greco-Roman culture, which cultivated soothsayers when the interests of the state were not thereby threatened. Astrologers, and other practitioners of the general occult skills, what Williams describes as "Magians," were frequently found in the imperial train and even in the close imperial circle. Striking an unusual note, he suggests they were harmless and even useful, since the occult dealing of the emperor was, by definition, no treason, being part of his dutiful care of the state.[4]

But is there no metaphysical map? Williams is sure there is, and sets out to make his own distinctions between the world of orthodoxy and the heterodox skills of the magians. He claims the interpreting of the future was not to be acceptable across the watershed of the incarnation, even though magi were seen to herald it in the Gospels. He celebrates the encounter between the Christ child and the Magi: "The Magians were the first conquest of the Child-God. . . . The first intellectual victory of the Faith."[5] Consciously or not, the church saw the magians in the Gospels as abandoning their art when they brought sacred and symbolic gifts. The practice of foretelling was at an end from that point. Williams explains why:

> [T]here could be no more foretelling, and that for two reasons at least. The first was that the future should not be foretold, since it depended on the will of God and the free will of men. . . . Secondly the future, apart from man's moral choice, could not matter. "All luck was good"; whatever happened was fortunate. Knowledge was not so much immoral as irrelevant to the reality of Love, loving and being loved at every moment. That was what did matter.[6]

But if at the beginning of the incarnation, magic was made captive in the adoration of the Christ child by the magi, the apostolic age was to be the history of conflict between practitioners of magic and practitioners of the Gospel: "The magicians, as such, were already being thrust into opposition to the Redeemer. . . . [T]hey were caused to desire to rival God."[7]

Williams evaluates the four categories of those who sought to operate by means of supernatural powers.

> The Doctrine of the Single Supernatural Will, and of the incarnation, had launched itself onto a world in which supernatural powers were believed to exist. It was believed that men could, if they wished, operate by means of these powers. The executants were in the main of four kinds: (i) there were the merely vile kind, the night-hags, the potion and poison makers, malefical wizards of the lower sort; (ii) there were the grander kind, such as the priestess in Virgil, learned in conjurations, who by knowing, as it were, the mathematical pattern of the universe, the proper balance of sound and movement, could control the heights and depths of things, change kingdoms and even terrify the gods; (iii) there were the diviners and astrologers, those who forecast the future and read the purposes of the stars.

This much one might expect. But his final category gives notice of his own experience of the world opened up to him through Waite and the Fellowship of the Rosy Cross: "and besides all these there were, it seems, some few to whom the magical art was indeed 'high-priestess of heaven,' who pushed on by pure learning, followed in honour and chastity towards a sublime union with the absolute power; there was a means of doing this, but it was very secret."[8] Here we have the precursors to the tradition out of which the Fellowship of the Rosy Cross was to emerge; they are treated with a seriousness that the other categories are denied. Whereas Yeats was to make a distinction between magic tricks and the magic of the artist, Williams offers a more sophisticated and historically subtle distinction between these categories.

In the rest of his book Williams traces these categories in his usual terse prose style, walking a careful line in his commentary on the metaphysics and ontology that lie behind what otherwise would be simple categories of dualism. But in his seventh chapter, "The Goetic Life," he gives more direct evidence of his tutelage under Waite.

The Centrality of Thomas Vaughan

One significant place of overlap between Williams and Waite is their mutual interest in Thomas Vaughan. Both Vaughan and the notorious Dr. Dee appear in each of their works. Vaughan plays a central role in *The Hermetic Papers of A. E. Waite,* a collection of papers brought together by Waite's biographer, R. A. Gilbert. The collection contains papers on hermeticism, Rosicrucianism, the Q'abalah, and "ceremonial union." There follow two brief papers on Robert Fludd and Dr. Dee, and a longer one on Thomas Vaughan. In the relevant chapters of *Witchcraft* Williams's focus of interest narrows to the same subjects.

Waite is particularly attracted to Thomas Vaughan because he appears to have achieved a level of "adeptship" that Waite found admirable: "[Vaughan] was exalted at once to a high throne of adeptship, and, as criticism of the opposite kind can scarcely be said to exist, he has remained so to this day."[9] Waite charts Vaughan's competence in magic and hermetic alchemy. With the same sensitivity as Williams, he is concerned to make a distinction between various kinds of magic. The categories of the elemental, celestial, and spiritual comprise the main portion of his inquiry. Vaughan, it was generally claimed, despised common processes of alchemy that would fall under the first heading, but he was nevertheless proficient in practical alchemy. He was aware of the power of the stellar influences that could be described as celestial magic, but Waite was most concerned with distinguishing subcategories of spiritual magic.

> It is plain that an alternative description of spiritual or divine magic is the root and experience which lies behind the mystical Doctrines of Theology. Having reached this point, it will, I conceive, be unnecessary to say that Vaughan's magic was a secret wisdom, distributed after definite manners and was not evocation or necromancy, dealing with

> angels or demons, trafficking with elementary spirits, the confection of talismans or sigils, or anything approaching, from whatever distance, the dregs and lees which have been gathered into the Keys of Solomon, Almadels, Arbatels and Grimoires. The intellectual fools of these subjects and devices he left to their foolishness, and the cultus-mongers of diabolism to the disease of their black arts.[10]

Waite uses Vaughan's work *Lumen de Lumine* to explore the distinction between material (as in "elemental" above) alchemy on the one hand and spiritual alchemy, that is, the transformation or transmutation of humanity, on the other. He is also concerned with distinguishing between Christian and non-Christian Q'abalistic theory.

Waite explains his criteria of discernment by which he unravels Vaughan's work:

> If a given cipher decodes in the official language of a theosophy which is already familiar, we have had our pains to no purpose, but we shall see at the end whether, in his concealed fashion, the author intimates anything concerning the *Rex Fidelis* by which his kingdom may be declared with power in the consciousness of the heart.
>
> Proceeding a little further in our reverse process, we shall come to understand more openly the sacred and religious nature of the metempsychosis[11]—or soul transfer—which is here under notice, because its alternative word is defined very simply as transmutation, and salvation itself is nothing else but a synonym of both. When it is understood that these three are one, their product is yet another familiar term which stands for them all—that is to say conversion, being a deep, mystical, substantial change, by which the hard stubborn flints of this world become chrysolite and jasper in the eternal foundation. It is the same process as that which is referred to in the old Rosicrucian counsel: *Transmutemini, transmutemini de lapidibus mortuis in lapides vivos philisophicos*—"Do ye suffer transmutation and be changed from stones that are dead into living and philosophical stones."[12]

In *The Figure of Beatrice* the same ideas occur. Two examples may be sufficient. Both Williams and Dante use the term "transmuted." On pages 79 and 80, Williams quotes from the *Convivio* Dante's own belief that "if Christ had not been crucified, but had lived for the full time possible to his nature, he would at the same age have transmuted his mortal body to an eternal." On page

112, Williams tells us that Virgil could hardly, without ceasing to be Virgil, have addressed himself with passion to the glory of the Virgin Mother. "But this is necessary, it is she into whose eyes the eyes of Beatrice are transmuted."

Vaughan is concerned with another transformation; he intends to carry his readers to the highest conception of religion, and shame those who have degraded the sciences of physics, astrology, and alchemy by their oversophistication and misapprehension that they are all aspects of the one science of sanctity. Although he takes Vaughan to task for an incompetent Christianizing of the Q'abalistic material,[13] Waite commends him for his clarity in expressing certain mysteries of the soul. He, along with Robert Fludd and Reuchlin the Q'abalist, was, according to Waite,

> conscious of an uninspired but feverish anxiety to probe the mysteries of Nature and carry to its last consequences the Hermetic doctrine that things which are above correspond to things that are below, that the macrocosm is summarised in the microcosm. There is a heart of truth in this fantasy, because the means of Divine Grace are abroad in Nature, though the correspondences between Nature and Grace are not understood in their confusion, but in their parallel distinction.[14]

Waite, for the personal reasons referred to in chapter 2, has concern about the potential for misunderstanding the distinction between magic wisdom that derives from the authentic Christian tradition. He concludes that although Vaughan elected to write "under the regrettable term of Magic" the way he handled eternal and divine things places him firmly in the category of "mystical philosopher."[15]

Williams, Thomas Vaughan, and the Hermetic Tradition

Williams is also concerned to pursue the essential distinction between the goetic and neo-gnostic alchemy. He analyzes the goetic as the path of the perversion of images, while alchemical exploration is part of the journey of affirmation. Recalling the evidence from one of the witchcraft trials, Williams describes the moment that the "tall woman" offered to Joan Weir to speak on her behalf to the Queen of Fairie:

> The invited mortal dallied with the thought. It needed but the sinking a little further into illusion than is customary to all sin, for by definition the very essence of sin is a deliberate perversity, and the perversity of the

> Goetic life was a temptation only to those peculiarly fitted for it—only perhaps to those peculiarly fitted for the religious life.[16]

Williams then describes the excesses of the goetic path, documenting with distaste the rituals of the black mass. In chapter 10, however, he moves from illusion to wisdom, and turns to Thomas Vaughan as his exemplar.

This chapter contains the outlines of Waite's influence condensed and reworked with the detail of Williams's critique. The tone of the writing changes and Williams develops a style that is less detached than before. He introduces Thomas Vaughan, Anglican priest, rector of a Welsh living, Royalist and brother of Henry Vaughan, and poet. He describes the apologia that Vaughan wrote in *Magia Academica,* which was published in 1650 under the authorial name of Eugenius Philalethes. In this book, magic is equated with wisdom:

> That I should profess magic in this discourse and justify the professors of it withal is impiety with many, but religion with me. It is a conscience that I have learned from authors greater than myself and scriptures greater than both. Magic is nothing but the wisdom of the creator revealed and planted in the creature. It is a name, as Agrippa saith, "not distasteful to the very Gospel itself." Magicians were the first attendants our Saviour met withal in this world, and the only philosophers who acknowledged Him in the flesh before that he himself discovered it.[17]

Through the mouth of Vaughan, with the accent of Waite, Williams proceeds to defend the relationship between a certain understanding of magic and the Christian tradition, and at the same time define and defend his own training and values experienced through Waite's influence.

Vaughan insists that this high art has always been in the world, and wise men of all generations had been aware of it: "The magicians had a maxim among themselves 'that no word is efficacious in magic unless it be first animated with the Word of God.'" Williams records Vaughan's scorn of the prejudice of ignorant critics: "Lawyers and common divines who knew not these secrets, perusing the ceremonial superstitious trash of some scribblers who pretended to magic, prescribed against the art itself as impious and anti-Christian, so that it was a capital sin to profess it, and the punishment no less than death."[18] The secret tradition, though, stakes its claim.

> In this confusion therefore the great magicians for long buried their knowledge in silence. The foolish imitated their knowledge, on a lower

> level, by charms, characters, circles, triangles and fantastic vocabularies, "but knowing not what spirit that was which the magicians did bind he (the common man) laboured and studied to bind the devil." And the great persecutors, also ignorant of the truth of the age-long operations, denounced and destroyed all alike. Until God deigned to excite certain great spirits to rediscover the hidden treasure.[19]

The recovery of the hidden treasure was exactly the task of the Fellowship of the Rosy Cross. Williams writes with conviction on the relevance of the old unitive maxim known as the Doctrine of Correspondence, "as above, so below," in order to justify the search for and guardianship of this hidden treasure. He sees it as the counterpart to the mystical tradition, which also searched for a single universal principle:

> All these occult students whatever they called themselves or were called, philosophers, alchemists, magicians—were concerned to discover a principle of operation in the universe. On the one hand, the search for that principle touched the methods of the spiritual Way and all that has been called mysticism; on the other, it was concerned with the transmutation of metals and the prolongation of life. Between the two lay every kind of debased science. . . . [M]uch of what we know concerning those things has been helped by the incitement felt by these scholars. The central passion, however, has been—like witchcraft itself—not so much believed as dismissed and not so much dismissed as despised. Yet the principle had in its day, a great imaginative appeal. It could be more or less summed up in the old maxim: "as above, so below."[20]

Williams was to return to the Doctrine of Correspondence, which became central to his thought, in several other places. In his essay "The Index of the Body" he considers the term "occult." Like Yeats, Vaughan, and Cornelius Agrippa, Williams pleads for a definition of the occult that stretches its meaning beyond the popular usage. In the following long but important passage he restates the tradition of Vaughan and Waite in language that contains many striking similarities to them:

> The word "occult" has come into general use, and is convenient, if no moral sense is given it simply as itself. It deals with hidden things, and their investigation. But in this case we are concerned not so much with the pretended operations of those occult schools as with a certain imagina-

> tion of relation in the universe, and that only to pass beyond it. The signs of the Zodiac were, according to some students, related to the parts of the physical body. The particular attributions varied, and all were in many respects arbitrary. But some of them were extremely suggestive; they may be allowed at least a kind of authentic poetic vision. Thus, in one pattern, the house of the Water-carrier was referred to the eyes; the house of the Twins to the arms and hands; the house of the Scorpion to the privy parts and the sexual organs; and the house of the Balances to the buttocks.
>
> It will be clear that these four attributions at least had a great significance. It will be clear also that in such a poetic (so to call it) imagination, we are dealing with a kind of macrocosmic-microcosmic union of a more serious and more profitable kind than the mere exposition by a debased astrology of chances in a man's personal life. It may be invention, but if so, it is great invention; the houses of the Zodiac, with their special influences ruling in special divisions of the spatial universe, may be but the fables of astronomy; it must be admitted that few certain facts support them. But they are not unworthy fables. They direct attention to the principles at work both in the spatial heavens and in the structure of man's body. Aquarius is for water, clarity, vision; Gemini are for a plural motion, activity, and achievement; Libra is for that true strength of balance on which the structure of man depends.
>
> With this suggestion, we are on the point of deserting the spatial heavens for something else. The like regions of the spheres, of which Patmore spoke, here begin to be transferred to the spiritual heavens. "As above, so below" ran the old maxim, but even that dichotomy is doubtful. The houses of the Zodiac, in this, do but confuse the issue, except in so far as they, like the whole universe, exhibit the mystery by which spirit becomes flesh, without losing spirit.[21]

This last phrase is central to understanding the thrust of Williams's theological and poetic concern. While distancing himself from the mechanics of astrology, which for obvious reasons he has already disclaimed, he nonetheless wants to identify with a metaphysical construct that allows him to retain his priority of the interpenetration of spirit and matter. Evidently he is concerned with finding a way of allowing the two categories to complement and inform each other rather than appearing to be in contradistinction to each other. Quoting Gerard Manley Hopkins's poem on the Blessed Virgin, which explores her qualities with vivid physical imagery, Williams makes the dramatic claim that "[t]he visionary forms of the occult schools are but dreams of the Divine Body."[22]

He is using the term "occult" here in its widest sense and referring to the wisdom traditions that have been alluded to. He suggests that it is in the hermetic wisdom traditions that one can better understand the correspondence between the material and spiritual.

He returns to the central Doctrine of Correspondence in his *Time and Tide* review of Vincent Taylor's *Forgiveness and Reconciliation:* "'As below, so above,' even among Christians the great experiences are often over-simplified and the words 'love' or 'forgiveness' are thought to be sufficient."[23] He refers to it also in his introduction to *The Figure of Beatrice* where he introduces the reader to the twin phenomena of the "Way of Affirmation and Rejection."

> As above, so below; as in him, so in us. The tangle of affirmation and rejection which is in each of us has to be drawn into some kind of pattern, and has so been drawn by all men who have ever lived. The records of Christian sanctity have on the whole stressed the rejection. This indeed can hardly be avoided in any religion—nor perhaps outside all religion; the mere necessities of human life—change, misadventure, folly, age, and death—everywhere involve it. But even more within religion the discipline of the soul, ordinary or extraordinary, enforces it. The general praise of ascetic life and even the formal preference of one good (such as virginity) to another good (such as marriage) have themselves imaged that enforcement. On the other hand such great doctrines as the Resurrection of the Body and the Life Everlasting have continually recalled the Affirmation; with every act of charity towards others, every courtesy towards others, and even permissibly towards ourselves. The very equalling of ourselves with others and of others with ourselves is a declaration of the republic of images. No doubt these doctrines, metaphysical or moral, are to be understood after a great manner and towards God. But no doubt also every way of understanding leaves them exact in themselves. After the affirmations we may have to discover the rejections, but we must still believe that after the rejections the greater affirmations are to return.[24]

If the balance of the interchange between macrocosm and microcosm was to be effective, the relationship between the two spheres needed to be as close as possible. Various strands in the orthodox and particularly in patristic spirituality had always sought union. Williams claims to have antecedents in an intellectual group of philosophers and adepts who pioneered their alternative route to union, one of which, in particular, took a different view of the body and its relationship with the soul. According to the formal teaching of the church the breach between heaven and earth was closed and the situation restored through the practice of conventional religious rites and duties: "The occult philosophers dreamed also of another means, a means not necessarily opposed, nor even alternative, but perhaps complementary or only auxiliary, but certainly practical, could the praxis be discovered."[25]

He adds a passage that hints of polemic and expresses a faint element of disdain, flowing perhaps from the self-confidence of the secure Gnostic, in pushing the credentials of this group a little further: "The desire and the design spread widely, and while the Wars of Religion devastated Europe, the intellectuals, in their own intellectual way, sought the Union, and (according to their capacity and interests) the various corollaries of the Union."[26] Williams had adopted a rather different tone in *Descent of the Dove* (1939), where his subject matter had not lured him into an exercise in esoteric apologetics. There he wrote more centrally within the Christian tradition. Discussing the Council of Nicaea, he makes it clear that the union between heaven and earth was brought about in the incarnation: "The Christian idea from the beginning had believed that his Nature reconciled earth and heaven. All things met in him, God and Man."[27] In the 1940s he appears to return more to the hermetic language and categories that were so dominant in his Taliessin cycle.

In the next step in his argument to establish the links between alchemy and orthodoxy, Williams turns to Dr. Dee. Waite was well aware of the links between Dr. Dee and the Rosicrucian quest, and he wrote a small though rather distinctive paper on him that R. A. Gilbert includes in his *Hermetic Papers of A. E. Waite.*[28] Waite obviously feels the need to set the record straight on the question of Dee's motivation and religious integrity. Williams provides a brief description of his life and his partnership with the dubious Edward Kelley, and quotes at length from Dee's letter:

> He defined his life's activities even more closely. The definition was in a letter to Archbishop Whitgift, so little did Dee suppose his activities anti-Christian, any more than, fifty years after his death, the Anglican rector Vaughan. In this letter—it was called *A Letter containing a most brief Discourse Apologetical,* he said that he had written it "not so much to stop the mouths, and at length the impudent attempts, of the rash and malicious devisors, and contrivors of the most untrue, foolish and wicked reports and fables of and concerning my foresaid studious exercises, passed over, with my great (yes incredible) pains, travels, cares, and costs, in the search and learning of true philosophy; as, therein, so to certify and satisfy the godly and unpartial Christian hearer or reader

> hereof; that, by his own judgement (upon his due consideration, and examination of this, no little parcel of the particulars of my aforesaid studies and exercises philosophical annexed), he will, or may, be sufficiently informed or persuaded; that I have wonderfully laboured, to find, follow, use, and haunt the true straight, and most narrow path, leading all true, devout, zealous, faithful, and constant Christian students, *ex valle hac miseriae, et miseria istius vallis: et tenebrarum Regno; et tenebris istius Regni, ad montem sanctum Syon, et ad coelestia tabernacula.*"[29]

When Williams writes, "so little did Dee consider his activities anti-Christian," he draws attention to the fact that while we have no real idea what doctrinal status Dee accorded himself, the populace in general and the establishment in particular held his Christian orthodoxy in considerable doubt. In 1555 he was arraigned before the Privy Council on a charge of blinding and killing children by magic. No less significant, though with a strong element of political machination, he was also accused of plotting by magic against the life of Queen Mary. In 1583 his house in Mortlake was sacked by the crowd. Williams makes a clearer distinction between the activities of the notorious Edward Kelley and his mentor Dee, "a great sincerity is predicable of Dee; of Kelley we may think what we will."[30] Not all commentators have taken such a sympathetic line.[31]

Williams attempts, following Waite, to offer definitions of magic that ensure a complete (possibly hermetic) seal between the alchemical explorations rooted in the wisdom tradition and goetic or theurgic elements. Dee and Vaughan are not dabbling in what might be popularly understood as magic: "In the historical sense of the word neither Dee's concern with spiritual creatures nor Vaughan's with alchemical works, nor that of any of their contemporaries correspond to Magic, of whatever kind. Yet both, and perhaps all, might claim that this is what lay behind the old kind, and was the only valuable thing in it, as Vaughan clearly did."[32] "Perhaps all" is a device for adding his own authorial affirmation to theirs. There is no obvious chronological or thematic link that would direct the historian at this juncture to the obscure world of Jewish Theosophy. But Williams, at this point in the chapter, takes that route, which is indicative of the significance of his own experience of the Fellowship of the Rosy Cross: the influence it had upon him and his predilection for its language and mythology. The Rosicrucian culture provided the mythology that he adopted in order to give expression to the ideas that comprised the Taliessin cycle. The integration of hermeticism into his own worldview allowed him to express a metaphysical outlook that enabled him to express the interpenetration of the spiritual and material. It is, of course, one of the foundations of Waite's own worldview, and Williams turns to it at this point in his argument. He refers to the source that he clearly had in the back of his mind while describing the origins of the hermetic movement. He moves from this brief excursion about the alchemists to Waite's central preoccupations, namely the Zohar and Q'abalism. Here we find Williams expounding in a rare literary moment on the roots of his esoteric training, drawing attention to the demands of the Q'abalah in general, and the Zohar in particular. He takes us back to the main expositor of Q'abalistic wisdom, Pico della Mirandola, who is now presented as a bastion of Christian doctrinal orthodoxy: "[Vaughan and Dee] would have assented, in faith and hope to Pico Della Mirandola's saying that 'No science gives greater proof of the divinity of Christ than magic or the Q'abalah.'"[33] Williams has Vaughan and Dee eschewing magic in the first text quoted from above, only to reintroduce it in different terms through Mirandola.

The caution that "[t]his is no place to search into the tradition of Jewish Theosophy" serves as an introduction to that very exercise. He recounts the tale from the Zohar of the reworking of the encounter between Balak and Balaam. Williams's argument in this chapter is not obviously helped by this excursus, although it does serve to inform us of his own preoccupations; and he does turn to it to establish the demarcation line between the goetic and the search for wisdom. We are introduced to the distinction between a sorcerer and a diviner, and at the end of the tale, the sorcerer is slain, with his bones turned to serpents aiding others in search of enchantments. He has been overcome by the "Tent of Assembly"—a reference to the "mystical Israel in a withdrawn state." The fate of Balaam is a warning to all those who follow in the "Way of Perversity," and such is the fate of Goetia.

Williams contrasts the Way of Perversity with the noble quest of alchemy. He introduces a comparative judgment between the esoteric wisdom traditions that depends upon the motivation and direction of the practitioners. A "great moral" is at the heart of this distinction. What inspired the alchemists was nothing less than a quest to take part in the potency of resurrection. "The old search into the relation of body and spirit was what partly preoccupied them. The mingling of fancies that had produced the obscene horrors of incubi and succubi is here for a moment reversed and becomes vivid in a noble manner."[34]

Williams appears to defend Vaughan on the rationale that, yet again, the "end" of sharing in union and resurrection is allowed to justify the experiments that are supposed to provide the "means" to achieve them. Not only Christian orthodoxy has remained chary of that equation. The attraction of Vaughan for Williams, however, is that Vaughan was preoccupied with the thought of the body of the resurrection ("at least occasionally"). Such is Williams's admiration for someone who is willing to take the body seriously in a metaphysical context that Vaughan's dream is justified. His preoccupation is with "the body of the Resurrection, 'the body of adeptship,' the body of energy and light, and yet a real body, as real and as related to that which is all we know at present."[35]

The justification of this alternative stream of religious experience and quest is that it is linked to events and perceptions within the mainstream tradition; it is both a commentary on and extension of them. The world of transmutation looked to the biblical tradition of transfiguration as a template for its own aims. The reference to the body of Resurrection displays the raw material that formed the theological conduit from which Williams was to emphasize the necessity giving prominence to the Way of Affirmation, in a culture so unsure of the *locus standi* of the human body. So we are referred to the illumination of the body of Moses coming down from Mount Sinai, and of course to the Mount of Transfiguration, Moses and Elijah on Mount Tabor. It should be noted that there is no great perception within the mainstream tradition that it was the bodies themselves that were shining. The illumination tends to be seen not as emanating from the body itself but a more general luminescence. This is Williams's point; and he adds a further link between numinous experience and the body: "the continual Christian Doctrine of the Heightening and Englorying of the Present Flesh; the illumination of that flesh seen in certain states of love—these are the justifications of the dream and even (could Vaughan's tracts be so understood, and could the operation be consummated) of the experiment."[36]

That Williams needs to turn to Vaughan as an exemplar of someone who took the body seriously in its relation to spirit is evidence of the impoverishment of the mainstream tradition and the fault, of course, that Williams himself seeks to rectify. If one wishes to level the criticism that he turned to the esoteric tradition in order to find the antidote to the imbalances of conventional faith, then this could be countered by his cogent charge that the church itself had fallen under the long shadow of the Persian dualist prophet Mani. Anne Ridler reminds us that "Williams is perhaps the Christian writer of all others in our time who has restored the body to proper place of honour. . . . [H]e held that we were all of us natural Manichaeans."[37]

Williams had made the point, in his essay "Sensuality and Substance," that there is little likelihood in our becoming amorously promiscuous simply because we have offered proper theological attention to the implications of physicality.[38] Williams is described by C. S. Lewis as having lectured to great effect at Oxford on chastity. Whatever the thrust of Waite's marital and sexual imagery in *The Secret Doctrine in Israel,* Williams affirmed the role of chastity in the tradition, but for different reasons than those who had more conventionally seen it as a remedy against the corruption of our physicality. He refers to Milton's speculation about angelic support for the chaste in *Comus,* and suggests that it is at least arguable that Vaughan thought he was talking about that. This is arguable perhaps, but not convincingly so. The text suggests that Williams thought so, too; for he then offers us a sexual imagery that derives directly from Waite, an overt theologizing of the sexual act: "The movement of the sex energy, the very flow of semen itself, was to be turned, purified, divinitized in Christ. Through the spirit and the soul, the Divine grace was to descend upon that Matter. It certainly was speculative and no practical imagination, but it was not Manichaean."[39] The only place one comes across imagery of this kind is *The Secret Doctrine in Israel,* but Williams does not develop the line of thought. He does warn of the lure of what he describes as "intellectual sensual exaltation" and locates it in the Faustian tradition as we have it through Marlowe, making a distinction between that and a proper theology of body.[40]

A second reference to both Waite and Rosicrucian culture comes in his introduction of the school of wandering scholar-adepts. In the following passage he makes the distinction between three strands of the esoteric tradition—the higher transmutations; the lower—alchemy; and the wisdom tradition.

> The high transmutations had their lower correspondences, and to these alchemy belonged. The more universal souls, like Cornelius Agrippa himself, aimed at all knowledge; leaning sometimes to believe that there was one general principle, one equation, one epigram, as it were, that would resolve all; in such power as in ancient times had been attributed to the Tetragrammaton. They moved through Europe seeking hints of it, founding companies or gathering scholars to help in the search.[41]

Williams himself incorporates variations of these at different points of his own development: (1) The lower correspondences, and in particular alchemy, are to be found in his first novel, *Shadows of Ecstasy,* which is highly colored in alchemical imagery and driven by a rather primitive admiration for an adeptship of what one judges to be an unsophisticated presentation of transmutation. (2) The intellectual wisdom tradition searching beyond the confines of the conventional is one that he himself personified, if with not quite the catholicity of Cornelius Agrippa. But his predilection for the esoteric search for the single principle places him in the center of the tradition of alchemical inquiry. There is a certain irony in the language he uses when he writes of the "lower correspondences." It was precisely the Doctrine of Correspondence to which he was to turn in order to justify his unitive approach to the interdependency of the material and spirit, and on which so much of his affirmative theology was based. The third element, (3) the founding of companies of wanderers drawn together by the same esoteric insights, would find its place in the establishment of his own order, the "Companions of the Co-inherence."[42]

In a book of few footnotes and of a total of three in this chapter, we find further evidence of Williams's dependence on Waite in this area. One of the three provides a reference from Waite's *Book of Ceremonial Magic.* Williams quotes Waite to make the point that in the so-called *Enchiridion of Pope Leo III,* a book purporting to contain prayers given by the pope to Charlemagne, the inclusion of devotional charms and magical secrets could not have happened "without apparently exceeding the devotional discipline of the Church."[43]

Any concerns that critics may have that Williams was insufficiently distanced from the goetic practices of what he calls the "Way of Perversion of Images"[44] should be dispelled by both the tone and the content of the dismissive critique with which he ends the chapter. He is dryly contemptuous of the kind of person who might attempt some of the rituals described, both of the state of the soul and mind, and believes it highly unlikely that anyone could easily find the stamina to survive the dullness, difficulty, deviousness, and danger of the rites. But he is more energized, though still dismissive, in his attitude toward more popular goetic culture:

> It is possible even now to feel a slight movement of the blood in reading the Ritual of Necromancy—of the spell "by the power of the East and the silence of the night, by the holy rites of Hecate," of the mastic and gum-aromatic, of the striking of the body, of its rising and standing, and of its faint responses to the questions asked. So Edward Kelley was said to have raised the dead in Wootton-in-the-Dale, and so the stories at least, had gone abroad in the days of Virgil and Apuleius. The dialogue of the Church is more tender, more human, and operative over all: "Rest eternal grant unto them O Lord." "And let light perpetual shine upon them."[45]

Williams has made his case for redefining the relationship between the esoteric and the Christian traditions. In the next chapter we will explore the intellectual mechanism by which he sets out to achieve their reconciliation.

CHAPTER SEVEN

The Integration of the Natural and Supernatural in Charles Williams

> Williams was a true hermeticist. Few writers can convincingly portray the immanence of divine energy and delight within the natural order.[1]

> Under the rays I studied arch-natural justice.[2]

Williams's vision of the demand for integration in the face of dualism pervades his work. In order to facilitate it he develops a language that will enable the fusion of otherwise dichotomous categories. Various scholars have proposed different interpretations of the relationship of the novels to one another in Williams's development. One more recent theory is Dr. Dennis L. Weeks's conclusion that the pattern in the development of the novels resembles that of the seven steps of co-inherence. This hypothesis is attractive for it is captivating and neat; however, the facts do not support it. (See "Dennis Weeks's *Steps toward Salvation*" at the end of this chapter.) A more fruitful and insightful avenue of exploration is to look at his use of the Waitean term "arch-natural," which demonstrates the flow of his developing thought over the period the novels' span, and which provides a mature synthesis of what would otherwise appear to be contradiction.[3]

Williams's views on the essential fusion of spirit and matter were evident in the works of his earliest period. Florence Conway was treated to walks with her fiancé and she was serenaded to the words of effusive enthusiasm on the Athanasian Creed.[4] In *Descent of the Dove* Williams describes the Athanasian Creed as a manifesto or "maxim" of the Affirmative Way: "It produces a phrase that is the very maxim of the Affirmative Way: 'Not by the conversion of the Godhead into flesh, but by the taking of manhood into God.' . . . [A]ll images are, in their degree, to be carried on; mind is never to be put off matter; all experience is to be gathered in."[5]

We are not able to analyze the chemistry of attraction that the Athanasian-minded Williams had with the Q'abalistic and Rosicrucian enthusiasm for the symbolism of the body, but one fed the other. The immature Williams found expression for both in material devices like the Grail in *War in Heaven,* or the stone in *Many Dimensions,* or the tarot pack in *The Greater Trumps,* all of which acted as conduits for the spiritual in his earlier novels; and the mature Williams allowed his theological sympathy with the material world to evolve into a means by which elements that stood in tension, contradistinction, or even contradiction were able to find a symbiotic resolution. Matter and spirit, romantic experience and spirituality, the Affirmative and Negative Ways are held together co-inherently within the Web of Exchange.

The influence of Waite is evident at the conceptual roots of the language that Williams uses. Of the odd words that Williams took over from Waite, "Messias" and "Graal" are familiar to readers and critics, but "arch-natural" has received little, if any, attention. The use of this unusual word, which is intended to avoid the polarization of natural and supernatural, draws attention to Williams's intention to find a metaphysical category that allowed him to achieve a fusion of the two categories. By this means he sets out to demonstrate his evolving sense of the co-inherence of all things. The novels show an aspect of this developing sensitivity of touch. The early novels use the device of special objects that mediate the supernatural and thus integrate it into natural experience. The later novels see this mediation as lying within the provenance of people rather than things. Not all commentators have seen this evolving fusion of category as central to Williams's development of thought expressed in the novels.

I propose that there is a form of development that has been overlooked, since its source has been unexplored and misjudged. It is the development from "Waitean" concepts, both conscious and subliminal, into a more fully developed and idiosyncratic style of thinking that carries the earlier worldview with it. This development incorporates it into a more powerful and coherent ideology that acts to restore a balance within the mainstream theological tradition that had until then been missing. Williams was constantly concerned to avoid unnecessary dualism. Dichotomies of category (categories that fell into duality) were anathema to him. By providing in his own later work a balance between what would otherwise be seen as opposites, he sets a pattern for a comprehensive and coherent theology that acts as an antidote to aberrations in the tradition, the most obvious one being the wholesale emphasis on the *Via Negativa.*

The initial template for this approach is found in A. E. Waite, and derives from the spirituality of Q'abalism that so valued the material and particularly the human body. Waite disliked the use of the term "supernatural," because its very antithesis to the natural suggested a diminution of the status of the natural, and a chasm between the two categories that distorted their proper interrelationship.[6] He took to using the term "arch-natural" as a way of avoiding to continue what he took to be a false distinction. Williams follows Waite repeatedly in this practice, for the same reasons. And one of the most important developments in the maturation of the novels flows from this apprehension. Williams develops a unitive approach within his understanding of co-inherence to the whole of creation that depends on his remedial understanding of the relationship between natural and supernatural, in his phraseology, the arch-natural.[7]

The "Arch-natural" and the Denial of Dichotomy

Williams is obviously more explicit about his concerns in his reviews, essays, and other works than in his fiction, and I will turn to them for evidence of his intentions; but as usual, the process of development begins with Waite. Waite uses the prefix on a number of occasions in order to make some form of distinction. So he writes of an "arch-natural" Eucharist when exploring the relationship between the Eucharist and the Graal mystery.[8]

In the same book he turns to the phrase "arch-natural" as a means of intensifying the concept of consecration.

> That is true of it in the uttermost which was said long ago by Paracelsus: "*Nihil tam occultum erit quod non revelabitur*"; but there are few with ears to hear it, it remains a voice in the wilderness crying in an unknown tongue. We know that according to high theology the substance is communicated in the Eucharist, normally in the symbolical manner, but, in cases, essentially and vitally according to true testimonies. It is therefore as if the elements were at times consecrated normally and at times by other words, more secret and efficient arch-naturally.[9]

A few pages later, Waite uses "arch-natural" where more conventionally one would have expected "supernatural" or "spiritual." Discussing alchemy and *The Theatricum Chemicum*, he writes, "We have on our part to realise that (a) there were two schools making use of the same language in a distinct sense, the one branch seeking the transmutation of metals and the art of prolonging life; the other branch investigating the mysteries of the arch-natural life."[10]

Williams wrote two articles that overtly address themselves to this central concern. The second, "Natural Goodness," deals explicitly with the natural/supernatural dichotomy. The first, in 1939, was written for *Theology,* the article entitled "Sensuality and Substance."[11] In both articles he pursues an argument for a unitive approach to body and soul, or spirit and matter in order to set up more clearly the parameters of their relationship in contradistinction to the unofficial Manichaeanism, where "the great world and energy of the body have either been deprecated or devotionalized; and by devotionalized I mean turned into a pale imitation of 'substance,' of spirit; thus losing their own powers and privileges without, in general, gaining any others."[12]

In "Sensuality" he presents with succinct clarity his orthodox and Athanasian arguments that the Christian Western tradition had underplayed with serious theological and aesthetic consequences:

> But the *Anthropos* in Christ was not "like" the Theos: it was nothing but itself. So the body is not "like" the soul; it is nothing but itself. The principle of our sensuality is unique and divine. It is no doubt, rooted in substance. "Soul is form and doth the body make" is a fine Platonist line. But soul ought not to be allowed to reduce the body to its own shadow—at any rate, in the Christian Church.[13]

His line of argument in the article, having exposed the deficiency he is addressing, is that the church owes a debt to its heretics in general, and because a recent biography had come out, he suggests to make his argument contemporary, to D. H. Lawrence in particular.[14] The value of heretical fellow travelers is that they share similar values but are free to criticize from outside the boundaries of the institutions' prevailing culture.[15] He had commended himself to Williams with the line: "The phallic consciousness is not the cerebral sex-consciousness, but something really deeper, and the root of poetry, lived or sung."[16]

Williams follows Ford Madox Ford in attributing Lawrence's reaction to the "inverted Puritanism" of his social class that made "nebulous glooming about sex" a "moral duty" and heroic (Ford's phrase). But this attitude Williams blamed on the failure of a Christianity that "refined the body into an unreal phantom" and embraced a "docetic" morality contrary to its own creedal theology.[17] But if it took the insight of Lawrence, to re-present to Christianity "the Way of Affirmation of Images" that it had deserted, Williams was glad to recognize a literary and poetic ally and make common cause with him.

> The movements for housing and social reform, the consciousness of the dispossessed masses, have already prepared the way as an accident of their own preoccupation. There is no likelihood we shall become more amorously promiscuous because the other preoccupation is heartened by the physical intellect, because we have more meaning to brood over. The great identity of the Anthropos will be preserved the better in the categories of substance and sensuality the more we attend to these categories as such.

Then he writes that wonderful and pungent phrase of prophetic criticism: "the hungry sheep look up for metaphysics, the profound metaphysics of the redeeming body, and are given morals."[18]

In "Natural Goodness" (1941) he turns more explicitly to the division of the natural and supernatural. He begins by making the point that natural and supernatural have unnecessarily come to be considered opposite rather than complementary. Supernature must include nature, and if we have misunderstood the place of matter, it is due to an apostasy of spirit. It is in fact primarily in the realm of spirit that the myth of the fall is located. Matter and nature have not sinned. From there, he suggests, with Duns Scotus, that even if there had been no fall, the incarnation would still have taken place, with the consequent implications for the place and value of the material that follow from such a hypothesis. If we are to make any distinction between matter and spirit, then it needs to be in the recognition that such sinning as took place was in the will of man, and the will of man was a spiritual quality. In Williams's view the supernatural therefore sinned; the natural did not. They should not be separated, but if they are, then, contrary to the popular judgment, our substance (or to avoid the Aristotelian usage that would refer to accidents here), our somatic being, has remained faithful, and the immaterial or spiritual has not.[19]

The next stage in the argument is to suggest that union with the godhead is obtained by acts. Some distinction needs to be made here, which Williams appears to make in restricted terms, to avoid the great Reformation debate over faith and works. His distinction is to define "belief" and "proper motive" as an act. No doubt if asked, he would reply that "responding to grace" was also an act. But from there he insists that an act is also an act; by which he means that the material arena is the place in which the journey of faith is acted out. This emphasis avoids the sentimentalizing or spiritualizing faith. It is intended to provide the framework for affirming the dynamics of salvation, the great acts of exchange and substitution that he will explore in his last two novels in depth.

However, another way of establishing that framework is the avoidance of the opposition of the categories of natural and supernatural. And this he does in

The Figure of Beatrice, published in 1943, one of his last major works, along with *Region of the Summer Stars* (1944) and *All Hallows' Eve* (1945). Intriguingly there has been, until *Beatrice,* no significant use of Waite's term "arch-natural," but in this, as some would have it, his most sublime work, he turns to it regularly.

Williams makes it very clear in the work that any linguistic terminology that contributes to the dichotomization of spirit and matter is to be avoided. For that reason, he wants even to avoid the use of the term "sacramental." He is examining Dante's use of the body and has referred to Wordsworth's well-known passage on the body becoming an index of delight:

> The great doctrine lies between the spiritualisers and the carnalizers—the idealists and the sensualists; it is explained away by both, yet for ever "it trembles yet it does not pass away." Nor, speaking generally, does it fare much better when it is called sacramental. Technically, the word might serve, but in popular use it dichotomises too much; it divides, while professing to unite and, in popular use, it throws over the light of the serious object a false light of semi-religious portentousness.[20]

At this point of conceptual frustration he turns to Waite's term, and uses it to describe the metaphysical state of perfection: "those other lovers' insights are themselves valid because that perfection is the arch-natural state of human beings, seen after that arch-natural manner."[21]

He later describes the visionary capacity of philosophy as "arch-natural": "Philosophy does it by reason, and she does it through vision. She is, as it were, the substance of spirit and the visibility of spirits; in that respect she is an arch-natural thing."[22] When Dante envisages the union of the animal, intellectual, and divine, in an entity almost "*un altro iddio incarnato,*" Williams comments, "This sentence again is a union of the vision of Beatrice-in-perfection and of the knowledge of philosophy-in-perfection. The actual Incarnation itself shows for a moment, arch-natural and not alien from our commonalty, a thing (as it were) all but seen happening, a marvel."[23]

When Williams looks for a term to describe the status of the emperor as Dante cogitates on the nature of earthly justice, he reverts to the same term:

> He is therefore the guardian of everlasting laws. He also is, in that sense, arch-natural, and not only Christ, but Beatrice, and the lady of the window and Dante, are subject to him. . . . [D]ante certainly had known a Republic also, however inadequate; he had known Florence. When he appealed to the Emperor against Florence he was appealing to the arch-

> natural against the natural. It is not to be supposed that he found any joy in it. *O misera, misera, patria mia!*[24]

The completeness of the feminine image has been presented in the light of philosophical analysis. Again Williams needs to find the complementary concept for natural:

> The girl had come like the True Light. The eleven fruits of nobility answer to the moral virtues (and correspond in the active life to the intellectual in the contemplative life). They are the marks of the soul-in-largesse, perfect in her temporal blessedness; which consists, as Dante now defines it, "*in operatione propriae virtutis*," "in the operation of his proper power." This operation would be the fulfilling of his function; his function is his vocation, and he follows it by this proper operation. But there had been something more. She had not only been so natural that the very earth and all habits of our mortal life are not more so she had also been so arch-natural that she had thrown light on the Faith itself. Faith began, and after faith the hope of that which we already foresee, and from that the activity of love . . . *fede* . . . *speranza* . . . *carita*. These are the theological virtues which lead to eternal life.[25]

In the *Making of the Commedia*, Williams fulminates against the "spiritualisers," whom he compares favorably with the ironists and the allegorists. They have denied the mortal identity of Beatrice, and turned her into "Theology" or "Grace" or "what not." She becomes unblooded, a vapor of the soul. And this evacuates the text of any interest for young lovers since there is no place to locate their own experience. The whole tenor of this spiritualization runs entirely counter to his thrust for integration; and through integration, application, "[t]he same miserable spiritualising has taken place in another myth, with Galahad the High Prince, the mystery of whose fatherhood in Lancelot has been forgotten."

While the *Paradiso* is not easy for beginners in romanticism nonetheless, to spiritualize Beatrice away from earth into pseudoromanticism is, in criticism, very like mortal sin. The passage of the two lovers into paradise as lovers who are integrating both body and soul in the journey of obedience, failed obedience, and subsequent repentance is one that Williams affirms:

> [T]he "glorious and holy flesh" is a part of its consummations; it is included in the painting of "*nostra effigie*" in the reflected light of the Second Circle at the grand poetic close. The passage through the Paradises

> is the true passage and history of Love—impossible to men and women because of sin, but comprehensible to the *"nobile intelletto,"* the intellect of the noble life, and even in a sense, after repentance, possible to it. It is the simple and arch-natural process of any two lovers—fortunate if they obey, infinitely unfortunate if they continue to disobey.[26]

Dante, in his journey, was not always in possession of love and courtesy, and again Williams is looking for a term to illuminate their nature: "These states are arch-natural certainly, in the sense that the knowledge of them does not depend (as is sometimes blasphemously asserted) upon our knowledge of their opposites. We are able to know good without knowing evil; I mean, that our nature is of that kind, though unhappily it has been so twisted that in fact we do not."[27]

Williams follows Waite in his choice of "arch-natural," but Cavaliero prefers the term "preternatural," meaning outside the natural, and comments on the distinction between a materialist view of the supernatural and the Christian unitive understanding that Williams represents:[28]

> The urge to belong to some body of secret gnosis, in order to assert and define one's own identity, provides frequent instances of how the concept of supernatural can be distorted by human insecurity. Such aspirations are materialistic at heart for they attempt the systematizing of the immeasurable. The declaration enshrined in the Athanasian Creed that the Incarnation constitutes a taking of the Manhood into God, rather than the conversion of Godhead into flesh, defines precisely the difference between a religious understanding of the supernatural and that held by occultists interested in magic and in manipulative spiritual ceremonies.
>
> While both theologians and students of the occult regard material objects as potential vehicles for the operation of the supernatural, the latter study them in the hope of understanding them and participating in their energy: theirs is a scientific spirituality. Theology, the divine science is contemplative; it focuses upon awareness of the indwelling divine order which constitutes beatitude. While affirming the hermetic belief in a materially operative immanence, it simultaneously recognises the utter transcendence of the absolute—Judaism's gift to Christianity. Failure to distinguish between these two responses, the hermetic and the religious, complicates the reactions of subscribers to materialistic philosophies when confronted say with Blake's matter-of-fact hold on spiritual things, and a systematic study of occult lore undertaken by Yeats. . . . Yeats's ambivalent commitments, and still more, the dazzling certainties of Blake, have be-

> come sources of embarrassment.... [E]ven late twentieth century readers, with their inbuilt simplistic reflexes of either/or where spirit and body are concerned (Blake's indictment of Bacon, Locke and Newton mythologizes the dichotomy) are resistant to these matters being taken seriously.[29]

Precisely by adopting the mythic categories of the hermetic, and attempting to synthesize the categories of natural and supernatural in his novels, Williams makes a bid for the intelligent imagination of the reader. By use of hermetic imagery, he intends to draw his reader into a renewed metaphysic that reflects the more accurate reality contained in the Doctrine of Correspondence, the fusion of immanence and transcendence, natural and supernatural, spiritual and material into an Athanasian synthesis that avoids illusory dichotomy. This process reaches its maturation in his last two novels.

Dennis Weeks's Steps toward Salvation

There have been other attempts to chart a pattern of development through the novels. An example of the most recent is that of Dr. Dennis Weeks in his work *Steps toward Salvation: An Examination of Co-inherence and Substitution in the Seven Novels of Charles Williams.* In his study Weeks suggests that the key to understanding the seven novels lies instead with the seven steps of co-inherence written as the manifesto for the companions of co-inherence. The constitution comprised seven propositions.

1. The Order has no constitution except its members. As it was said: "Others he saved, himself he cannot save."
2. It recommends nevertheless that its members shall make a formal act of union with it and of recognition of their own nature. As it was said, "Am I my brother's keeper?"
3. Its concern is the practice of the apprehension of the Co-inherence both as a natural and a supernatural principle. As it was said "Let us make man in Our image."
4. It is therefore "*per necessitatem,*" Christian. As it was said: "And whoever says there was when this was not, let him be anathema."
5. It recommends therefore the study, on the contemplative side, of the Co-inherence of the Holy and Blessed Trinity, of the Two Natures of the single Person, of the Mother and Son. of the communicated Eucharist, and of the whole active Catholic Church. And it is said: "*figlia del tuo figlio.*" And on the active side, of the methods of exchange, in

the State, in all forms of love, and in all natural things, such as childbirth. As it was said: "Bear ye one another's burdens."

6. It concludes in the divine substitution of the Messias all forms of exchange and substitution, and invokes this Act as the root of all. As it was said: "He must become, as it were, a double man."
7. The Order will associate itself primarily with four feasts: the Feast of the Annunciation, The Feast of the Blessed Trinity, the Feast of the Transfiguration and the Commemoration of All Souls. As it was said: "Another will be in me and I in him."[30]

Weeks begins his analysis by exploring the meaning of the seven steps, and then sets out to prove that each of the novels treats either or both theories of exchange and substitution as they align with his seven steps of the "Companions."[31] While providing us with a useful study of the material in the novels where they express substitution and co-inherence, Weeks is inclined to see more intellectual organization than there may be evidence for: "Williams saw his first novels, up to *Descent into Hell,* as foundations for Co-inherence and Substitution."[32]

It is more likely that, although the novels of course contained the two ideas essential to Williams's outlook, they do not work through them as methodically or consciously as Weeks implies. The fact that there are seven in number is likely to have been given more significance than it ought to bear. In a letter to his wife dated December 3, 1944, on the eve of the publication of *All Hallows' Eve,* the seventh novel, he wrote implying he had plans for a further novel, an eighth: "Every so often one of my indistinguishable pupils emits a sudden remark, such as one last night who said of symbolism in literature that it was like the rope in *Descent into Hell.* Perhaps it's not a bad thing that there is another novel coming out; Perhaps after the Prose Arthur we will do another novel and do it better."[33]

In a reminiscence of her husband, Florence (Michal) Williams wrote in April 1955: "It was during one of the last weekends Charles was ever to spend at home that he spoke to me of his post-war writing. . . . [T]hen he said, 'And I shall write one more novel which my faithful public will not like I think. This time it will be a straightforward one. There will be no black magic, no dancing figures, and no supernatural beings wandering though its pages.'"[34] If Williams had lived to write his eighth novel, Weeks's hypothesis would clearly be inadequate. The evidence of these letters shows that it is misplaced. Even without the evidence it requires too systematic an approach from Williams. However, there is clearly some development, and a number of different commentators have offered their insights.[35]

CHAPTER EIGHT

The Second Phase of Maturation

The Later Novels

The Extension of Axes of Correspondence in Descent into Hell

> The young shall save the old and the old the young
> the dead the living, and the other living the dead.[1]

> The supreme achievement of hell is to make interchange impossible.[2]

The integration Williams has been developing can be most vividly demonstrated by contrasting the central characters in the last two novels with the central characters in the earliest fiction that Williams wrote. Pauline, Margaret, and Stanhope in *Descent into Hell* represent a mature Christianized adeptship of co-inherent integration, whereas the fate of Wentworth in the same novel clarifies the consequences of metaphysical decay in a markedly different way from the antiheroes of the early novels. In *All Hallows' Eve* Williams provides a stark and compelling definition of metaphysical corruption in his depiction of the profane as perversion. In this way he avoids using the classical notion of hell in stark opposition to heaven.

Williams bases his views upon the notion of the Doctrine of Correspondence, so linking the metaphysical dimension with the physical. His dependence on Waite for the embryonic concept from his earliest works has been established. However, the concept is developed in a striking way over the period during which he wrote the novels.[3] One can find early signs of a development away from the primitive celebration of adeptship in the hermetic mold exhibited by Considine in his earliest fiction. His is replaced by a new adeptship of a different kind, that of the remedial, substitutionary, and enabling figures like Anthony in *The Place of the Lion*, Chloe in *Many Dimensions*, and most notably,

Sybil in *The Greater Trumps.* The emerging pattern of the role that these new adepts play comes to fruition in *Descent into Hell.* The link between the dimensions of being that may, risking a certain primitive spatial clumsiness, be called vertical, now becomes horizontal as well. The notion of correspondence is extended socially and interrelationally between figures in the drama. Williams no longer restricts his focus to the metaphysical dimension of above and below, nor related only to the alchemical journey of the individual into ultimate union with the godhead; it has been enlarged laterally to include community. To this end the plot includes the juxtaposition of different characters for whom the most important task is their reconciliation.

There are a number of different fault lines requiring the healing of reconciliation: between Pauline and her *doppelgänger;* then subsequently between Pauline and her martyred ancestor Struther; Mrs. Margaret Anstruther and the dead workman; Wentworth and Austin Moffat; and two contradictory notions of the self, as well as time and space. Among them all, Prospero-like, Stanhope exercises his metaphysical drama, weaving his aesthetic magic through the developments of plot, and expressing this new adeptship—the magus of co-inherence and substitution. Stanhope's task is also alchemical, but he practices an evolved alchemy more concerned with transfiguration than transmutation. He brings about change within the community. The change along the lines of the original correspondence is intended to mirror the greater and deeper reality of the wider universe, described more conventionally here again as "supernatural." Transmutation cannot take place where change is impossible. But transmutation has become alteration, and alteration becomes a notion of change that involves one in the life of ultimate redemption. The language of change is now the language of transfiguration. Pauline is faced with the adept of degenerate occultism, Mrs. Sammile—otherwise Lilith. Mrs. Sammile represents the occult culture where knowledge and control become the dominating skills of the adept; a culture in which change is only a function of the adept's determination to control people and events. Lilith, as she is, attempts to lure Pauline with the false distorting knowledge of her trade.

> She laughed again at the useless attempts to explain. The sterile silence of the hidden cave exposed itself, and the single laughter of the girl ran over it, and after the laughter the silence itself awoke. As if the very air emanated power, the stillness became warm; a haze of infinite specks of gold filled the darkness as if the laughter had for a moment made its joy, and more than its joy, visible.

> The sombre air of the chill city of the plain was pierced by the joy of the sons of God which exists even there. Lilith shrieked and flung up her arms; and a sudden thin wail followed the shriek, the wail of all those dead who cannot endure joy.[4]

The notion of changed humanity points us in the direction of this joy. Williams appears to suggest that one of the problems encountered in homosexuality is that it provides artificial freedom from the enforced changes that parents experience at the hands of their offspring. In an ambiguous passage he may be comparing that biological sterility with the sterility of those who do not know how to love "another" of whatever gender. Where there is no community of love, there is no alteration.

> He said: "The Lord's glory fell on the cities of the plain, of Sodom and another. We know all about Sodom nowadays, but perhaps we know the other even better. Men can be in love with men, and women with women, and still be in love and make sounds and speeches, but don't you know how quiet the streets of Gomorrah are? Haven't you seen the pools that everlastingly reflect the faces of those who walk with their own phantasms, but the phantasms aren't reflected and can't be. The lovers of Gomorrah are quite contented, Periel; they don't have to put up with our difficulties. They aren't bothered by alteration, at least till the rain of the fire of Glory at the end, for they lose the capacity for change, except for the fear of hell."[5]

Williams does not use the Waitean term "arch-natural" here. He turns to this term only in 1943 with *The Figure of Beatrice,* but here he does find other ways of expressing the same concept. When Stanhope is discussing the role and nature of the chorus with one of the many young women, Williams resorts to the word "different."

> "The main thing is that they are non-human."
>
> "Spirits?" said the Watteau young lady with a trill of pleasure.
>
> "If you like," said Stanhope, "only not spiritual. Alive, but with a different life."[6]

The "different life" is the life where vertical correspondence, "as above, so below," is mirrored existentially and relationally by what may be called a lateral correspondence. This lateral correspondence requires the integration of fractured relationships, and extends through both time and space. Williams accentuates the task of interrelating by having his characters coexist in space, if not in time, while windows into time are opened. Dichotomy is confronted wherever it is found. Williams will echo the language of adeptship to describe the task of integration. Both Stanhope and Margaret Anstruther are presented as skilled adepts of union. The vagrant, who is finally ready to move beyond purgatory, is described as representing a more universal need, as being in need of a reconciliation beyond himself. The vagrant is used by Williams to develop notions of dichotomy and transmutation.

> No dichotomy of flesh and spirit distressed or delighted him, nor did he know anything of the denial of that dichotomy by the creed of Christendom. The unity that creed has proclaimed against experience, against intelligence, that for the achievement of man's unity the body of his knowledge is to be raised; no fairer stuff, no other alien matter but this—to be impregnated with holiness and transmuted by lovely passion, but still this.[7]

The novel charts how the integration of co-inherence both does happen and, in the cases of Wentworth, Sammile (if she is treated both as a person as well as a mythic representation of evil), and Adela, does not happen.

Pauline Anstruther: The Quest for Transfiguration, Reconciliation, and Integration

In Pauline Anstruther this double axis of correspondence can be most clearly seen. She has two tasks of reconciliation to achieve. The first is the act of reconciliation in which she is able to carry the fear of her ancestor; this is a reconciliation that takes place at the junction of different times and spaces.

This act is accompanied by her own internal journey of reconciliation or, better, integration. This will result in a kind of transfiguration of her whole self. This transfiguration lies at the heart of Williams's understanding of the romantic vision, where a lover sees the beloved momentarily as God sees them. The vision below mirrors the reality above. In this case the task of reconciliation is presented through the encounter with her *doppelgänger,* as it is termed in the novel. Paradoxically, the *doppelgänger* will constitute what in Jungian thought functions as a type of shadow of Pauline's character. But here Williams takes Jungian typology and inverts it. For the shadow here is not a dark, repressed, complementary figure to Pauline, but an inverse shadow that presents her with the illuminated, redeemed potentiality she carries within her. The inverted shadow is the illumined Pauline, whereas the "conscious Pauline" acts the hidden, repressed, and threatening or threatened life of the conventional shadow. Reconciliation between the dark and light embodiments of Pauline still needs to take place. When it has happened and she has encountered and surmounted her own internal fear, she embarks on the more conscious choice of bearing the fear of her ancestor in the face of the flames at his martyrdom. As she achieves this, Williams presents her not as transmuted but as transfigured, showing how he has grown beyond the default hermetic culture. He carries the remedial insights of hermeticism into the language of orthodoxy. In this transfiguration both axes of correspondence are fused into one.

The process of change takes place in her as she makes choices on her journey. Intimations of an illumination accompany her transfiguration. In Pauline's encounter with Mrs. Sammile, she is tempted with the prospect that she will never have to do anything for others anymore. This assault on the entire nature of substitution and co-inherence is recognized and resisted. As she does so, she is aware of the "glory of exchange." "Perjury on her soul and in her blood if now she slipped to buy sweets with money that was not hers; never till it was hers in all love and princely good, by gift and gift and gift beyond excelling gift, in no secrecy of greed but all glory of public exchange, law of the universe and herself as a child of the universe."[8] Her oath to Stanhope holds her in the face of temptation: "An oath, an oath, an oath in heaven, and heaven known in the bright oath itself, where two loves struck together and the serene light of substitution shone, beyond her understanding, but not beyond her deed."[9]

She will make the same journey of initiation into liberation and freedom of exchange as Felicitas, the Carthaginian whom Williams documents in *Descent of the Dove.* When facing martyrdom she bore a child in prison and screamed with pain; her jailers asked her how if she shrieked at *that,* she expected to endure death by the beasts: "She said: 'Now *I* suffer what *I* suffer; then another will be in me who will suffer for me, as I shall suffer for him.' In that Felicitas took her place for ever among the great African doctors of the Universal Church."[10] Pauline will face not the pain of childbirth but that of existential terror. In her act of mutuality with John Anstruther she will set in motion the entrance into the mutuality of the dynamism of exchange that releases the possibility of transfiguration.

When she sits in the dark with Margaret Anstruther, the phrase "mortally illumined" presumably refers to electricity, in contrast to the metaphysical black darkness referred to in the immediately preceding passage. But at the moment of *dénouement,* when she both carries John Anstruther's fear and retrospectively locates the origin of her own fear in his, the image is one of transfiguration. Her other self, which she has now at last encountered,

> wore no supernatural splendour of aureole, but its rich nature burned and glowed before her, bright as if indeed mortal flesh had become what all lovers know it to be. . . . [T]he glory of poetry could not outshine the glory of certain fact, and not any poetry could hold as many meanings as the fact. One element co-ordinated original and translation: that element was joy. Joy had filled her that afternoon and it was in the power of such joy that she had been brought to this closest propinquity to herself. It had been her incapacity for joy, nothing else that had till now turned the vision of herself aside; her incapacity for joy had admitted fear, and fear had imposed separation.[11]

Separation, or more accurately, alienation, is indeed the antithesis of transfiguring co-inherence. Pauline will experience more illumination as she shares in the co-inherence of all things. At the point where the world of the spiritual necromancy of Gomorrah dissolves, Pauline confronts Lilith, who is crouching on the ground. The image is once again the language of transfiguration.

> The angelic energy which had been united with Pauline's mortality radiated from her; nature, and more than nature, abhors a vacuum. Her mind and senses could not yet receive comprehensibly the motions of spirit, but that adoring centre dominated her, and flashes of its great capacity passed through her, revealing if but in flashes, the single world of existence.[12]

Transfiguration has grown out from transmutation, and by this change the unitive world of existence is perceived, free from all dichotomy or division.[13] Pauline has changed. Her dullness and fear, which were rooted in her sense of separation and dislocation, have been transformed into radiance and holy energy. Willingness to change is a prerequisite for making the journey from Gomorrah toward Zion.

> The lovers of Gomorrah are quite contented, Periel. . . . [T]hey aren't bothered by alteration, . . . for they lose the capacity for change, except for the fear of hell. They're monogamous enough! and they've no children—no cherubim breaking into being or babies as tiresome as ours; there's no birth there, and only the second death. There's no distinction

> between lover and beloved; they beget themselves on the adoration of themselves, and by themselves too.[14]

The hand or influence of Q'abalism through Waite also stretches into the novel at this point. God blessed Adam, who originally was presented as containing Eve, because "they" were male and female united for the purpose for the fulfillment of creation; according to the Elohim that purpose was to increase, multiply, and replenish the earth.[15] The sex here involves no begetting, no exchange, no interdependence, no adoration of the Creator with whom one becomes co-creator in the procreation of children. Williams offers a theology that improves on the Q'abalistic preoccupation with the responsibility for peopling the earth with souls, and he delineates the psychological and spiritual implications of sterility in terms of his presentation of the imperatives of exchange and co-inherence. Wentworth's immersion in autoeroticism is sinful precisely because there is no act of real exchange with another.

Pauline discovered during her vivid dream of separation and search that "while she hurried she changed."[16] She changed from an overpowering fear that others would notice her to a determination to catch up that shadow of herself that fled her.[17] Lilith epitomizes the spirit of Gomorrah when she attempts to lure Pauline into accepting her inaccurate promises to fulfill unnamed desires.

> The absolute and entire sufficiency of existence rose in her . . . she could ask for nothing but what was—life in the instant mode of living.
>
> "Change," said the shape. "I don't change."
>
> Pauline cried out: "And if it changes, it shall change as it must, and I shall want it as it is then."[18]

Pauline makes the journey of the novitiate. Adeptship lies elsewhere.

Margaret Anstruther: The New Adeptship of Substitution and Union

Margaret Anstruther mirrors Stanhope in his role as an adept of substitution and union. Although she is close to death, her adeptship generates no ambition for the extension of her life as Considine's had. She prepares for death expecting to discover its joy. She shares vicariously the adeptship of poetry—a language of metaphysical knowledge: "She knew that since [Stanhope's later plays] were poetry, they must mean more than her individual being knew."[19]

One observes obvious parallels between the figure of Stanhope and Williams the author. Both are poets with a vision of transformation through poetry, so the reader may evaluate the suggestion that "when she was dead she might be able to say Stanhope's poetry properly"[20] as something of a lapse from the best standards of literary taste. However, this aspiration should not hide the point that poetry is now the language of the new adeptship. Where before undifferentiated energy was the mark of the adept, it is now energy of knowledge, and knowledge with a purpose for expressing the purpose of reconciliation in the face of disintegration.

> In those places the movement of human life had closed—of human life and human death, of the death in life which was an element in life, and of those places the Hill in which she lived was one. An energy reposed in it, strong to affect all its people, an energy of separation and energy of knowledge. If, as she believed, the spirit of man in death saw truly what he was and had been, so that whether he desired it or not a lucid power of intelligence manifested all himself to him—then the energy of knowledge was especially urgent upon women and women here. . . . [S]he felt, as if by a communication of a woe not hers, how the neighbourhood of the dead troubled the living; how the living were narrowed by the return of the dead.[21]

Wentworth will have the opportunity of contact with the unquiet soul of the vagrant, but, having never acknowledged the unity of the republic, will merely ignore it. Some reconciliations are not acceptable because they are misleading or inaccurate. Williams uses Margaret's vigil for the dead both to excoriate the egocentricity of spiritualism and also to locate the more recent preoccupation with psychoanalysis into the displaced failure of the social and religious metaphysical understanding of death. In a scathing passage that encompasses not only the specifics of spiritualism and psychoanalysis but also acts as a critique of the whole of contemporary culture and its accompanying truncated metaphysic, he comments:

> But where superstition and religion failed, where cemeteries were no longer forbidden and no longer feared; where the convenient processes of cremation encouraged a pretence of friendship between the living and dead—might not that new propinquity turn in fearful friendship in the end? It was commonly accepted that dead were anxious the help the living, but what if the dead were only anxious for the living to help them? Or what if the infection of their experience communicated itself across too

> narrow a grave? Men were beginning to know, they were being compelled to know; at last the living world was shaken by the millions of spirits who endured that further permanent revelation. Hysteria of self-knowledge, monotony of self-analysis, introspection spreading like disease, what was all this but the infection over the unpurified borders of death?[22]

Margaret would endure the exposure of self in the searching light of reality because she had learned and progressed from the Greek maxim of "know thyself" to the Christian of "know love." In an extraordinary passage of visionary experience Williams describes Margaret's purgative experience of the mountainside, modeled it seems on Waitean liturgical and Rosicrucian imagery.[23] It begins with the Hill of St. Albans that grows:

> Mountains or modes of consciousness, peaks or perceptions, they stood; on the slopes of each the world was carried; and the final height of each was the separate consummation of the whole. It was, as the apprehended movement upon each of them died away, in the time before the dawn that they rose there, nor had the sun risen though they were not in darkness. Either a light emanated from themselves or some great sun drew towards them from its own depth.

The dross to be cleansed becomes fugitives fleeing from the light:

> At the increase of the sun there grew also an increase of fugitive sound; and she became aware of a few wandering shapes on the heights about her. Some climbed on; others, instead of welcoming the light as lost mountaineers should do, turned to escape it. They seemed all, even those who climbed, grotesque obtrusions into that place of rock and ice and thin air and growing sun, a world different from theirs, hers and not hers.[24]

Her early years are referred to in language that fits both the monastic and gnostic contexts, as a "novitiate." Williams continues to use language that is polysemous: both hermetic and orthodox. When the dawn of union with the godhead arrives, it will be to effect "one last throb of piercing change under its power."[25] Since her novitiate she has come to know her own being as deeply interconnected with the rest of humanity. It is from this illumined Christian adeptship of knowledge that she is willing to reach out and be part of the means for effecting a reconciliation with the unquiet spirit of the vagrant.

> She had no work of union within herself to achieve; that was done.[26] But this man died from and in the body only. Because he had had it all but forced upon him, he had an opportunity to recover. His recovery had brought him a chance of love. Because he had never chosen love, he did not choose it then. Because he had never had an opportunity to choose love, nor effectively heard. . . . [H]e was to be offered love again, and now as salvation.[27]

In the vision she has as she prepares for death, Margaret sees the stark divisions acted out as Pauline flees her illuminated *doppelgänger,* and the unquiet vagrant flees the mocking mob. Margaret is to be the instrument of reconciliation for them both, and heal the fractures of the psyche they carry with them. Pauline will find her way toward the vagrant and her ancestor under Margaret's tutelage. The vagrant will be offered help directly by her. "The three spirits were locked together in the capacity of Margaret's living stone."[28] The stone is another alchemical symbol, connecting not so much with the image of the stone of power, but with the imagery of mountains invoked within and beyond the novel.

Wentworth, the Decadent Adept

The consent of the individual is significant. The vagrant finally consents, as does Margaret. Wentworth refuses to break his isolation and accept co-inherent reality to the very end. "The envious man identifies the kingdom of heaven with himself and by a frantic effort to retain the outward manifestation of the kingdom, destroys it within himself, and with it his capacity to see outside himself."[29] The comparison between Wentworth and Persimmons provides a means by which to gauge Williams's development between 1930 and 1937. Whereas Persimmons had secret skills and insights that he used to satiate his appetite, yet his desires were part of what vindicated him, Williams has now a more sophisticated moral evaluation of the nature and role of desire. Simply to desire either knowledge or experience is no automatic link to the godhead despite it constituting an attractive trait in Persimmons. Wentworth will direct his desires away from integration. They will lead him on a journey of steady disintegration to hell. The structure of his exploration will mirror that of Pauline; but whereas she will effect a reconciliation with her transfigured other self, Wentworth will create his own, in this case feminine, *doppelgänger,* an "anima" of projected self-satiating introversion.

Some moments of choice carry within them not only the practical choice to be made but also the taking of a direction that contains an element of moral virtue, or lack of it, within. One of these moments when his desire lures him toward destruction comes when Moffat is offered his knighthood. He was presented with an opportunity for vicarious joy. Williams charts the gradations of moral choice with careful accuracy. If joy cannot be managed, there is the possibility of an effort toward the intention of joy.

> The infinity of grace could have been contented and invoked by a mere mental refusal of anything but such an effort. He knew his duty—he was no fool. . . . [H]e could enjoy; at least he could refuse not to enjoy. He could refuse and reject damnation. With a perfectly clear, if instantaneous, knowledge of what he did, he rejected joy instead. . . . He preferred anger. . . . He invoked envy, and it obliged him.[30]

The way toward disintegration is opened up, and desire or at least the direction of desire is the key. Wentworth, finding facts not conducive to his comfort, decides to reject them. The false Adela is invoked, and the perversion of the vision of romantic love is enacted.[31] The vision could not be adored; instead it perplexed. It was to offer a false integration, neatly described as "she in him and he in him."[32] The pattern of rejection is in place, and his refusal to acknowledge or take part in the interdependency of all things expresses itself next in his rejection of the vagrant:

> He sprang forward and up, to drive it away, to curse it, lest it interpolated its horrid need between himself and his perfection. He would not have it: no canvassers, no hawkers, no tramps. He shouted angrily making gestures; it offended him; it belonged to the City, and he would not have a City—no city, no circulars, no beggars. No; no; no. No people but his. No loves, but his.[33]

If "salvation lay everywhere in interchange,"[34] then by his refusal, Wentworth exposes the consequences of sterile independence. His descent into hell is written with a precisioned, growing horror that reflects the steady fracturing of his involvement with the world beyond his immediate self-interest. The descent is written in terms of the disintegration of the lateral axis of correspondence. At each point where he might find a secure engagement with anything that lies beyond the self, his withdrawal from the city, or from the others, takes the ultimate entropy of his soul a step further. The opposite of co-inherence is fragmentation, and that process accelerates. At the point where he might accurately assess the detail of the uniforms of the *masqué* he is overwhelmed by the sight of the real, but to him false, Adela. A huge sound combines with the sight and imprisons and splits him.[35] This splitting becomes the pattern of his engagement with his surroundings. Where there was one Adela, as his succubus, there are now two. He retreats from involvement with the community, because they want something from him. For Williams this denial of dependence is a denial of being. While Adela stared at his odd behavior, he withdrew into his recesses and refused to be wanted. "Like the dead man on his flight down the hill, he declined communion."[36]

J. J. Kollmann observes in her chapter "Complex Rhetoric for a Simple Universe" that by the time of writing *The Greater Trumps* Williams was questioning the line of demarcation between the dimensions of natural and supernatural and that by the time he wrote *Descent into Hell* the concept of a universe that is totally co-inherent became the central vision.[37] However one argues the nuanced gradations of development during this period, it is evident that the process of exploration to integrate notions of nature and supernature colored Williams's development from his first novel. His perception and handling of the relationship between natural and supernatural evolved and became markedly more subtle as he matured. In order to make his point that the metaphysical is bound up completely with the physical, he abandons his earlier reliance on the magical devices, and instead begins to draw with precision the web of interrelationship. He explores both the consequences of its development and its fracture. The axes of lateral correspondence now match the importance and significance that the vertical had. While Wentworth's change is the reversal of the alchemical quest, it is also more than that. It involves the decay and corruption through the process of change—the de-godding as opposed to the in-godding. His isolation complete, the opposite of transfiguration takes place within him. His final disintegration at the encounter with Moffat at the club exposes the truth that his notion of a self in which he could take refuge from all the other selves is also utterly inaccurate, and in a passage of chilling finality, he sits at the end, looking up an avenue of nothingness as little flames lick his soul.

> Eros need not for ever be on his knees to Agape; he has a right to his delights; they are part of the Way. The Division is not between the Eros of the flesh and the Agape of the soul; it is between the moment of love which sinks into hell and the moment which rises to the in-godding.[38]

The development of Williams's quest for integration can be viewed by reference to his treatment of ideas relating to the self, time, and space.

The Integrations of Self, Time, and Space

Between *Shadows of Ecstasy* and *Descent into Hell,* Williams's concept of "the self" has also undergone refinement. For Considine, the notion of self was closely interwoven with divinity. Whether or not this arose from the culture of adeptship, early existentialism, or simply immaturity, Williams has refined his writing on the nature of self. Narcissistic self-regard, Considinian egotism, or sheer self-indulgence are sharply distinguished from a form of self-giving that is rooted in a recognition of our identification with one another.[39]

When comparing the experiences of self, known by Wentworth and the vagrant, Williams describes the spectrum between these two universal perversions: "The self-worship of the one was the potential source of cruelty, and as the self-loathing of the other was the actual effect of cruelty; between them lay all the irresolute vacillations of mankind, nourishing one and producing the other . . . [s]ave only those whom holy love had freed by its revelation of something ever alien from and conjoined with the self."[40]

The identification of the self with "the other" is fundamental to a perception of what lies behind what Williams called the universal rule.[41] That there are the deepest of connections between individuals is expressed in the web of co-inherence. This interconnection is also what is meant by the lateral axis of correspondence. Substitution is the most natural practical expression of this interdependence. Each axis has become an essential concomitant of the other. "The central mystery of Christendom, the terrible fundamental substitution on which so much learning had been spent and about which so much blood had been shed, showed not as a miraculous exception, but as the root of a universal rule."[42] More developed definitions of the notion of the self are found in the technical languages of theology and particularly in psychology, with an especially important distinction between the Freudian ego and Jung's "emerging self" as part of the process of individuation. Williams develops an increasingly orthodox theology of the self once he moves some distance from his primitive Considinianism. He analyzes Wentworth's succubus as a perverted attempt of the self to love the self improperly, and notes that that kind of love expresses itself in the idolatry of self, and "over the idol tyrannises without purpose." Human experience requires "the most exquisite delight in the interchanges of romantic love."[43]

At the moment when Mrs. Sammile begins a discussion on the virtues or otherwise of poetry, she places herself at odds with Stanhope not only over the perception of the importance of poetry but over the nature of the self. Two forms of magic, in its widest sense, are in conflict here, and two adepts.

Mrs. Sammile is a practitioner of Goetia, and Stanhope a magus of the Affirmative Way; he is a poet and has an understanding of the alternative power of co-inherence. But no overt struggle takes place between the two alternative adepts, as in either of the first two novels. Even a small hint of dualism is unacceptable to Williams at this stage of his development. When Mrs. Sammile asks why he makes such a business of enjoying himself, turning poetry into labor instead of settling for mere enjoyment, Stanhope replies, "because sooner or later there isn't anything to enjoy in oneself."[44] This distinction between the self that enlarges as it engages creatively with other selves is contrasted with the self that diminishes and falls into oblivion. Mrs. Sammile will shrink or diminish as she gives herself to the role as Lilith:

> Their enchantress sat there, the last illusion still with her, the illusion of love itself; she could not believe her breasts were dry. She desired infinitely to give them suck. Oblivion had failed. Her dead had returned to her; her living were left without her. . . . But she sat there cut off from the earth she had in her genius so long universally inhabited, gazing, waiting, longing for some of the living to enter, to ask her for oblivion and the shapes with which she enchanted oblivion.[45]

Wentworth's experience mirrors hers and is hers. She is the principle of negation, a climax of the representation of the Doctrine of Evil as private evil. Williams has delineated alternative approaches to the notion of "the self" and details the consequences of choice in forensic detail—diminution or integration. Pauline's integration of the two aspects of herself, one with the other, and Wentworth's mutuality of seduction with his succubus demonstrate the two possibilities. One is an integration that enables interchange, the other a disintegration that disables it.

While Williams consistently reconciles the dichotomized spirit and matter, he is at pains to present the different dimensions of time and space as aspects of the interchange as well. His sense of the metaphysical incorporates the interpenetration of both. The most obvious example of this phenomenon is of course the interaction between Struther and his descendant Pauline, partly because "his blood was in her and made demands upon hers,"[46] but also in her experience of the hollow in Stanhope's garden. Out of this hollow there sprang the knowledge of the dead whose unrecompensed lives had gone before. Pauline is made aware that if the joy she experiences is to have any life, it must be reconciled with the agony that had been. "Unless hollow and shell were one, there was only hollow and shell."[47] Further than that, the device that

Williams uses to allow the encounter between the joy and agony, Pauline and Struther, is the notion of interchanged devotion operating to bridge or connect different moments of time. The narrator muses, "If centuries meant anything, perhaps they didn't—perhaps everything was all at once, interchanged devotion. Perhaps even now he burned, and she and her friends danced, and her grandmother lived and died, and Peter Stanhope wrote his verse, and all the past of the hill was one with its present. It lived; it intermingled."[48] In this apprehension, those who surround her are transfigured, and she accepts the necessity of interchange of time and space, and the opportunity it gives to allow the expression of that fundamental universal rule of substitution by those who have attended to the transmuting and transfiguring experience of love. If this reconciling perception is not evident to us, its inaccessibility is a function of our own divided consciousness: "The past existed still in its own place, since all the past is in the web of life nothing else than a part, of which we are not sensationally conscious."[49]

The web of life held time and space together in equilibrium, but part of Williams's idiosyncratic insight involved his perceiving both time and space as made up of a quality of elasticity that allowed a certain fluidity between the two: "Sometimes where time varies place may be stable, or where places intermingle, time is secure, and sometimes the equilibrium of both, which is maintained in so many lively minds, swings into the place of the dead. A single clock tick or a single door opens in two worlds at once."[50]

Williams was to use this elasticity of time and space frequently. C. S. Lewis was to use a similar device with his door into Narnia in his children's stories. Williams's more adult context is a means of allowing it to be more than the engagement between normality and a mythic culture. It suggests that interdependence penetrates further than the parameters of the insights of three-dimensional rationality, and by integrating time and space in this elastic way, it is a means of diluting the dualistic appearance of separation between spirit and matter.

Stanhope, the New Poet Adept

In the way in which he juxtaposes Stanhope and Wentworth, Williams has moved a long way from both Roger and Considine, and even from the Archdeacon and Persimmons. Wentworth has few features that would attract the sympathetic identification of the reader. There is no heroism in him. He works only a magic of his isolated imagination to create his succubus, whereas it is Stanhope who takes on the role of a magus of the new co-inherence. He has elements in his character that invite the reader to make connections with Williams himself. He also was "the optimist who hated it,"[51] and "while never negligible, was often neglected. He was everyone's second thought, but no one's first."[52] Williams used the name Peter Stanhope as a pen name on the title page of *Judgement at Chelmsford*[53] and as Hadfield points out, sometimes in letters.[54] He is presented as poet, and as both magician and magus, and these amount to his functioning as an adept of his art. Adeptship is no longer confined to the artistry of hermetic manipulation, as it had been with Considine. He even uses the old hermetic terminology explicitly when he wrote: "it would have been small use for any adept, however much greater than Peter Stanhope, to have offered his service to Wentworth, where he sat in his own room with the secret creature of substantial illusion at his feet caressing his hand."[55]

Like Yeats's, Stanhope's adeptship was to be one of enchantment. It would be capable of achieving the thing to which it addressed itself. The prologue of Stanhope's play at its dress rehearsal "sounded annunciatory. It called its world together and prepared union. . . . [Pauline] recognised the awful space of separating stillness which all mighty art creates about itself, or, uncreating, makes clear to mortal apprehension."[56]

Pauline supposes in a flight of imagination that Stanhope had seen something more terrible than a vision of his own *doppelgänger.* She imagines that he had contemplated the nature of the world in which such visions could be, and that the entwined loveliness of his verse was a mirror of its being. A high level of insight and artistry is attributed to Stanhope. In the conversation that follows, he acts as a combination of adept, priest, and psychotherapist as he offers to engage in the offering of substitution by which he will carry her fear, thus enabling her eventually to carry that of her ancestor. Although Williams is careful not to deify Stanhope, he comes close when he has Pauline respond that "she had been commanded; a god had been with her—not Peter Stanhope, but whatever answered him for her depth."[57] But this adeptship is closer to a more conventional Messianic model than is the old alchemical one.

All Hallows' Eve: *Profanity as Perversion and Inversion*

> There is but one dichotomy: that between those who acknowledge that they live from the life of others, including their enemies, and those who do not.[58]

Williams's metaphysical development has traveled from an alchemical preoccupation with transmutation, drawn down the vertical axis of correspondence, to a lateral integration of the web of co-inherence. This has become a vision of union, with others and through others, in the godhead. In his last novel Williams draws the lesser dichotomies (such as fantasy or illusion and truth) into the wake of a central one, the moral dichotomy that has at its heart interdependent, co-inherent exchange, both across humanity and creation, and between humanity, creation, and God. *All Hallows' Eve* explores moral dichotomy in a context where the central struggle appears in terms of the polarities of the sacred and the perverse. Christendom has been more familiar with the categories of sacred and profane being held in contradistinction to each other. But Williams will not have this. It builds into our view of the universe that essential dichotomy that his whole thrust of his metaphysical critique is determined to resolve. Profane is derived from the Latin, *pro fanum,* "before," or "outside," the temple. In Williams's assessment this division into sacred and profane is an inaccurate reading of metaphysical reality. It will inevitably dichotomize. Any distinction between outside and inside is likely to create a dualism of opposites. Williams's critique is that this false opposition, which undermines the unitive nature of a more Christian metaphysic, can be avoided by replacing "profane" with "perverse." *All Hallows' Eve* examines the nature and practice of perversion. Williams would also describe hell not as an opposite but as twisted heaven. Williams writes, "The arrangement of Purgatory is not the exact opposite of hell—though it is so in general—and that because Hell is not the mere opposite of heaven. Heaven is the absolute thing; Purgatory, the approach to it, is in proper relation to it; but the improper relation of hell is twisted. All the sins are a twisting of the virtues."[59]

Magic assumes a further and more refined role in this novel. This plot is no longer dependent on magical things: the "Graal" from *War in Heaven,* the stone from *Many Dimensions,* the tarot from *The Greater Trumps.* The use of magic has been to create a language of myth that allows the reader to suspend belief in the material and accept, in terms of the functioning of the imagination, the interpenetration of natural and supernatural. The morality underlying the practice of magic is now internalized and located in people rather than projected onto objects. The myth has become more refined.

Charles Moorman suggests a rationale for Williams's use of the mythical. He sees the contemporary interest in myth as psychologically reflecting a need and a search for order and certainty in the midst of the apparent chaos and disorder of the twentieth century.[60] He argues that Williams's use of myth is a way of universalizing or generalizing the situations in which he presents his characters, in order to allow the reader to gain a more immediate identification with the particular issues presented. In that sense, Williams's novels become a series of morality plays, albeit ones in which the morality evolves as the novels move into a more finely honed metaphysic carried by the myth. Moorman explains,

> It seems to me that myth is used in the novels . . . [t]o universalise what is basically a highly improbable situation and therefore highly specific fictional situation. Thus, I fancy, Williams hits upon myth as a means of generalising the specific problems of his characters. . . . [Myth] becomes a medium of approach by which a modern situation is given depth in time and in universality and so gains in weight and significance.
>
> In poetry the situation is reversed. Instead of starting with a specific contemporary, though frankly supernatural situation, and leading through that situation to the mythical patterns that make it universal, Williams begins with the terms of the myth itself and ascribes to it a broad pattern of meaning designed to enlarge our understanding of the contemporary world.[61]

In chapter 9, we examine how Williams turns to the language of the hermetic and the occult in order to ascribe this pattern of meaning and supersede the limitations of a metaphysic truncated by a materialistic culture.

In the earlier novels Williams has relied on the hermetic and the magical to establish the axes of correspondence, and the interpenetration of the natural and supernatural. Having developed this unitive worldview by the time he wrote *Descent into Hell,* where he does not use magic at all, he now returns to the myth of magic and the language of the goetic. He does so in order to expose how co-inherence may be more clearly recognized as well as how it may be undermined. By the practice of perversion, co-inherence itself is set in greater relief. Had he not written *All Hallows' Eve,* it would be tempting to suggest that he had laid aside hermetic attractions once the fully developed notion of exchange and substitution that make up co-inherence had been so clearly expressed in *Descent into Hell.*[62] This would be to underestimate the extent to which he depended on his particular variant of myth to achieve for his reader the level of metaphysical insight he intended to convey. Moorman compares Williams with Eliot and Lewis in their dependence on myth to make particular to their cultures their apprehension of a more universal metaphysical vision.

> Williams recreates the whole [Arthurian] myth; Lewis lifts out portions of it, *(That Hideous Strength)* and Eliot who fuses into single images allusions both to myth and the contemporary scene in order to form

> ironic identifications of the fertile life of the past with the grim life of the present, in the Fisher-King-Waste-Land myth.
>
> Our contemporary dilemmas and frustrations are seen by these men in relation to the universal issues of morality and religion of which they are parts, and they are presented in terms that are meaningful to all men at all times. And by means of this sort of aesthetic distance, these writers achieve not less, but more relevance to our own age. Certainly no one could deny that these men are concerned with marriage. *Shadows Of Ecstasy, The Greater Trumps,* The Arthurian poetry, (—*That Hideous Strength* and *The Cocktail Party*—) all have as a principal theme the relationship of husband and wife in the contemporary world.
>
> Each of these writers seeks to return to the religious values symbolised in the Grail quest, to find some means of redeeming the time. In Charles Williams, this desire takes the form of a plea for universal charity, for a social code based on the Pauline conception of divine love. C. S. Lewis would seem to advocate the return to doctrinaire orthodoxy, to the principles and practices of the historic Church. Both practice what Williams would call the Way of Affirmations. The third, T. S. Eliot, follows the Way of Rejections. After the *Waste Land,* Eliot's work retreated further and further from the world into a mystical vision. . . . Each in imposing the order of myth upon the disorder of his age, has suggested a way out of the contemporary waste land.[63]

The waste land in *All Hallows' Eve* is the place of perversion, but also more than that. George L. Scheper suggests that perversion may be better understood by the notion of parody.

> Moralistic literature tradition is inextricably bound up with dualities, and thus with the Manichean tendency. Whereas the mode of parody of the sacred is more consonant with Charles Williams's monistic metaphysics: things are either good, or misapprehensions and caricatures of the good.[64]

Scheper proposes that the framework of the novel is liturgical and that therefore the way to read Williams in this novel is to suggest that magic parodies liturgy, as the magician parodies Christ. The baptism of Betty, the iconography of the two paintings, and the "real presence" to one another of Lester and Betty all set up a liturgical leitmotif within the narrative. In this novel the magician functions to parody the liturgical symbols, if one accepts Scheper's analysis, and also the metaphysical monism both within and beyond the liturgical elements. The three Simons are a parody of the Trinity, for example. Scheper is particularly cogent when he argues that the concept of the parody of the sacred is helpful in finding a critical stance for reading Williams that serves essentially as a genre-concept.[65]

There is something out of the ordinary about the use of the goetic in Williams's hands. In most other contexts it finds its place more naturally in a dualistic framework. In *All Hallows' Eve* it acts to provide a unified metaphysic, where the essential elements are co-inherence and its perversion. However, this idea can be taken further. While perversion and parody are certainly helpful concepts to interpret this novel's moral polarities, they do not take into account a distinctive facet of the dynamic of the novel that has to do with movement. Williams shows an apprehension of the movement of things in time and space, but with a particular direction. He describes the flow of all matter being drawn into ultimate union with God and the whole of creation. The alternative, as it is displayed in *All Hallows' Eve,* is a movement of reversal or inversion.

There have been hints of this metaphor of flow in earlier works. In *War in Heaven,*[66] the Archdeacon is aware of it in the Grail. In *Descent into Hell* when Stanhope's play is to be performed, not only would the press be there but "the world seemed to flow towards Battle Hill."[67] In the later novels Williams uses different art forms for the artistry of his adepts: Stanhope was a poet; Jonathan Drayton is a painter. His adeptship as an artist is not exactly parallel to that of Stanhope but nonetheless it is used to enhance and describe the metaphysics that lie behind the material. Even if Jonathan Drayton does not see himself as an adept, Simon the Clerk is aware of the status and power of the artist as an interpreter and an adept. "You belong to yourself and to me. Great art is apostolic. You must not lessen yourself. You are to be a master."[68] Drayton will not offer himself as a part of this Faustian pact, but acts nonetheless as seer or metaphysical interpreter. At the end of the novel, Williams is reluctant to see art as capable of acting as a conductor for evil in any efficient manner: "It was the nature of the world to produce not so much evil as bad art."[69]

Drayton's two paintings, one of London and one of Simon the Clerk, are described as being set back to back in the studio in a deft touch that is both spatially and metaphysically descriptive. One painting acts as an agent for light, and the other for a glimpse of "dark deadness, . . .—a sort of massive dullness—much like your mass and light: only the opposite."[70] This becomes contradiction rather than duality, in the same way that Simon himself is later described as "frightfully definite and completely indefinite at the same moment—an absolute master and a lost loony at once."[71] The two paintings express further contradictions. Drayton's painting of London is a study in light as a metaphor for the incarnate Logos. ("Word" will be another concept central to the metaphysics of the plot.) Here is Williams's description of the light:

> A beam of wood painted amber was more than that; it was light that had become amber in order to become wood. All that massiveness of colour was led, by delicate gradations almost like the vibrations of light itself, towards the hidden sun; as localised it certainly was. "Here lies the East"; does not the day break here? The day did, but the light did not. The eye, nearing that particular day, realising that it was leaving the whole fullness of the light behind. It was everywhere in the painting—concealed in houses and in their projected shadows, lying in ambush in the cathedral, opening in the rubble, vivid in the vividness of the sky. It would everywhere have burst through, had it not chosen rather to be shaped in forms and to restrain and change its greatness in the colours of those lesser limits. It was universal and lived.[72]

What is almost an anthropomorphism attributed to light is a deliberate way of connecting with kenotic associations of both creation and incarnation, and stands in stark contradiction to the imposing dominations of the magus. A further element of contradiction is provided by a quotation from Sir Joshua Reynolds, who once "alluded to 'common observation and a plain understanding' as the source of all art."[73] Art is not to be used as a gnostic science—in contrast to the schools of secret arts Simon attended in Renaissance Paris.

But the critical difference is found when Richard Furnival is meditating in front of the two paintings (presumably no longer back to back) and he sees that the essential difference between them has become one of movement. The narrator describes, "There, in the middle of this room, lay the city, ruined and renewed, submerged and gloriously re-emerging. It was not the sense of beauty, but the sense of exploration that was greatest in him. . . . [I]t moved forward as the other painting retired. The imbecile master and his companion were swallowed up in the distance, but this was swallowing up distance. There was distance in it, but it was all one. As a painting is."[74]

Within the novel there is a drawing into unity of all things, except where the influence of denial or perversion is to be found. In *The English Poetic Mind,* Williams describes this denial as it is found in Milton's Satan.

> It is the choice which so many men have made, the preference for the existence of their own will as the final and absolute thing as against the

> knowledge (whatever that may be) of some "great commanded good." The only choice which a man can make in that crisis is between submitting to that good or refusing to submit to it, and if he refuses, he does so precisely because he can hold divided empire with heaven's king. Every bold baronet in the old stories did the same thing. He cannot get rid of the good, he cannot destroy it. He can only know and refuse, and hate it, and be equivalent to it.[75]

Simon the Clerk does have ambitions to be more than equivalent, but Williams's metaphysical monism exposes the flaw of fatal illusion lying at the roots of his enterprise.

In *The Figure of Beatrice,* Williams had written that "all the images are moving sweetly into God."[76] Here, however, we are presented with a study of an inverted movement, a movement away, and into diminution. Transmutation has become only metamorphosis. As Richard inspects the painting of the clerk, it appears as if the worshipers had become insects in the painting. He asks himself if the change might be the raising from beetle to human, but he also saw that metempsychosis was the other way. Any miracle that there was appears as one of lowering and loss. This dynamic of reversal or inverted movement is found at the heart of the process of goetic magic itself. In contrast (at least to Simon the Clerk), the incarnation is described Q'abalistically as the utterance of the perfect tetragrammaton:

> It had been a Jewish girl who, at the command of the Voice which sounded in her ears, in her heart, along her blood and through the central cells of her body, had uttered everywhere in herself the perfect Tetragrammaton. What the High Priest vicariously spoke among the secluded mysteries of the temple, she substantially pronounced to God. Redeemed from all division in herself, whole and identical in body and soul and spirit, she uttered the Word and the Word became flesh in her.[77]

Simon the Clerk is introduced to the reader as having been brought up in the Parisian hiding places of necromancy, in the reign of Louis Quatorze, in a milieu that is resonant of both Rosicrucian and Q'abalistic traditions. But he is distinguished by his desire for fame and domination, and it is in these terms that we are offered an interpretation of the incarnation. Another Jewish sorcerer had attempted domination and apparently failed, as Simon learned the tale. It was not Jesus but St. Joseph, that is Joseph Bar David, who is taken to be the sorcerer, who, "clothed in angelic brilliance had persuaded a woman

. . . [t]o utter the Name, and something more than mortal had been born." But it had ended in failure. Joseph vanished, and the "living thing that had been born of his feminine counterpart had perished miserably."[78] The difference between this highly theological account, albeit an inverted one, and the narration of Considine and his attempts at domination delineates how far Williams had come in moving toward an orthodox Christian metaphysic between his first and last novel. Here the magic has no glamor, unless it is the horror of perverted drama. The eradication, even of charm in the characterization, extends to Simon's being unable to smile, but only able to manage a mere constriction, an ignorant grimace.

Simon's process of inversion and reversal found expression as he stripped away the meaning from words, though they fought against him, so that as his smile became mere grimace, the words became mere vibrations. These were small spells associated with the power of the word. His highest achievement of inversion would be the reversed tetragrammaton itself. The whole process of incarnation would be not merely parodied but also inverted as he set about drawing one from that world and sending one to that world. "He would thus have a double link with infinity. He would begin to be worshipped there."[79]

The whole character of the incarnation is turned on its head. Where Christ empties himself of protection and omnipotence, and makes a journey that clothes him in vulnerability and solidarity with vulnerable people who are not in control, Simon seeks power, and uses that power to replace and supplant vulnerability and the exchange of love.

> His servants had, at his will, attempted his death and he had foiled them. But so doing, he had refused all possibilities in death. He would not go to it, as that other child of a Jewish girl had done. That other had refused safeguard and miracle; he had refused the achievement of security. He had gone into death—and the Clerk supposed it his failure—as the rest of mankind go, ignorant and in pain. The Clerk had set himself to decline pain and ignorance. So that now he had not any capacities but those he could himself gain.[80]

Magic becomes an agent of dissolution, not of real creation. When Simon sets about to ape Simon Magus who sent his servant into the underworld to serve him, Simon plans to send Betty, his own daughter. This act of commission will involve no act of creation such as occurred at the incarnation, where spirit and matter converged into one unitive life. Instead it would be a compulsory dissolution of the bonds between soul and body. Where the incarnation drew all things together in a metaphor and agency for unity, this would be a "making forever all but two of what must be at bottom forever one; the last fact of known identity alone remaining."[81] The same movement of inversion can be found in the parody of the creation of the Adam. Instead of breathing into the dust, Simon, with overtones of Judas, kissed his dwarf-woman creation on the mouth, sealing in those spirits who had entered.[82] This novel has no room for prevarication. Magic is described as a powerful tool, albeit a lie.[83] When Lester and Evelyn are bound together in the dwarf-woman, magic is credited with having achieved coherence, but not co-inherence, which is utterly inimical to its nature.

At the end of the novel, the movement proceeds in antitheses, for the two streams flow in different directions. In a passage of visionary lucidity Williams describes the river Thames, encapsulating the flow of time and space toward its goal of divine union and, incorporating the painful fact of the contradiction of separation in death.

> The Thames was dirty and messy. Twigs, bits of paper and wood, cords, old boxes, drifted on it. Yet to the new-eyed Lester it was not a depressing sight. The dirtiness of the water was, at that particular point, what it should be and therefore pleasant enough. The evacuations of the city had their place in the City; how else could the City be the City? Corruption (so to call it) was tolerable, even adequate and proper, even glorious. These things were also facts. They could not be forgotten or lost in fantasy; all that had been, was; all that was, was. A sodden mass of cardboard and paper drifted by, but the soddeneness was itself a joy, for this was what happened, and all that happened, in this great material world, was good. The very heaviness of the heavy sky was a wonder, and the unutilitarian expectation of rain a delight. . . .
>
> [O]n earth men see through lucidity to density. To her now all states of being were beginning to be of their own proper kind, each in itself and in its relationships, and not hampering the vision of others. So the Thames was still the Thames, but within it the infinite gradations of clarity deepened to something else.
>
> A sense of division, as if it was at that point that the lucid river flowed into the earthly river,[84] so that beyond that point the way divided and the source of the Thames was one thing and the springs of the sustaining tributary another. At that point, or indeed at any; but always the same division at each. She was suddenly afraid.

> O vain all meetings vain! "A million years" not one moment; it had been the cry of a child.[85]

This endorsement of the goodness of all things, the wholesomeness of all matter within the flow of providence, is set against the inverted flow of the clerk's goetic inversion. The false Trinity collapses onto itself, threatening to sink into a metaphysical black hole of destruction, as the false images of Simon gravitate back toward their center. With the climax of this novel comes the most mature expression of Williams's metaphysical monism. Dichotomy has become antagonism, and antagonism is expressed as either the perversion of love or the inversion of the eschatological convergence of time and space.

CHAPTER NINE

Vocabulary and Imagery

The Doctrine of Correspondence, Macrocosm and Microcosm, and the Index of the Body

> Talaat ibn Kula of Ispahan
> taught me the measurement of man
> that Euclid and Archimedes showed,
> ere I took the Western Road.[1]

Williams's reversion to explicit hermetic imagery in his mature poetry enables him to create a unifying myth and metaphysic that he developed. In his essay "The Index of the Body" he justifies hermetic language as the means of exhibiting the mystery by which spirit becomes flesh without losing spirit. He argues that the human body presents both an index and a pattern of wider creation, and he uses physical imagery to connect with a wider metaphysical reality. The hermetic interest in mathematics is linked to Williams's continuing fascination with geometry, expressed in his Doctrine of Euclidean Love. His Arthurian poetry provides its fullest expression.

The measurement of man was also, for Williams, the measurement of the universe. Williams shared the hermetic conviction that there was a connection between the macro and microcosmic dimensions. At the heart of this concern lies the preoccupation with a single unifying principle to describe the universe and our experience of it; or, as in Williams's case (that flowed from his awareness of co-inherence), to also describe the principle of interconnection:

> This idea is practically that of the microcosm and the macrocosm: the idea that a man is a small replica of the universe. Man was "the workshop

> of all things," "a little world." "*Mundus minor exemplum majoris Mundi ordine, filius totius Mundi.*" It is a very ancient idea; it was held before Christianity and has been held during Christianity; it was common to Christians, Jews, and Mohammedans and, for all I know, the scientific hypothesis of evolution bears a relation to the union of the two.[2]

While this notion of the interrelation between the macrocosm and the microcosm was a common part of Renaissance culture, one specific line of influence on Williams would have been that of Thomas Vaughan interpreted through Waite. In *The Secret Tradition of Alchemy* Waite describes the centrality of Vaughan's Doctrine of Correspondence:

> I have intimated that Vaughan was an occult philosopher, and as such he carried the warrants of his school at the period for an explanation of the cosmological universe. To this end he had the one Catholic and Hermetic axiom for a root principle of philosophy, being the Doctrine of Correspondence as established by the Emerald Table. It is not only of universal acceptance in all branches of Hermetic Theosophy, but it is the very root of mystical religion which explains nature by Grace, man by God, that which is without by that which is within, and the things that are seen by means of things that are invisible. It is par excellence the universal sacramental doctrine.[3]

He later criticizes those who at the beginning of their wisdom exceed their measure, and "declare in the macrocosm who should declare in the microcosm only."[4]

The significance of the human body within the Doctrine of Correspondence lies in the understanding that "man is the measure of the whole creation . . . [a]nd what we discern intellectually is in the likeness of the truth of things."[5] Williams was to become even more explicit: "The Sacred Body is the plan upon which physical human creation was built, for it is the centre of physical human creation. The great dreams of the human form as including the whole universe are in this less than the truth. As His, so ours; the body, in this sense of an index, is also a pattern."[6] And later, "the imperial structure of the body carries its own high doctrines—of vision, of digestion of mysteries, of balance, of movement, of operation."[7]

Williams's essay "The Index of the Body," which appeared in the *Dublin Review* in 1942, is particularly helpful in directing us toward the foundational ideas that lay behind his dramatic and artistic preoccupation with the human form. In this essay he returns to the primacy of the epigram "as above, so below"—deriving from the Doctrine of Correspondence—and acknowledges the esoteric schools that provide its pedigree, notably astrology and occult study. Rather than provide definitions, he directs his reader beyond whatever preconceptions are evoked by the language to his concern that it provides us with "a certain imagination of relation in the universe." This is the key to understanding the influence of the so-called occultism in his writing. It operates as the function of imagination. In much the same way as Yeats was to invoke enchantment in order to fulfill his role as an artist, so Williams turns to a structure of thought that enriches and acts as a catalyst to the imagination: in particular to what he will refer to as the "imagination of relation in the universe." Connection is all. It lies at the root of his developing insight into the interrelatedness of all things, co-inherence. He explains how it was that the body presented itself as a symbol of a wider reality:

> The idea went through many changes, but its general principle remained: that man was the rational epitome of the universe. It led, of course, to many absurdities, and (if you choose—like any other idea) to some evils. Some writers catalogued painstakingly the more obvious fantasies: hair was the grass or the forests; bones were mountains; the sun was the eyes, and so on. Astrology, if not based on it, at least found the idea convenient; however we may reject that ancient study, it had at least this philosophic principle mixed up with it—that each man, being unique, was a unique image of the universe, that the spatially greater affected the spatially lesser, and the calculable influences of the stars were only calculable because each man represented and reproduced the whole.[8]

His arguments turn to a justification of astrology as offering a provisional pattern to interpret the vicissitudes of life.[9] At this juncture Williams merges the two themes that have been traced to both Waite and the Q'abalistic literature: the importance of the body for intellectual and spiritual revelation by virtue of the Doctrine of Correspondence between that which is "above" and that which is "below"; and the profound symbolism of human sexuality and romantic love acting as a model of the further anticipated union between divinity and creation. The human body becomes an index of the mystery of creation; we can read back from it into the intentions of the cosmic author; but it also operates as a pattern. The living out the holistic life in the body displays the preferences and the concreteness of God in and through his creation. Williams suggests that

> [w]e carry about with us an operative synthesis of the virtues; and it may be held that when we fall in love (for example), we fall in love precisely with the operative synthesis.
>
> "Grace was in all her steps, heaven in her eye"
> In every gesture dignity and love"
>
> is much more a definite statement of fact than we had supposed; footsteps are astonishing movements of grace.[10]

Williams rejects the Socratic and Cartesian dualism between body and spirit that leaves us with the concept of the organism as a "dead carcass activated by a living ghost," and in doing so offers us the service of helping in the redemption of the Christian tradition from the fracture of dualism. He suggests instead that "the imperial structure of the body carries its own high doctrine."[11]

Brian Horne comments that

> Williams's espousal of the theories outlined does not arise out of a careful and detached consideration of the Doctrine of the Creed or the writings of the Old or New Testaments, but out of a poetic awareness of certain facets, frightening in their power and beauty, of human experience. By the strange alchemy of his own creative powers this personal vision is translated into the "rich and strange" structure of a theological system.[12]

Williams's theological system was to provide for an apprehension both of the body and of romantic love, which became the means of perceiving a metaphysical pattern that derives from our observations of the patterns found on earth and in matter.

He applies this unifying frame of reference to the Incarnation.[13] The essential unity of creation, the unity of love, and the means of reconciling division itself are brought together in the Incarnation. Although there may be difficulties in perceiving an overarching unity in what appears to be temporal and spatial diversity, he writes of

> a unity no more divided by two thousand years than by two seconds. We certainly have to separate them in thought, because of the needs of the mind, as we have sometimes to divide form and content in poetry. But the poetry is in fact one and indivisible, so is the fact; so even is the doctrine. The thing as it happens on the earth and in the world, the thing as it happens on the earth and in the soul, are two stresses on one fact; say one Word.[14]

Williams rejects dichotomizing categories in whatever form they may come: spiritual and physical, sacred and profane. He celebrates the goodness of matter, and both creation and eventuality as holy fact. Using the human body as a visual and visionary antidote to dualism, he carries his treatment of it throughout his writing. The novels and poetry are peppered with references to the phenomenon of dualism.[15]

Shadows of Ecstasy provides an early example in Williams's writing where metaphysical insight is generated by the geography of the body:

> But he never understood it as now, suddenly he understood Rosamund's arm when she leant forward to give a plate to her sister; somehow that arm made him think of the Downs against the sky. There was a line, a curved beauty, a thing that spoke to both mind and heart. . . . Well she was only human, she couldn't be perfect; and then she stretched out her arm again and she was perfect, she was more than perfect.[16]

And again—"Rosamund's arm had lain like a bar of firmamental power across the whole universe."[17]

But in *All Hallows' Eve* the reference to that which is material is rooted in a more developed metaphysic that conjoins it to the sacred. Williams goes on to explain this in relation to the lines, "Whose speech Truth knows not from her thought / Nor Love her body from her soul,"[18] as he writes that

> he had never before so clearly understood that sense of Lester as now when that second line must be rationally untrue. But his sleep had restored to him something he had once had and had lost—something deeper even than Lester, something that lay at the root of all magic, that the body was itself integral to the spirit.
>
> He had in his time talked a great deal about anthropomorphism and now he realised that anthropomorphism was but one dialect of divine truth. The high thing which was now in his mind, the body that had walked and lain by his, was itself celestial and divine. Body? It was no more merely body than soul was merely soul; it was only visible Lester.[19]

The body is also the place where the most serious doctrines of Christendom are experienced.

> All that can really be hoped is that some semi-attentive reader, distrusting or despising what he reads, may turn from it to consider in

> himself the nature of forgiveness; so and only so can this consideration hope to be of any use. . . . [D]iscussion and speculation are amusing enough; there are twenty four hours in every day and they have to be got through somehow. Any fool can invent theologies of the Fall and when fools were interested in theology, they frequently did; nowadays they are more interested in economics, or strategy or "ideals." Any fool can know how or what God, from his pure self-existence, knows, creates or sustains. . . . [T]he easy talk of mental stress being worse than physical may occasionally be true; only occasionally. Most men would prefer a month's mental distress to a month's serious neuralgia. It is in our bodies that the secret exists. Propitiation, expiation, forgiveness are maintained *there*—when the mind has explained them away—the need and the means and the fruition.[20]

The body was not the only focus of this central Doctrine of Correspondence. The body is also used to offer a rationale for the Eucharistic theology that Thomas Cranmer needs to create in order both to meet the political needs of the moment, and to express a metaphysic with the profundity to reflect the reality of the Eucharist. The Archbishop of Canterbury addresses the Lords:

> My Lords, King Henry had it in mind to make
> a ritual for communion, that men should find the natural
> moving all ways into the supernatural,
> and the things that are below as those above.[21]

The Lords accept the theory but turn it on its head and claim an idolatrous and inaccurate reflective correspondence with ultimate reality; they say, "We are the things below as the things above."

In *The Forgiveness of Sins* he again is clearly working from a more fully Christianized Doctrine of Correspondence when he sets about once more to obviate the need for any distinction between natural and supernatural: "It is said of Shakespeare that he wrote the whole supernatural life in terms of the natural, and it is true that he is the great protagonist of the natural life without apparent need of the supernatural. . . . [T]he one thing that could be deduced was that man's human nature was made on the same principle as his supernatural."[22] In keeping with these later insights, images of the body are much more frequent in his later work. Both in his prose essay "The Figure of Arthur" (part of the *Arthurian Torso*), where he offers his own introduction, and the poetry of *Taliessin through Logres,* the body acts as an aperture through which one can glimpse a wider reality and see into the metaphysical heart of the universe.

In a critique of the excesses of courtly love, Williams affirms, despite its excesses, that it represented a tangible and cogent experience that was more than sexual and more than romantic, and that, whatever aberrations it had given rise to, it remained representative of continuing romantic and religious experience. And so for Lancelot:

> The physical beauty of Guinevere appeared to him a thing literally transcendental. This is, no doubt, what the code taught him he ought to feel and in any case how he ought to behave. It will not do however to forget that a great number of lovers have felt like this. To codify—almost to institutionalize—is perhaps unwise, but the folly (if it is a folly) does not abolish the original reality; any more than the imbecilities of some of the disciples of Wordsworth about flowers and mountains alter the fact that Wordsworth and many others have been moved and exalted by flowers and mountains. The body of the beloved appears vital with holiness; the physical flesh is glorious with sanctity, not her sanctity, but its own. It is gay and natural to genuflect to it. Such an experience may exist before marriage, in marriage and after marriage; it is the *stupor* of which Dante wrote and which we, when we read of it, immediately recognise. The code was no doubt an invention, but not the passion that led to the code. That it sometimes led—and leads—to adultery no more disproves its validity than the fact that it may lead to marriage or renunciation proves it.[23]

In contrast to Williams's celebration of these epiphanies, the apophatic tradition has always been chary in the extreme, lest sensuality overwhelm spirituality. Williams is under no illusions of the danger of this, and his turning to Lancelot as his example of the authenticity of the courtly love tradition would be implicit recognition enough of the inherent dangers of adultery. But Williams is also explicit: "The two elements of a proper worship and (pace the adultery) a proper sensuality are too close together for our taste. The maxim for any love affair is 'play and pray: but on the whole do not pray when you are playing and do not play when you are praying.' We cannot yet manage such simultaneities."[24]

Pythagoras, Euclid, and Wordsworth—The Doctrine of Euclidean Love

Williams's preoccupation with the body as an index was also informed by the hermetic incorporation of the mathematical and geometrical. The hermetic tradition was influenced by religious scientists like Roger Bacon, whose expertise and interest straddled both metaphysics and mathematics. Bacon's interests and analyses set the direction and tone of later exploration. It was he in particular who was to direct attention back to the mathematics of the Greek schools of philosophy. The intellectual lineal descent was Neoplatonist and Aristotelian. Between the tenth and twelfth centuries, most of the Greek world had been recovered from the guardianship of Arabian culture, and a scientific and intellectual revolution followed. Thierry of Chartres (1110–56)[25] affirmed the growing centrality of mathematics when he wrote that "the creation of number was the creation of things."[26] His mathematical and theological excitement was followed by Robert Grosseteste (1168–1253), first chancellor of Oxford and also bishop of Lincoln, who insisted that "God disposes everything in number weight and measure." Margaret Wertheim, in her history of the science of this period, claims that in it we witness the double process of the Pythagorizing of Christianity and the Christianizing of Pythagoras.[27] Grosseteste's disciple Roger Bacon (1214–92), a Franciscan mathematician, helped ensure that hermetic and alchemical pilgrims would turn to Pythagoras and Euclid for an interpretation of the relationship between matter and spirit. Bacon wanted to use geometry as a pragmatic aid to evangelism. He was convinced that if painters were to learn geometry and produce three-dimensional paintings (with perspective), the consequence would be that people would see the miracles before their very eyes, and believe.

A sensitivity to the importance of the geometrical found its way through the normal hermetic channels into Waite's work. *The Secret Tradition of Alchemy* contains numerous references to Pythagoras. Williams was clearly affected by this awareness of the geometrical and his own interests were stimulated along similar lines. Hadfield, reflecting on the fact that Williams's thought is also characterized by an interest in the geometrical and the mathematical, comments: "Williams had for years been meditating on geometry in the body, reason and intelligence in the flesh."[28]

Particularly in his later poetry, Williams interprets metaphysics through the physics of the geometry. In *Taliessin through Logres,* and "The Coming of Palomides," Palomides sings in celebration of a vision of the queen's arm in which he sees Archimedes, Euclid, love, and straight lines conjoined in her limb:

Blessed (I sang) the Cornish Queen;
for till today no eyes have seen
how curves of golden life define
the straightness of a perfect line,
till the queen's blessed arm became
a rigid bar of golden flame
where well might Archimedes prove
the Doctrine of Euclidean Love,
and draw his demonstrations right
against the unmathematic night
of ignorance and indolence.[29]

In case the Doctrine of Euclidean Love had not been properly celebrated before in English poetry, Williams offers elucidation of the Euclidean imagery. From the side of her body,

fiery circles leap
round finger point and shoulder; arc
with arc encountering strikes a spark
wherefrom the dropping chords of fire
fashion the diagram of desire.

The flaming of heart and thought constitute the base of this equilateral triangle, and so he continues, developing the geometrical conundrum and offering us the solution: "lo on the arm's base for a sign / the single equilateral trine." The arm is the solution to the identification of the equilateral triangle, and he continues in his search for images of unification. He blesses the hour when the intellectual power first apprehended this dimension of reality and saw "that proceed which naught divides / through their great centre, by the stress / of the queen's arms blissful nakedness, / to unions metaphysical." The effect is a unification of diverse power:

blessed the unity of all
authorities of blood and brain,
triply obedient, each to twain,
obedience in the mind, subdued
to fire of fact and fire of blood;
obedience in the blood, exact,
to fire of mind and fire of fact;

to mind and blood the fact's intense
incredible obedience,
in the true equilateral ease.[30]

Both Hadfield and Ridler (each had access to Williams's own notes) inform us that an image in Wordsworth's *Prelude* had become a primal concept for Williams. Wordsworth dreamed of an Arab, riding fast over the sandy wilderness, racing the incoming sea that threatened to overwhelm him, while carrying a stone and a shell, which represent Euclid's *Elements* and poetry. Wordsworth has the Arab say that Euclid was "The one that held acquaintance with the stars, / And wedded man to man to soul in purest bond / Of nature, undisturbed by space or time."[31]

Space and time are conjoined in Williams's thought in numerous ways. The Doctrine of Exchange will allow—in fact, require—free movement within space and time. Not only is this doctrine a device Williams frequently used in his novels (particularly as he pursues the development of the notion of "exchange" in the last two novels), but in his later work, Williams is explicit about the way in which the resurrection and the presence of Christ supersede our perception of space and time. In *The Forgiveness of Sins* he notes that "Resurrection is something other than spiritual survival. It is the continuation of the physical in the highest degree; the continuation of the past into the present."[32]

However, this is not a license for unlimited time travel in the categories of either the theological or the poetic. He makes clear that there are certain limitations in the way in which the interpenetration of time and matter may be apprehended or used.

> In sorcery as in sanctity there is no return. The master of any art who abandons the method of his mastery and falls back on prentice habits runs a fearful risk. No lover of any kind, not even the lover of himself can safely turn from maturity to adolescence. His adolescence is in his maturity. The past may be recalled and redeemed in the present, but the present cannot be forsaken for the past.[33]

The geography of the body, steeped in its astrological associations, and the geography of nature, informed by the approach of Wordsworth, and William Blake—both of whom exerted considerable influence over Williams's thought—combined to provide Williams with a scheme of imaginative connectedness that he used to trace his metaphysics. Williams explains in his notes on the Taliessin cycle that in that myth "there was imagined a union of geography, physiology and metaphysics."[34] The opening of the cycle speaks to us in exactly those resonances:

> Carbonek, Camelot, Caucasia,
> were gates and containers,
> intermediations of light;
> geography breathing geometry,
> the double-fledged Logos.[35]

Shideler, in exploring the use of images in Williams's poetry, draws our attention to what she calls "a startling concatenation of identities—nature and social organization, sound and light, justice and mathematics,"[36] which Williams uses in his biography of Francis Bacon. For our purposes here, it is the combination of mathematics and geography that is important, and the way in which Bacon invests them with notions of justice. "The principles of nature correspond to the rules of government; the practice of music to the habit of affection, the delight of quavering music with the playing of light upon water; commutative and distributive justice with arithmetical and geometrical proportion."[37]

In his play *Thomas Cranmer of Canterbury,* several images can be found by which Williams traces the interplay of service, love, justice, and fate:

> Mystery is there to be resolved by the soul's mathematic.
> There are two classes of men—godly and ungodly;
> those who desire experience of the only good,
> those who refuse it. Children, will you refuse?[38]

Though mathematics was a metaphor for accuracy, that essential concomitant of hermetic art, Williams also recognized that there was an even higher expression of accuracy: "Love was even more mathematical than poetry; it was the pure mathematics of the spirit. . . . [I]t was the means as it was the end."[39] Elsewhere in the play, the enigmatic dramatic device "The Skeleton" describes his role as "A moment's geometrical formation of fate; / a functioning spectrum of analysed eternity. / Eternity always insists on being analysed."[40]

One of his later and more developed works, *Descent of the Dove,* opens with a geometrical formula to express the trigonometry and metaphysics of the Incarnation:

> The beginning of Christendom is, strictly, at a point out of time. A metaphysical trigonometry finds it among the spiritual Secrets, at the

> meeting of two heavenward lines, one drawn from Bethany along the Ascent of Messias, the other from Jerusalem against the Descent of the Paraclete. That measurement, the measurement of eternity in operation, of the bright cloud and the rushing wind, is in effect, theology.[41]

His later poems "Taliessin through Logres" and "The Region of the Summer Stars" both bring together these various hermetically rooted affirmations into a vivid focus. In his poetry he obviously chooses and requires a mythical framework, and Williams turns to hermetic culture to provide it. Charles Moorman has already been quoted above describing the effect that myth had in the novels and poetry. He suggested that myth in the novels became a medium of approach by which a modern situation was given depth in time and in universality, providing a greater weight and significance; but that in poetry the situation was reversed. Instead of starting with a specific contemporary and supernatural situation, and leading through that situation to the mythical patterns that make it universal, Williams instead began with myth itself and developed from it a more general pattern of meaning. The purpose of myth was to enlarge our understanding of the contemporary world.[42] The poems that Williams wrote are permeated with aspects of the hermetic and occult in its broadest or cultural sense; with the significance of the body as a guide to the soul; with the language of accuracy and proportion expressed in the terms of mathematics and geometry.

The Myth of the Body in the Arthurian Poetry

Williams had found the Christian myth of the incarnation as the central mystery of life. In adapting the myth of Arthur and the myth of the Grail, he himself re-shaped it then in poetic terms. The supreme examples of imagery for Williams were the human body as it images the human spirit, and human love as it images divine love.[43]

> Taliessin saw the curved bottom of the world.[44]

Williams's most explicit dependence on physical imagery is evident in the Taliessin cycle. We are confronted with how overtly the metaphysic of the cycle of poems is based on the union of geography and physiology in the end papers to the first edition of *Taliessin,* where the geography of Europe is reinterpreted by means of the human body.[45] Here we find another example of Williams taking a principle he encountered within Q'abalistic Rosicrucianism and making something of it that was both similar and yet involved a distinctive evolution. We are not presented with Waite's frontispiece of a human outstretched and the values of "mercy, severity, beauty, victory and glory"; instead we have a metaphysics of European history, as well as one of the whole nature of humanity.

> In that myth there was imagined a union of geography, physiology and metaphysics. The boundaries of the ancient Roman Empire under Byzantium were conceived as forming the shape of the human body, and also of more than the body—of the whole structure of man. Byzantium itself was the informing soul; and the head, with the conscious brain lay in King Arthur—which was called Logres and afterwards Britain. . . . [The body] taken in the feminine (as opposed to the masculine of the Emperor himself), the breasts were in Gaul (and the great historical development of Christian doctrine), the hands lay in Rome (whether for the armies and roads or for the offering of the Eucharistic Sacrifice by the Pope), and the buttocks were in Caucasia. . . . [Caucasia] meant . . . [i]n the poem a kind of free natural life . . . [p]rimitive society, unromanticised sex.[46]

The imagery of hand and arm in particular operate in a dramatic and vivid way. The poem in which this vision is explicitly worked out, "Taliessin, The Vision of the Empire," is woven with physical imagery. Physics and the morality implied in Williams's metaphysics are fused in a vision of the human body:

> Strength articulated itself in morals
> of arms, joints, wrists, hands;
>
> The organic body sang together
> the Acts of Identity adored their Lord;
> the song sprang and rang in Byzantium.[47]

The poem ends with what is a form of or homage to the "*Benedicite omnia opera*" found in Cranmer's Book of Common Prayer, and much used in the Anglican Office of Morning Prayer. It celebrates the works of God in a doxology that turns to a language of limbs:

> O you shoulders, elbows wrists,
> bless him, praise him, magnify for ever;
> you fittings of thumbs and fingers,

bless ye the Lord;
sockets and balls on knees and ankles
bless ye the Lord;
hips, thighs, spine in its multiples,
bless him, praise him, magnify him for ever.[48]

In "The Coming of Palomides" the imagery is set within the Euclidean framework, introducing the geometrically defined Euclidean love:

O what long isosceles
from finger point and shoulder flies
towards me, and distant strains my eyes
along the twin roads there to prove
the Doctrine of Euclidean Love;
let the queen's grace but yield her hand
to be by such strong measure spanned—

In the summer house of the Cornish King
suddenly I ceased to sing.
Down the arm of the Queen Iseult
quivered and darkened an angry bolt;
and as it passed away and through
and above her hand the sign withdrew.[49]

In the poem that follows, "Lamorack and the Queen Morgause of Orkney," the queen's physiology is again the instrument of both bruising and catastrophe:

Hued from the livid everlasting stone
the queen's hued eyelids bruised my bone;
my eyes splintered, as our father Adam's when the first
exorbitant flying nature round creation's flank burst.

Her hair was whirlwind about her face;
her face outstripped her hair; it rose from a place
where pre-Adamic sculpture on an ocean rock lay,
and the sculpture torn from its rock was swept away.

Her hand discharged catastrophe.[50]

Taliessin in the rose garden in "The Region of the Summer Stars" continues Williams's immersion in the culture of the Grail. He uses the Arthurian imagery and narrative to provide a setting for the poet Taliessin to both play a part in the struggle for and describe the dynamics of the kingdom of heaven through this myth. The verses contain a number of lines that use the imagery of arms, but a wider imagery also adds to the impact of the physicality. Once again Williams is fusing human and spiritual love, the body and the spirit in his vision of Guinevere. The linking of the happiness of the woman who feels Galahad rise in her flesh with the immersion of her flesh and Christ, and the consequent healing of others, is brave indeed:

> At the entrance to the long rose path he saw
> the sensuous mode, the consummate earth of Logres,
> the wife of Arthur, the queen of the kingdom, Guinevere.
> Hazel-lithe she stood, in a green gown;
> bare against the green her arm was tinged
> with faint rose veins, and golden flecked
> as the massed fair hair under the gold circlet of Logres.

And:

> The phosphor of Percivale's philosophical star
> shines down the road of Logres and Broceliande;
> happy the woman who in the light of Percivale
> feels Galahad, the companion of Percivale, rise
> in her flesh, and her bright flesh in Carbonek with Christ,
> in the turn of her body, in the turn of her flesh, in the turn
> of the Heart that heals itself for the healing of others.[51]

In the early *Taliessin* text the arm acts as a conduit for joining earth with the heavens:

> The sevenfold stars fell fast
> down a naked arm
> into a naked breast—
> the stars that the Emperor cast.

And in lines 45 to 48 of "Taliessin's Return to Logres," as revised for a book publication (*Taliessin through Logres*, 4), the crooked arm becomes the sickle of judgment on the landscape:

Beyond the farms and the fallows
the sickle of the golden arm
that gathered fate in the forest
in a stretched palm caught the hallows.

In the *Christendom* version of this same poem, the last two lines have been replaced by lines combining the geographical-anatomical element: the catching is accomplished by the "hand / of the Logrian horizon's arm." Williams was clearly ready to submit this for publication, but in the end turned instead to "the sickle of the golden arm" as above. Nonetheless, the striking imagery of the "horizon's arm" demonstrates his line of thinking and the extent to which he was willing to go in his attempt at synthesizing various aspects of geometry and anatomy in his overall imagery of physicality.[52]

In her essay "Co-inherent Rhetoric in *Taliessin*," Angelika Schneider explores meta-images in the poetry. She reminds her reader that the discovery of cell metabolism, intracellular communication, and the genetic code give the metaphor of organic unity on which the image of the human body is based an even greater aptness than the poet knew. She offers a commentary on the integration of the parts of the body and the politically and economically integrated parts of the empire, suggesting that they allow Williams to put forward a complex of images with a single word. As a comment on his technique, this is a helpful summary. Her interpretation of the significance of Jerusalem and its connection with the genitals may not encompass all the relevant associations. Her suggestion is that since sin is not caused by sex but propagated by it, since the tendency is passed down from one generation to another, the myth of the origin of evil must be enacted in Jerusalem. (This sounds too much like St. Augustine's flawed and dreadful notion from his misreading of Genesis and Romans, that original sin was communicated by the sexual act of making love, and thereby associating sexual intimacy with sin in the church's mind in perpetuity.)Waite suggests a different interpretation of the significance of Jerusalem. Jerusalem contained the temple, and the temple is understood as the spiritual union of male and female apart from any fleshly union. "It symbolised therefore the mystery of sex at its highest."[53]

Waite even suggests that any man proclaiming the Divine Unity, in the words "Jehovah is Elohim" above and below, twice a day, is thus rebuilding Jerusalem in his heart.[54] Although this theological insight might press this train of thought further than it can reasonably go, it does have the attraction of uniting heart and genitals in a way that provides us with the maturest image of integrated unity. However this may be, Jerusalem claims the genitals by virtue of the redemptive role of sex in Waite and *The Secret Doctrine in Israel.*

Schneider adds that it is also because the genitals are the organs of generation, and Jerusalem is the birthplace of three world religions, and the site of the gravest contention among them.

She does offer us a constructive analysis of the use of the arm in the poem.[55] The arm is part of the human body and shares in the body's role as an image of organic relationship and as a means of awakening and communicating love. The arm as an image of the body and a channel of love is explicated in "Bors to Elayne: The Fish of Broceliande," where the fish of Bors's love enters Elayne's body through hand and arm.[56] Taliessin's arm and hand, the instruments whereby his poetry is written, also give the signal for the charge that decides the battle of Mount Badon in Arthur's favor[57] and open the way for the establishment of Logres as the union of political order and religious truth.

In "The Star of Percivale" the joined arms of Taliessin and the enslaved girl are "bands of glory" imaging spiritual union in mutual love.[58] The arm of an enslaved person serves as a central image in the two succeeding poems as well. It conveys the signal of ascent from rebellious bondage to the freedom of voluntary acceptance in "The Ascent of the Spear,"[59] and forms a channel of revelation to Taliessin in the complex imagery of the "Sister of Percivale." Here the figures of the slave girl and of Blanchefleur are superimposed, breath of trumpet blast and muscle of water bearing arm, blended in an encompassing and profound insight into the nature of all being.[60]

As one critic comments, "This catalogue of the multifarious uses of a single image in the Arthurian poems may suffice to show how its significance is developed and enriched in the course of the work, making of one simple element a many faceted network of meaning, a subordinate pattern within the larger pattern of the whole, in itself a representation of co-inherence."[61] The myth and symbolism of the body is, as we have seen, part of the means by which Williams looks to establish a fusion of the dualities of body and spirit. He continues this process in his use of a wider hermetic imagery in his Arthurian poetry to which we now turn.

The Hermetic Imagery in the Arthurian Cycle

Angelika Schneider also reviews the role of magic in the poetry. We have noticed that both Yeats in one regard and Williams more generally make a special plea for magic to be interpreted within the context that the author intends it to be used. Schneider identifies magic, accompanied by myth, as another of the important meta-images. Logres is actually founded by Merlin's rites of magic. He is given power to use magic to oversee its development. His magic allows Galahad to be protected at birth and to be cared for by nuns, so that he may achieve the Grail, and one critic comments, "This, the apotheosis of the work, signifies the possibility of individual salvation through exchange and substitution in spite of Logres' failures to achieve the reign of God in human society. Merlin's magic makes possible the full realization of the individual's potential through total participation in the co-inherence."[62]

Williams utilizes magic in contradistinction to its lower uses as documented in *Witchcraft*. Magic, with its sense of a universal language of apprehension and descriptive of inner reality, becomes a language of salvation. The magic pentagram is the blazon of Percivale, who represents "the contemplation of the images,"[63] the spiritual intellect,[64] and love coupled with rational insight, which is the means of the divine vision. This brings into relief the argument over the role of magic. Heath-Stubbs condenses the issues in his astute observation: "Magic is the prime symbol of the abuse of spiritual power. It stands, and perhaps has always stood, in the same relation as do wilful lust and perversion to love, and usurpation and tyranny to the legitimate exercise of power in government. Indeed, in all Charles Williams's work, these three aspects of the same thing are, by implication, closely linked."[65]

This may be true of magic as it was portrayed in the later novels, but not of its use in poetry. Brian Horne suggests that magic as it is portrayed at the beginning of Williams's literary life should be distinguished from the way Williams depicts magic at the end of his career. The novels were full of occult associations, but the magic in Taliessin was "natural, from the earth."[66] This distinction is helpful. It confirms the journey Williams made from the gravitational pull of the Waitean hermetic underworld to a more intellectually evolved and poetically polished use of hermetic culture. By this means he structured a mythical framework that enabled him to create a culture in which co-inherence, exchange, and the interpenetration of spirit and matter could flourish without any hint of dualism.

A further differentiation is needed. The novels incorporate hermetic metaphysics, but goetic magic is anathematized in them. The imagery in the later poetry is hermetic rather than occult in its popular sense. Shideler observes that the Arthurian cycle was Williams's prime attempt to embody to the full extent the consequences of his vision of co-inherence for the conduct of human life.[67] Williams could best achieve this by using the tool of occult or hermetic imagery. Williams was perfectly clear, in his own mind at least, that the word "occult" meant simply "hidden," and in his usage, he declined to give it a moral sense, unless he was deliberately referring to the goetic. His use of the term was not so much "with the pretended operations of occult schools," but "with a certain imagination of relation in the universe."[68]

Hermetic and apparently occult images are found throughout the Arthurian cycle. Roma A. King Jr. has summarized the essential elements of the usage of occult imagery in a chapter in *Rhetoric of Vision* entitled "The Occult as Rhetoric in the Poetry of Charles Williams" and I will rely on it in what follows. For reasons suggested earlier, in order to avoid confusion by association, the wider term "hermetic" will be used here where otherwise "occult" might seem more natural.

The difficulty Williams faced in his poetry was finding imagery that brought matter to life. Wordsworth had imbued nature with an energy or a force that carried associations of the numinous, but Williams needed imagery that went further. In *The Figure of Beatrice* he turned to Wordsworth as an example of how poets see clearly, in comparison to Dante, who would claim the same for philosophers. The passage does more than that; what is observed are the implications of the power of words.

> "Visionary power," wrote Wordsworth,
> "Attends the motions of the viewless winds
> Embodied in the mystery of words:
> There, darkness makes abode, and all the host
> Of shadowy things work endless changes—there,
> As in a mansion like their proper home,
> Even forms and substances are circumfused
> By that transparent veil with light divine,
> And, through the turnings intricate of verse,
> Present themselves as objects recognized
> In flashes, and with glory not their own."[69]

Williams as poet and seer viewed material things as resonant of the numinous. Matter, as well as words, was the place of endless change that reflected the transmutation and transformation of humanity. For that reason he needed to use corporeal imagery to draw out the implications of a spirit-infused creation. The Q'abalah provided just such a schema. In his poetry, by its application, he was able to anthropomorphize the material. The "Sephirotic Tree" is a diagrammatic representation of the spiritual journey of humanity in search of reunion with God. The last of the Sephiroth, or stations, Malkuth, lies at the base of the tree, representing either the earth or the kingdom. Williams used it to locate "women in the world's base." Malkuth is feminine, the estranged bride of Kether, the first Sephira, the male God with whom she awaits reunion.[70] A passage in "Taliessin in the Rose Garden" is reminiscent of the annunciation and Mary's visit to Elizabeth. It is a paean in praise of holy women:

> Happy the woman who in the light of Percivale
> feels Galahad, the Companion of Percivale rise
> in her flesh, and her flesh bright in Carbonek with Christ,
> in the turn of her body, in the turn of her flesh, in the turn
> of the Heart that heals itself for the healing of others,
> the only heart that healed itself without others,
> when our Lord recovered the Scorpion and restored the Zodiac.
> Blessed is she who can know the Dolorous Blow
> healed in the flesh of Pelles, the flesh of women.[71]

The scorpion represents sexuality. The restoration of the zodiac, the patterned order of meaning is linked to the Q'abalistically informed need for the reintegration of sexuality and spirituality in the kingdom of Logres. Dindrane opens the eyes of Taliessin in Aquarius. The queen's majesty exhibits the glory to the women of Logres; and all this "brings to a flash of seeing the women in the world's base."[72] The Q'abalistic worldview allows for an integration of the feminine, spiritually and materially. The most focused expression of this was of course the co-inherent interdependence between mother and child in the Incarnation, but the use of the Sephirotic Tree allows Williams to extend the integration of the two in a more varied imagery.

King suggests that, since Williams saw matter and spirit as two modes of one absolute unity of being, "he saw the occult as the instinctive expression of man's elemental need for ultimate unity, a unity consummately expressed in the Christian revelation."[73] Williams uses two central mechanisms of transformation with a Christian interpretation, the pentagram and the Sephirotic Tree. King suggests that they function as images. In fact they are more than images; a stronger definition is needed. They are certainly symbols and perhaps almost sacraments (despite Williams's reservation about the term), since to some extent they also affect what they represent.

The pentagram is a familiar image in Western magic. Its rationale is that four of the points represent the four elements, while the fifth stands for the surrounding spirit. When the fifth point is directed upward it signifies blessing. For Williams, its capacity for integration of spirit and matter also allows it to act as a tool to represent and affect co-inherence. When it is placed in conjunction with Percivale, who also acts as a symbol or sacrament of co-inherence, the effect is the more intense. Williams uses this conjunction to symbolize personal and communal integration when he has a serving maid of the castle say in "The Coming of Galahad," "This morning when the Saracen prince was christened / dimly the Lord Percivale's pentagram glistened / in the rain-dark stones of his [Palomides's] eyes."[74]

Palomides represents more than the conversion from Islam to Christianity. He represents all systems that contain a metaphysical dualism at their heart. Williams describes the first step in a long spiritual journey that has involved moving from the Islamic rejection of the integrity of the material to the co-inherence of Christianity. The combination of both Percivale and the pentagram at this juncture offers an affirmation of the process that has ensued in Palomides's conversion from representative disintegration to co-inherence. In the concluding lines to the poem Taliessin speaks of proofs, creeds, songs, and roofs. These are located in the planets of Mercury, Venus, Saturn, Jupiter, and Earth is placed between them. Together the planets compose five undimensioned points (line 104). However, the undimensioned points would, if joined, form a pentagram, the image of co-inherence, and Taliessin's clear view of it is a premonition of the imminent cosmic victory of co-inherence over division.

The Christianization of the hermetic imagery is given lucid expression in "The Coming of Galahad." In "Taliessin in the Rose Garden" the poet warns, "Well are women warned from serving at the altar, who . . . [s]hare with the Sacrifice the victimization of blood."[75] Pelles the Grail King with his bleeding wound inflicted by the Dolorous Blow and Blanchefleur, who died from giving a cup of blood to save another, are all involved in some way in the restoration; they are incapable of completing it. All find their fulfillment in Jupiter, described as the heavenly planet with the deep red scar, the bleeding wound. Jupiter thus, resonant with the associations of Calvary, becomes the fifth and upper point, the surrounding spirit that brings the undimensioned points into co-inherence. Christ integrates, and the figure of the pentagram stands for the completion that flows from the atoning sacrifice.

The second symbol or sacrament of transformation is the Q'abalistic Sephirotic Tree. King offers a working description of the tree.[76] Its stations or branches are the stages through which one is required to pass in order to close the breach between oneself and God. They involve a Jungian dialectic between opposing forces that reflect the polarities of gender and spirit and matter, but knowledge of only four of the ten Sephiroth is requisite here: Malkuth (feminine, earth); Ysod (masculine, air); Hod (feminine, water); and Netzach (masculine, fire).

In "The Death of Palomides" Williams resorts to the image of the Sephirotic Tree, which becomes a means of transformation within a Christian ontology. Palomides remembers his experience of two Jews sitting by a fire intoning the names of God. "The first mathematics of Ispahan trembled before the intoned formulae." They pronounced Netzach:

> Sharply I shouted into the sound: "Netzach?
> What is Netzach?" Together and deeply they answered:
> "Netzach is the name of victory in the Blessing:
> For the Lord created all things by means of his blessing."[77]

Achieving the state of Netzach signals victory over the natural elements and admission to a higher plane of humankind's consciousness and spiritual awareness. Beyond Netzach is Tipereth. Beyond Tipereth is God. Netzach is only achieved by bringing together the opposing powers in dialectical balance. The pattern of the encounter in the poem is Williams's process and pattern in microcosm. Palomides, who as a Muslim represents a culture of dichotomy, encounters Jewish mysticism in the form of Q'abalistic ideology. The two Jews bear witness to the belief that God created the world by the help of Hebrew letters. Waite describes the tradition that claims that after their "emanation" the archetypes, of which the letters on earth are a reflection, remained concealed for 2000 years before the Holy One proceeded further with his work. In Waite's words,

> When he willed so to do the letters came successively before Him to shew cause why each one of them should be utilised as an instrument of the task. . . . [T]he letter "Beth" was chosen, but not because it was the initial of the word "Bara" meaning to create nor yet because it is that of "bereshith," or "In the beginning" which the book of Genesis opens, but because it is the initial of the word "Barach," to bless.[78]

This affirmation laid the foundation for a theological endorsement of matter, allowing the integration of matter and spirit, and so preparing the way ultimately for the Incarnation: "That Thou only can'st be Thou only art."[79] The Q'abalistic imagery of the Sephirotic Tree becomes the conduit of a theological process that leads to and affirms the Incarnation, and the resolution of all things within the metaphysical monism of the One God. When Taliessin claims that he "was Druid-born and Byzantium trained,"[80] Williams's own development is re-presented. "Druid-born" suggests a natural, primal inheritance of the hermetic; "Byzantium trained," the drawing of the hermetic into the culture and framework of Christendom, a poetic and theological art fused in a symbiosis of ancient and orthodox, each informing the other.

While the strains of the Druidic in Byzantium have caused the orthodox anxiety, Williams is unequivocal in his perception that the ultimate metaphysic is known in the Incarnation. Williams, through Taliessin, as artistic "Druid" has but set the words of orthodox Christian revelation to a more flexible, accessible, and balanced tune:

> Poor, goetic or theurgic, the former spells
> seemed beside the promise of greater formulae;
> poor—control or compact—the personal mastery,
> the act of magic, or the strain of ancient verse
> beside the thickening dreams of the impersonal Empire
> and the moulded themes of the Empire.[81]

Williams was to set his own challenge for personal mastery, as well as reliance on the promises of the greater formulae, as he was to struggle to reconcile the contradictions that emerged in his private life, which we examine in the next chapter.

CHAPTER TEN

The Quest for Integration: "*A Century*" *and Correspondence from the Later Years*

The potential difficulties inherent in this affirmative romanticism, and the limits on integration, were encountered by Williams himself, when the vision intruded from outside the confines of his marriage. He turned to the culture of myth to provide interpretation and safety. The mythologization of relationships provided ways of interpreting the experience safely and creatively. Myth became a safety valve that both interpreted vision and contained it. The myth of Phyllis Jones, with whom he fell in love as "Celia," and that of his wife, Florence Conway, as "Michal," offered the personal experience to which the Dantean structures of Beatrician vision gave expression. To equate one with Beatrice and one with the "woman at the window" may be to force Dante's template too crudely on Williams, but the parallel is nonetheless present. In these myths he sought protection, reality, and finally integration. In his poetry, these myths allowed him to express the dynamics of his metaphysics in a way that freed him from the constraints of his own culture. We are driven to ask questions about the way in which his own quest for Christian integration in the face of misapprehended dualism might work in the grueling practicalities of our human mess. The discovery of his letters to Celia (Phyllis Jones) set alongside his last letters to Michal (Florence), his wife, allow us to do just that.

The central task of this chapter will be to analyze the hermetic influence that functioned to give coherence to Williams's pattern of thinking in mythical terms. The myth expressed itself in the correspondence with both Celia and the last letters to his wife, both of which were penned from 1940 to 1945. Williams's personal reputation has not been enhanced by the public apprehension of his marital difficulties. In fact, much as his immersion in hermetic culture has caused what I hope to have shown to be unfounded criticism, so his moral standing has been affected by the difficulties that his love for a second woman engendered. He may not have left his wife, and he did not subject himself to the trauma of divorce, but a taint still attaches. Perhaps moral probity may depend more on how the individual acknowledges and confronts difficulties of this kind, than on their simple existence. Two critical questions would then be first, what the nature of his affection for Phyllis Jones was; and second, how he dealt with it. Critically at this juncture, the issue of his own personal reconciliation of his myths arises. Since his thought and art were directed toward an ultimate co-inherence, the question of whether some kind of integration was achievable in Williams's own fractured romantic and marital experience presents itself.

One also needs to reorder and redraw the biographical details that relate to Phyllis Jones, in particular, and to "Michal," his wife. Two tasks present themselves. The first and simpler is the revision of the biographical details as they appear in the correspondence to Phyllis Jones of 1935–1943, and also in "A Century of Poems for Celia" (dated 1926–27), which function as an introduction to the relationship. The original manuscript of these poems is now lodged in the Bodleian, but it has received no critical attention. They chart the early and formative stages of the relationship between Williams and Phyllis Jones, or Celia, and they describe in more detail the nature of the vision that Williams perceived.

We have seen how the influence of hermeticism provided Charles Williams with a vision of reality that invited integration, particularly of the spiritual and material. This holistic metaphysic was directed particularly at the fusion of the romantic and the religious, following the pattern that Waite had established in *The Secret Doctrine in Israel.* But it went further than that. It aspired as a principle of coherence to find a way of uniting both the affirmative and negative spiritualities that provided the two poles of theological and experiential interpretation in Christian spirituality and artistic vision. Co-inherence springs directly out of this unifying intellectual and aesthetic coherence. His dictum "This is Thou; neither is this Thou" attempted to bind together transcendence and immanence. But how practical a possibility was this? To what extent was Williams able to implement this restitutive hermeticism in his own life and achieve this aim of integration in his own affairs? Or to put it another way, if one of its attractions was to root theological reflection in the praxis of human experience by incorporating the romantic into a wider metaphysical framework of reference, could it succeed in practice?

The key to this question lies in biographical study. One of the aspects of his life that biographers find difficult is his relationship with Phyllis Jones and the disintegration that it represents for his marital experience. There remain important omissions from his biographies, and thus they need amending. The most important gap is the continuation of his relationship with Phyllis Jones beyond her marriage to Billie Somervaille and her exodus to Java. Hadfield had access to letters written to her in Java, and asked Phyllis Jones about the resumption of a literary epistolary relationship. Phyllis had asked by letter "Am I still Celia?" and Williams had replied: "The answer is that you are. Quite clearly, quite certainly, you are all that I ever said. I always saw you. . . . [I] cannot bear to think that you should think of those letters, those poems, as being past. They are as much as you will have them be—from me now."[1]

Phyllis Jones kept letters that Williams wrote to her from the period 1935–1943. Most of the letters written in Oxford after her return from Java, before she lent them to me, were not known to exist. One clear effect they have is to contradict Hadfield's analysis of the period after 1938. She writes:

> In the last year or two Phyllis Somervaille's marriage had broken down, and early in 1938 she returned from Java with her daughter Penelope Celia. She lived in London, and did occasional editorial work for the O. U. P. This sometimes brought her in to the Production office or the Library. She and Charles had very intermittent relations. He did not look for any renewal of the vision nor did he deny the past.[2]

In fact the correspondence shows the opposite. There was a renewal of the vision and a continuation of the relationship until as late as 1942, albeit expressed in correspondence punctuated by lunches.

The Chronology of Contradiction

Williams observed in his preface to *The English Poetic Mind* that, "The following essays are based on two convictions: (1)Troilus and Cressida is of a great deal more importance than has generally been allowed, (2) the central crisis in Troilus is in direct poetic relation to the culminating crisis in Wordsworth's account of his own history in the Prelude."[3] He was using a study of the handling of the experience of crisis by the great poets partly as a way of looking for a solution for the contradictions in his own experience. He described something of that experience more fully in the introduction to the letters of Evelyn Underhill. She had come to the point of conversion to Roman Catholicism, only to be balked by an encyclical condemning of the very theological modernism that had underlain the integrity and direction of her journey. Williams wrote:

> One is apparently left to live alone with an Impossibility. It is imperative, and in the end possible, to believe that the Impossibility does its own impossible work; to believe so, in whatever form the crisis takes, is of the substance of faith; especially if we add to it Kierkegaard's phrase that, in any resolution of the crisis, so far as the human spirit is concerned, "before God man is always in the wrong." That is not, by itself, the complete truth; we should have to add to it the opposite and complementary phrase that, also before God, man is always in the right; but the other is more important for our own sense of any resolution. The only rightness there is in the Impossible itself.[4]

Williams's own experience of unresolved "impossibility" was the rekindling of romantic vision by which he fell in love with Phyllis Jones, a young employee at the Oxford University Press. The impossibilities stacked up one after the other. The most obvious difficulty was the emotional betrayal of his marriage, in particular after having made a small name with his early poetry (most obviously, *The Silver Stair*), in celebration of his love for his wife. There was the impossibility of consummation given his strict adherence to the metaphysics underlying Christian morality. The final "impossibility" that he needed to face arose when she moved on to become the lover of Gerry Hopkins ("Alexis"), another colleague in the press, and then made two subsequent marriages.

Hadfield describes the relationship with a hesitant sympathy. In the same way that the Rosicrucian influence was underplayed by her because she found the concept uncongenial, so also she underestimates aspects of his relationship with Phyllis Jones for a similar reason. Most important, Hadfield underestimates the scale of the relationship and was ignorant of the later correspondence, which continued long after she believed some form of closure had been reached. Other commentators like Shideler ignore the Celian experience altogether and concentrate on the Dantean rationalization of the Celian experience. Beatrice was Dante's lover and not Williams's, and so functions to provide a commentary on the theology of romantic love without any undertones of moral discomfort. But intellectually and emotionally Williams's Dantean vision was fueled by the Celian vision, which acted as a bridge between his experience as a young man with Michal and his later mature theologization of the *Divine Comedy*. More personally, the tragedy of having fallen in love and continuing to love someone outside the marriage and who remained inaccessible in every way, except as the recipient of poetry and spiritual or personal direction, marked the second half of his adult life.

The assumption with which Hadfield leaves the reader is that of the fading away of a midlife crisis. Michal Williams's response was understandably even more brusque when she refers to the matter in correspondence after her husband's death.[5] The reality was more complex, and the relationship raises the question of whether or not by the end of his life Williams managed any reconciliation of this dichotomized romantic, emotional, and religious experience. Hermetic mythological culture had furnished his relationships with a structure that defined them. If one of the functions of hermetic culture, as I have suggested, was to facilitate integration philosophically and religiously, the issue of whether or not he managed some form of integration of his own fractured personal experience is of particular interest.

"Celia" acted as the controlling romantic and emotional myth for him from 1926 until 1942, replacing or augmenting the romanticism of his marriage to "Michal" or Florence. A brief outline of the relevant dates is needed to clarify the biographical facts, and to allow an examination of the accuracy of the dates attributed to "A Century."

In 1924 Phyllis was appointed to a position in the library. In 1927 Williams wrote the first of the three masques, *The Masque of the Manuscript* for his colleagues at Amen House. *A Masque of Perusal* followed in 1929, described accurately by Hadfield as being "darker in colour." In a letter to Raymond Hunt in a "sketch of an autobiography," he wrote that their "great period" was from Sept. 1926 to Apr. 1927: "After that, everything went wrong—except, of course, the Holy Ghost."[6]

The first issue that "A Century" poems present is their supposed typewritten date on the manuscript of the collection, and the accurate charting of the relationship consequent upon it. Phyllis Jones provided the date for the typist and repeated it in subsequent interviews with me. This date, however, is unavoidably the object of much scrutiny, and among scholars it is heatedly debated. Hadfield refers to a crucial letter from Williams to Phyllis Jones in *Charles Williams: An Exploration of His Life and Work.* In the letter dated approximately 1929 (for reasons that will become evident) Williams writes:

> What a year. I don't really go back much—or rather only vaguely—before the end of last June. And the first Tolstoy. And then . . . the lecture. And the second Tolstoy. Do you remember offering to take me to the "Ghost Train"? Yes, you liked me a little then. But instead I took your arm—which to me was like a weekend at Brighton—and we talked about Almighty God. . . . [I]t was only the second time in my life I had taken—even as

> remotely as that—a woman's arm. And certainly it was only the second time that the idea of kissing her crossed my mind—as it did at Victoria. And took four months to eventuate, Blessed be He! . . . All is but a prelude. We begin something new—and that is also a prelude. Will next year be sharper, sadder, but as precious as the past?[7]

The period that the letter refers to suggests a different date for the work under dispute. There were two Tolstoy centenary exhibitions. Tolstoy was born in 1828 and consequently they took place in 1928. The Oxford University Press had an exhibit at the exhibition,[8] and Williams took Phyllis Jones to see it. If the letter referring to his taking her arm and wanting to kiss her, for the first time, is associated with the exhibition, then nothing of a deeply personal nature can have preceded it, making the dating of 1926/27 tenuous at best. The cycle of poems acts as a form of poetic diary to describe the way in which the relationship began, developed, and was redefined in those crucial twelve months, and offers internal evidence of its development:

> The second autumn cannot be the first—
> . . . [i]n her
> *Soul, body, intellect, are not what they were.*[9]

There are alternative possibilities. The dating depends of course on what Williams meant by their "great period." If it was the period of the greatest depth of their encounter, covered by the poems, then it suggests the relationship first erupted in the late summer or autumn 1926. But it may be that "great period" refers to a period of friendship and nonromantic intimacy before the vision bit. That would allow a dating of autumn 1928. As will become clear, the relationship appears to have had an intense and romantic mutuality in the early months of that year. "A Century" charts the hesitation, frustration, and final withdrawal of Phyllis from an affair that had developed further than she was willing to go. Physically the poems and letters chart the exchange of kisses. But no doubt it was the emotional intensity and, as becomes clear, the controlling possessiveness of Williams, which became most uncongenial to her. Her withdrawal caused Williams intense pain and desolation,[10] and is reflected in a moment of poetic, critical self-examination that is one of the most powerful and moving pieces of this cycle.[11] A form of *modus vivendi* appears to have been achieved by the end of the cycle.

There is evidence on both sides of the argument. In "A Century of Poems," which is the context for great period: No. 56 is entitled "At a Rehearsal of the

Masque"; No. 57, "With the Sonnets Concluding the Masque"; and No. 58, "On the Proposal that in a Second Masque, She Should Present the Soul Ecstasy, and on Her Objections." The first masque, *The Masque of the Manuscript,* was performed on Apr. 28, 1927.

However, one of the difficulties with accepting the earlier date is that it suggests that it was three years before Fred Page disclosed the fact of the relationship to Florence Conway, "Michal," with the trauma that ensued. Given that the relationship flowered intensely for a year, such a delay would seem a little odd. If, however, it flowered between 1928 and 1929, then 1930 is still sufficiently close to the eruption to make the 1930 date of disclosure reasonable. Hadfield documents that 1927 was the year that Phyllis Jones's mother sold her house, with Phyllis moving to a flat in Upper Bedford Place. Hadfield is not clear if it was 1930 or in 1933 that Fred Page disclosed to Mrs. Williams the fact of her husband's adoration of Phyllis. The interview with Phyllis (now McDougall) confirmed the date of 1930. If Phyllis McDougall was wrong about dates for "A Century," she may not be reliable elsewhere. In fact 1930 was the year she broke her leg in a riding accident, which would lend some weight to her claim to be sure. It was also the year and occasion that Williams then discovered that she had moved on to become the lover of Gerry Hopkins, his colleague who inhabited an upstairs office. In 1926 in writing *The Black Bastard* Williams had modeled Isabel on Michal. In 1930 he was writing *Many Dimensions,* and he had chosen Phyllis for the character of Chloe.

The three verse plays, written between 1929 and 1930, were *The Witch, The Rite of the Passion,* and *The Chaste Wanton.* (These plays were published by Milford as *Three Plays* in 1931.) All three are presentations of the death of love, and this common theme suggests that they were written in the aftermath of Phyllis's withdrawal from the affair. How long after remains unclear.

Williams was seriously ill in 1933, and was rushed to hospital suffering from intussusception.

In Sept. 1933 Phyllis moved from the library to production under Miss Peacock. The next serious crisis arose in the autumn of 1934, when it appeared that Phyllis would be leaving the press on one Friday that September and that she would be marrying Billie Somervaille, whom she had known since moving from home to Bedford Square in 1927. He had been studying to become a company secretary at the time. He had since moved to Java, having found employment with an oil company. Billie Somervaille had come home on leave and Phyllis had agreed to marry him and move to Java. Both Williams and Hopkins were severely shocked by the news.

Hadfield has had access to some of the correspondence Williams sent to

Phyllis during those years, but most of the letters were retained by Phyllis and lent to me. They add to the picture considerably. Phyllis's return to England in 1938 was no surprise to Williams.

What is not clear from Hadfield's commentary is that Williams continued to write to her on her return. His last letter is dated August 1942. In her interview, Phyllis McDougall confirms that her son, Roddy, was born in the Radcliffe Hospital in Oxford in 1942, and that that year was the last time she saw Charles Williams. The question arises as to why there appears to have been no communication between them after 1942. What then becomes clear is that Williams turned back to his wife in the last three years of his life, and invested in her the full emotional and spiritual resources of his imagination and intellect.

The Celian Moment

Hadfield offers the reader a description of the unfolding of Williams's relationship in general terms. This contains no examination of its beginnings in "A Century," no recognition of its extension beyond a few letters in the "Java years," and only a brief reference to the "Celian Moment" as he wrote about it in his introduction to *The New Book of English Verse,*[12] with a reference to an accompanying letter to Phyllis when he sent her a few pages of the introduction. Hadfield simply briefly refers to this letter in which he describes to Phyllis the Celian moment. Shideler ignores the relationship and Cavaliero writes an intellectual history of Williams with few references to the underlying drama of his personal life. He does not even attribute Williams's description of the Celian moment to Phyllis Jones in his brief reference to the introduction to *The New Book of English Verse.*

Yet, as Williams makes clear in his letters, the Celian experience dominated his personal life and his poetic and imaginative thinking from 1926 to 1942. In this lies the importance of making accurate reference to the relationship with Phyllis Jones, and analyzing her effect as a catalyst and an inspiration for the myth of Celia that was to expand and deepen into his treatment of Dante in *The Figure of Beatrice.*

Hadfield quoted from a letter in 1935 in which Williams asks Phyllis to read the book through from the beginning,

> because then you will come upon what I have called "the Celian moment" in the proper order. You will know that it is, for me, a definition of all that the great vision of you was. . . . [I]ndeed it seems to me that it was the

> most marvellous visibility of the potential and the actual in you—in your beauty, your power, your goodness, your intelligence, your love—that was your peculiar greatness. . . . [Y]ou were in fact—I wrote you a poem about it didn't I? at once the stone and shell of Wordsworth's vision—geometry and sound—exact definition and reverberating loveliness.[13]

He described it in the preface to *The New Book of English Verse:*

> The Celian moment (so to call it) has a double vocation–as love and as poetry—and retains for us a passion in both. It is the moment which contains, almost equally, the actual and the potential; it is perfect within its own limitations of subject and method, and its perfection relates it to greater things. It is the moment of passion, and it is described both for love and for poetry, in Marvell's Celian poem, *The Match.* (p. 330)[14]

In a later letter dated November 4, 1935, Williams writes further about the Celian moment and the rationale behind his selections of poetry in *The New Book of English Verse.* Both for its tone and its detail, it is worth reproducing in full.

> AMEN HOUSE
> 4 Nov. /35
> My Dearest, dearest Celia,
> There go to you by this week's mail two books—Dorothy Sayers' new one, *Gaudy Night* (and I only hope dozens of people aren't sending it), but it was a matter of allegiance for me to send), and my own anthology, of which you have seen the Introduction. I think perhaps you will not dislike or reprove, as it were, the Introduction or the Notes, where the Celian moment appears again—twice, though you very likely may not want to be bothered about it just now. I have collected as many Celian poems as I could find of value, and Whitehead[15] is only in the Notes for our sake. Marvell's Match I love because of "and that was Celia." In January I am speaking to a Univ. Literary Society at Cambridge—on Poetry and the Celian Moment: when I will launch the phrase vocally on the world. It is an easier January engagement that yours, but, if I succeed in planting it in criticism, then at least another thing which springs from you and all you did shall be held of value. And you will remember that it is meant—one side for poetry, and one for you.
>
> The book itself has certain things in; there is hardly a page without some description of you, but also there are a number of our joint loves.

> There is, on page 261, "by our first strange . . ."; on page 389—admire, my blessed, God's providence and me—"who think too little and who talk . . ." I put Congreve's phrase into the Introduction for your beloved sake. There are chunks of your Prelude and my Paradise Lost. There is "Unknown Eros," though there is not "my nightingale." And there is nothing of beauty or goodness or intelligence from beginning to end that does not mean to me something of you—nor anything of their opposites that has not been exposed as fought or hated in and by you. As you will know how I wrote a poem once on the Wordsworthian stone and shell which identified them with your hands in Holborn, and said how one was the mathematics or meaning of things and one was their beauty and sound. Or words to that effect. And certainly they catch me still, on many and many a night, on the very point of real sleep, and thrust me upwards again into wakeful-ness. But as for the book, darling, there is one thing you will have to forgive, I know, and (if you are kind) take the burden off of yourself—or rather the indecency—and that is the Acknowledgements.[16] But there are no "overtones" or "undertones" there; they mean exactly what they say, and no more, and there is but one Celia; and not outpourings or offers or petitions or tributes since you left here. . . . I will not say deflected, for they have never had any power or chance deflecting, but have come near shadowing the least fact of you, of you, of you: nor have any of them ("perhaps I should say 'alone!'") been able to produce even any satisfaction to them. One by one I dismiss all "my young women" to be "Kings and priests over themselves"—and (very properly) all of them go. There was but one who would not: to whom, for ever, as far as she will be with me, be ascribed, as is most justly due . . . and so on.[17]

The introduction to the book traces through poetic experience the different names of the vision of the poet for the beloved. Myra, Amaryllis, Chloe, Dianeme, Amoret, Stella, Ianthe, and from Marvell, Celia. The Celian moment functions to describe both the actual experience of the love for one woman and the potential universality that encompasses the whole poetic spectrum of women. Williams notes its bifunctionality, existing both for the sake of the romantic experience itself and for the sake of poetry. He traces and distinguishes the Celias of the Elizabethans, Johnson, and Percy. The "moment" appears in both early Shakespearean comedy and in Milton's "bruited Neaera of Cambridge." Both Swift and Pope treated it for its own sake as love, and for the sake of their poetry. Shelley offered some illumination and Coleridge transformed the concept into that of Christabel and the Abyssinian maid. For the nineteenth century Williams adjudged the experience to have lost its "overtones." But the greatest defect of the age was the failure to explore the metaphysics that lay behind the experience, or as Williams put it, "It was still bright with something of angelic light, from 'the top of speculation'; few then explored the angelhood."[18]

In the last few pages of the introduction Williams both sketches the trail of the Celian moment as it is presented in the volume but also gives a clue to what he means by "exploring the angelhood." The persons who utter and presumably experience the universality of the Celian moment become superpersonal by the mere intensity of their personalities, and further, by the breaking down of the parameters of "normal" experience, they take on the knowledge of refusal and rejection of hell. In this perception it was Milton and the metaphysicals who went beyond Shakespeare, for his "people were able—they were compelled—altogether to die."[19] But if Shakespeare did not offer the full spectrum of hell, he did renew the Celian moment with a new perfection: "it hovered on the edge of more than humanity when a kind of earthly-immortality rang in Ariel."[20] When analyzing Kipling and Yeats, Williams explains what role he himself attributes to the exercise of myth. In poetry, even Christianity is a myth, and the use of myth serves to introduce the element of metaphysical exploration and speculation to accompany what would otherwise be a less dimensioned interpretation of human experience. The book ends with the death of Gerard Manley Hopkins, because, "It is the moment of the close of myths. Flecker and Francis Thompson delayed the end; Eliot recovered Agamemnon; Chesterton infused them with the ceremonial of the apocalypse, but if the poets use myth, it is by private compulsion in the face of cultural rejection. Pan is dead."[21]

In this lengthy introduction Williams offers an apologia not only for the interaction of myth and the exploration of metaphysics but also for his own use of the myth of Celia in his personal experience. The influence of hermeticism blurred the false distinction between secular and spiritual, between the material and the transcendent. This affected Williams in two ways. It had the advantage that he was able to interpret the experience of romantic love as moments of lucid theophany. It had the disadvantage that he was unable to make the necessary distinctions in his own experience of it between the exploration of the spiritual potential the experience carried latent within it and his own erotic and romantic inclinations. Throughout "A Century," these two categories of experience continuously overlap in a way that is confusing and damaging to the integrity of each.

"A Century of Poems for Celia": Amen House (1926?)–1927 (1928?) Chronology and Myth

The interpretation of the collection of one hundred poems is helped by considering the following three issues.[22] There is a chronology of the relationship; the unfolding of the separate myths; and the interweaving of the erotic and spiritual responses to the relationship.

The first two can most easily be taken together. Williams, who clearly kept copies of his poems to Celia, is offering an anthology from the range written over a year. In the prologue he writes with a style that is close to affectionate doggerel:

> I will choose out a hundred poems for you
> of all I have written since our love was new,
> of all that, in this sudden burst of days,
> I have written for your pleasure and your praise
> which is your easy setting by of pleasure;
> therefore I have written this song for you to treasure.

The very first poem deals mockingly with Alexis's (Gerry Hopkins's) latest novel. The second is entitled "On a thwarted invitation to lunch: also, on a question about the Rosicrucians." Hadfield has described Phyllis Jones as eager to learn, and the discovery that Williams was an authority with experience of an esoteric group exercised an attraction.

> We should have sat and chatted you and I,
>   of Christian Rosycross and of his creed,
> of other masters, of the dark and high
>   symbol and doctrine—how the final Deed
> is only reached by hearts and lives that bleed,
>   Messias, or the little feathered bunch
> frozen in winter by some leafless weed.
>   But I was going to ask you out for lunch.

Williams clearly felt himself to be an older man without the immediate attractions of her contemporaries and finishes with the wistful lines:

> Go, Celia, where your best appointments lead:
>   The people whom you know (I have a hunch!)

are young and gay and of your own fair speed,
  but I was going to ask you out to lunch.[23]

Certain of the poems have prophetic touches to them. "On having left her suddenly" has the couplet: "Dark symbol! Celia it shall be / you who shall one day drop me."[24]

No. 33, "On Flirting with Alexis," also has a tinge of prophecy, and offers an indication of Williams's feelings; he has evidently become engaged and he seems to suffer from jealousy:

I do not blame Alexis; he was wooed—
  wooed by what invitation, o by what
challenge of womanhood, the maiden snood
  deftly arranged, the whisper, the hard lot
  of the fair damsel in the paltry cot
(that is the library), keeping it trim—
  and he must haste to help you at a trot:
but Celia, need you so encourage him?

ENVOY
Ask, princess, ask your conscience, if the slot
  of that strong lion should provoke your whim
to lure it forth: I should not care a jot
  but Celia, need you so encourage him?[25]

Whatever pressures Phyllis thought she could escape from when she agreed to marry Billie Somervaille, it cannot have been unconnected with evading both Williams and Hopkins. In "On a Letter Warning Her to Be Careful Lest She Came to Shipwreck," Williams writes of the consequences of attracting a series of lovers, however playfully. A degree of jealousy remains:

Alexis, Colin, Urban love me, each
in his degree, and I love in return.
and all of them have much to learn and teach,
and I have much to teach and much to learn,
among my peers; nor lower nor more high
than any of this republican brotherhood,
but their sweet sister, their fair friend am I.
Shipwreck, I shipwreck? So she smiled and stood.[26]

In No. 36, a clerical visitor refers to Celia as a "good lady," which provokes a mockingly reverential pastiche of possessive defensiveness:

But "this good lady"! Celia! this
foot, this impetuous mind and heart,
this agile victory over Dis
this mouth that smiles at every smart
this winged procession from your soul,
across the dark and ruddy world,
this beauty, shining from the whole,
in your slim hands and hair new curled!
Celia a lady? Celia good? What else?
what other is the truth each sonnet tells.[27]

There came the point, inevitably perhaps, when she began to resent the claims on her that the poetry and his attitude explicitly made. Williams responded to her shot across his bows with "On the Word 'My'":

If I should say *my Celia* should the word
  as many implicits of evil bear
as in the ruffian language of the herd,
  snorting possession over all things fair?
Ah think not so; it hath a double sense,
  but freedom either way its meaning lights . . . .
So long, my Celia, shall the word endure.
as you allow, since that *my* means *your.*[28]

It was a penchant of Williams's to choose nicknames for those he knew well. It also allowed for the easier operation of a mythology that suited the relationship. In No. 48, "On Her Names," Williams explains that although she took the name Phillida at her baptism, she grew to song in "Celia." But he adds:

then
the insulting habit of your style
  found in the Arabian tales another mask
where many a fair Circassian dared revile
  the appointed governor of her daily task.[29]

Inevitably she asks what "Circassia" means, and Williams offers it to her as a second dimension of myth by which she is described:

What is Circassia? Child, 'tis fantasy,
  'tis faerie of the ever dreaming mind,
mimicking its own great disdain, to be
  the thing whereto its daylight life is blind;
'tis capture, bondage, 'tis the infidel
  loosed on the holy places of all love . . . .

'tis Celia, but 'tis Celia in a dream.[30]

The Circassian state, which he elaborates on in the following poem, No. 50, seems to involve the category of submission and mastery that Lois Lang-Sims was to enter to become the slave girl Lalage. If those critics who have attributed a degree of sadomasochism to Williams have a point, it is the Circassian state that offers a platform for their anxieties. Celia is an alternative myth of romantic vision:

The Celian and Circassian states
  exist on common ground,
but say, what difference between
  those august names is found?

This—the Circassian changes not,
  how marvellous soe'er,
immortally rebellious and
  continuously fair.
. . . .
But O the Celian State proceeds
  from change to growing change,
and all it hath of permanence
  doth still more widely range.
. . . .
The Celian and Circassian States
  on common ground abide,
and daily the Circassian maid
  shall fault and I shall chide.

But O with what a marvelling thought
  I see the stars ascend
at evening through the Celian air,
  my sister and my friend.[31]

The three myths come together in a remarkable way when Williams chides Phyllis for some apparent resentment of Williams's attitude and behavior. She appears to no longer want to "play." In "On a Morning Meeting," he writes:

Do I detect a certain flagging
  in the daughter of Maia's tread?
Have the jests and general ragging
  wearied already that golden head?
What! Does Circassia find it tiring?
  what! does Phillida find it dull?
What! has Celia put off aspiring?
  have all of them ceased to be worshipful?[32]

In the next poem, "On Her Forgetting Certain Pencils," he explains the different dynamics attached to the three mythic personae (if one includes "Phyllis"):

Since Celia, on the best hypothesis,
  cannot forget, being all three perfected,
and since Circassia, though she work amiss,
  works with a joyous and deliberate head,
it must be Phillida who so left void
  work she is nigh but is not paid to do—
Phillida the official, the employed,
  the B.Sc. and the librarian, who
kept all three pencils over the weekend;
  and how shall Phillida be charged with it?
Celia might be implored, Circassia penned
  in chains; but neither for their peer is fit;
who—is she?—by subordination gagged,
  is neither begged nor bullied, but just nagged.[33]

The myth of Circassia is justified in the following poem, "On the Wars of Circassia," along the lines that Cavaliero pursued in his exploration of the principles of spiritual direction when he introduced the letters to Lois Lang-Sims in *Letters to Lalage.*[34] Submission is the key to a higher purpose. The key phrase here is "the centre which is you," which suggests Williams understood quite clearly the limits of the myth and its purpose. He intended Phyllis to as well. To good effect he introduces both the siege imagery and austere morality of Bunyan's Holy War:

Think that by this the centre which is you
rides more advanced among the watching stars,
for from this wild submission you renew
admired defiance in more potent wars.

So, when the dark drum of Diabolus
begins throughout your shattered streets to roll,
you, trained to honour and to battle thus,
shall save the inmost places of Mansoul.[35]

In the poems numbered 50, "On Possibilities," and 56, "At a Rehearsal of the Masque," he makes further distinctions between Phyllis, Celia, and Circassia. But by No. 70, "On an Unexpected Departure," the crisis of her rejection is breaking the surface. She has, it appears, walked out on him and taken over the dynamic of control:

I learn another etiquette; the mode
of a new land, and mightier I discern:
patience, O practised in that loftier code:
I too, I too, shall learn . . . .

Only if, ere the learning is at an end
my mind grows darker for a little while,
pardon.[36]

In No. 71, which has no title, he rationalizes her withdrawal and consequent fractured relationship. But in No. 72, "Daydreams," he writes an extraordinary poem of humiliated self-analysis and deprecation. It takes the form of confession:

All this unhappy afternoon
I have been dazed by an evil moon
that floats within me and turns my dreams
into visions nearer the truth, it seems;
I am not I, and if we talked
of God or poetry as we walked,
it was that they should be panders both
to an old man, full of lust, and sloth,
crawling and peeping and slinking about
behind those masks and only to find

for his greasy slimy and feverish mind
the thought that pleases him; in what guise
so'ever, 'tis that he hath longed to surprise.
If I chat of Wordsworth or of Donne
it is that old man that I put on;
if I speak of eternity,
it is that old man grows in me;
if I seem to talk of your soul
I am grown whole to that old man's whole,
who in his own manner enjoys your youth:
and this I know at last is truth.

. . . [t]he great fat crocodile lifts his head
and drags himself forward with feet outspread
on the compost of damned souls that is hell,
and each body breaks like a breaking shell;
and above, O how far away none knows,
glimmers the faint light of the Rose:
and the crocodile snaps at it, and again
with all his horrible mouth in vain
stretches and snaps, and far away
the Rose folds up, and the Night and the Day
are perfectly closed—but over me
the crocodile waddles eternally.[37]

He continues to write however. In No. 73, "On Her Practice," he likens himself to a bound child, one who is unconscious and bruised. But her fingers strove to pluck the bonds away. In No. 74, "On a Gesture of Affection," he had asked her for a sign of affection, which she had given. He seems pathetically grateful. By No. 78, "On Her Past," he defends himself against having caused her any harm:

Yet this at least, princess, I cannot say:
  "She had been happier were it not for me";
you raised no ignorant eyelids on the day
  of man's ill-hap and waxing misery;
your blood was not unheated; not at peace
  your gracious spirit moved above the dark,
and in my most unmeant and dear increase

I spoiled no vision and I quenched no spark.
This, this at least Immanuel shall declare,
Howe'er he judge my motives and my will;
this, this at least himself he deigned to share,
using my nearness for his heavenly skill;
though either of each other now are rid,
Celia, that shall not ruin what I did.[38]

The resolution to the crisis is found in "On the Knowledge of Love." It contains the required synthesis after his declaration of love, attempted control, and her consequent rejection. Her rejection appears to be a renunciation of the erotic element, or desire, in their relationship. He returns to the hermetic vision—romanticism infused with spirituality as mediated by the poets. This appears to be the only acceptable way to relate to her now. A combination of circumstances and ideology have forced it on him:

Love that the poets teach I practise still;
however poorly, yet I practise it.
and therefore will I have therein my will
toward you, and set it all in order fit.
For first to love and then to order so
that nothing injudicious is therein—
this is the art which man was set to know,
and therefore hath relation to his kin.
But having known desire, it cannot be
that knowledge should be subject to desire
a second time, nor to captivity
return what to pure freedom doth aspire.
Only as I love others, I love you;
ah in you first that choice I saw and knew.[39]

Although No. 89 is not the last poem in the cycle, it does offer a conclusion and a diagnosis of the year of passionate engagement. He feels contrition for having overstepped some boundary in their personal relationship. He recognized that it was no longer acceptable to her, and he has rationalized what has happened. If an element of control exists in the relationship, it is Phyllis who is exercising it. He reverts, as he began, to the safety and stability of addressing her as "Sister":

Sister, an end is now; a grave delight
  closes the fantasy and the frenzy both;

If I should err again, if you should err,
  it is not purposed, no nor permanent;
  this is the newer friendship that we meant,
and aught beside does but for an hour stir.

  . . . I never was so wise as this before
  no, not when my first youth began to adore
Love, and beheld his full divinity shine.
For that was heaven brought down to earth, but this
  earth raised to heaven, since heaven is nought but He:[40]
  littler desire in either, but to see—
because to see is lovelier than to kiss.

And if it wholly perish, if this year,
  you meet me in the entry, and less sweet
  it seem than when some newer friend you meet,
it will not therefore have been less than dear:

it will not therefore have been less than He
  in whom all death is, and all life made new,
  to whom be ascribed, as is most justly due,
all praise, dominion, government, equity.[41]

The Infusion of the Romantic by the Erotic

The religious overtones of the last lines raise the issue of the influence of hermetic culture on Williams's romanticism. In Waite's Q'abalistically inspired writing the body becomes the key to incorporating a wider spiritual dimension. The inspiration this gives mandates the poet in his celebration of the material as revelation of the spiritual. The difficulty it produces is that it does not allow for any obvious demarcation between the spiritual and erotic. Throughout "A Century" Williams exhibits this confusion.

He is never quite clear what she is to him. He uses "sister" and "friend" initially. "But O with what a marvelling thought / I see the stars ascend / at evening through the Celian air, / my sister and my friend."[42] In No. 40 she is "sister," and in No. 48, "child." After the crisis, he returns to "sweet sister, fair salvation, dearest friend."[43] But the main area of confusion is between the spiritual, romantic, and erotic.

When writing a poem in honor of her eyelashes, the lifting of which he acknowledges as "my Lord," he infuses romantic longing with religious overtones:

> *The fringèd curtains*—O if Prospero
>   had looked on those and not Miranda's eyes
> and seen the shadow that their lashes throw
>   under the darkness where your meaning lies!
> O if the youthful prince whose heart declared
> *the lifting of her eyelash is my lord,*
> had seen yours lift, and all the purpose bared
> which are in those large deeps of meaning stored.[44]

While starting with physical attributes that carry an ambiguity, he moves on rapidly to an overt religious imagery that still carries within it overtones of erotic and romantic attraction. In "At Mass on Ascension Day," it is not clear what the operation of great alchemy is transforming. But the critical final line, "In thee Love runs and yet does not make haste" clearly reflects a religious love, but with overtones of human loving. No distinction is made.

In No. 44 he employs a religious theme, "At Mass on Ascension Day," choosing provocatively to use the pronoun "my" again, but grounding its use in the language of spirituality rather than romanticism. His fascination with her is signaled in his use of the word "alchemy" to describe her growth and change into the image of God:

> "I have known you for the image of your Master."[45]
>
> Sleep'st thou, my Celia? asleep, but ere sleep closes
> let one faint dream assure thee all is well,
> while the high ritual here itself disposes
> to the redemption of his Israel.
> Most holy, and most happy, and most blessed,
>   he who admires (ah let it be by thee!)
> the presentation of a creed professed,
> and operation of great alchemy.

See how thou art with this strange virtue graced:
In thee Love runs and yet does not make haste.[46]

Her praise is set in another poem, No. 57, called "With the Sonnets Concluding the Masque," in religious language with overtones of the Virgin Mary:

O no, in this too you are free from sin,
generous immaculate,
. . . [y]our perfect movement gave him what he sought,
a gateway for his entrance.[47]

He continues in the next poem with lines that are close to idolatrous:

. . . [t]he only soul that does not mirror God
because reflection is in every quest
  but the quest ends in that great period
where you are all and all are you! O mute,
O sacred wisdom holy beyond speech.[48]

The attribution of holiness is intensified and the spirituality cloaks both romanticism and eroticism.

The avoidance of Phyllis and the adoption of Celia in Marian mode is the mechanism by which he holds the sensual romanticism within the cover of spirituality of piety. The hermeticism allows for veneration of the body. In other circumstances the erotic quality of the physical attributes would be more obvious.

In No. 68, the title suggests a religious theme, "On Her Growth in Grace." In fact it reverts to being a conventional love poem devoid of any religious imagery:

. . . [i]f you grew
a small flower in your garden plot . . .

and if, one joyous eve of spring,
you to your garden wandering out,
found a high bush of colour fling
a rain of fragrance all about.

. . . [h]ardly by others seen,
but seen but known, but loved, by you.

... [w]ould you not with a startled mind,
a trembling breast, a beating heart,
gaze at it from behind the blind.[49]

In the depressive confession of "Daydreams" he admits that this confusion was deliberate, though it seems more likely that the motivation spanned both consciousness and the unconscious.[50] If it was mere strategy, as he accuses himself of, it is unlikely he should revert so overtly to it after the crisis has past—"Christhood" and "kiss" are found in the same verse in poem No. 82, line 3—though it is not clear if this kiss is that which has the irresponsible overtones of Eros, or more ominously the fatal encounter with Judas in Gethsemane:

Celia I see the Christhood that you are,
I put your work on and am made agen:
O wear it ever spirit.
... [A]ll's done; kiss me; this is the end,
sweet sister, fair salvation, dearest friend.[51]

He continues to synthesize the religious and romantic when in "On Looking Forward" he appears to compare his first experience of love with this second. The first appears to carry overtones of the incarnation; the second, the deification of humanity in orthodox theology:

For that was heaven brought down to earth, but this
  earth raised to heaven, since heaven is nought but He:
  littler desire in either, but to see—
because to see is lovelier than to kiss.[52]

Hermeticism finds its way back as the controlling category for his vision when he writes the epilogue, and sets it in terms of transformation and alchemy. Her journey is to be one of inward change, with the poet as the poor companion who observes and celebrates, and in the best traditions of courtly love, serves from afar:

And she was one who walked in loneliness. . . .
[s]he found no peace in all her range
and modes of loving, till she knew to change
all things within herself; she would not cease
from utmost labour till the utmost Peace,

finding fulfilled all that its need demanded,
within her soul transforming it, expanded.

She was more beautiful when she loved than light
astonishing the green leaves of Spring; her flight
upward was like her motion forward, rare
as any sun-directed folk of air
alchemical or actual; going gaily,
she set her foot upon the dragon daily.

and therefore one who saw . . . .
[w]rote for his pleasure first, then in her praise,
then as a poor companion upon the ways
that go unto the end beyond all choosing,
these poems for her laughter and her musing.[53]

In a later letter, Williams summarized the experience of contradiction he had encountered in her:

> What you have, Celia,—what you are, rather,—is one of those curious and marvellous beings whose lure is the refusal, whose invitation is the denial, whose hand of union is the sword of separation. It is the type which hides in some of Shakespeare's boy-heroines (spiritual in you, theatrical in them). It is what I have meant by babbling about your virginal aloofness. It is, I think, not a common type (and incidentally it was always my childhood's dream, my adolescent vision). . . . [Y]our abandonments and play do but emphasise it—but woe to the wretch who doesn't realise it. I think you might easily be, because of that, a delirium to some minds.[54]

She certainly produced both delight and delirium in his mind, as the following letters to her demonstrate.

The Unseen Letters to Celia

> Of all my sins I count least the taking of that adoration.[55]

The unseen letters comprise material that spans the years 1935–1942. Phyllis McDougall kept them secretly in a private box. These letters resemble much of Williams's other correspondence, having been written in his appallingly difficult hand, under the influence of neurasthenia. They varied in length and content. In my interview with her, she gives a clue as to why she, now Phyllis McDougall, had kept the material secret from A. M. Hadfield. "When the bombing started, Alice Mary went to stay with her brother abroad, so she wasn't aware of anything that happened in Oxford during that period."[56] It seems that Phyllis McDougall was glad to keep some privacy from the eye of the biographer.

The letters show that the integrity of the vision of Celia stayed with Williams to within three years of his death. It may be that it stayed to the end, but since he ceased to write to Phyllis McDougall in 1942, it cannot be ascertained. We do know, however, that having ceased to write to Phyllis, his letters to Michal develop a quality of emotional intensity that they lack before that date. To use the parallel of Dante, one could say that Williams had both the vision of Beatrice and the subsequent woman at the window: both Michal and Celia. At the level of beatific vision, they are both aspects of the face of God. At the level of human engagement, the visions were of two women; one of them he was married to and the other not. The vision itself carries its own integrity and integration; whereas the nature of the human relationships by which the vision comes does not. If Williams was tempted to neglect what he had seen in Michal for the fresher, though inaccessible, vision of Celia, it would not have been surprising. The correspondence offers evidence that the integrity of the vision itself drew him to find a reconciliation between the two manifestations of his perceptions relocated within his marriage by the end of his life.

The letters to Celia range from chat to inarticulate colloquy, from emotional support to spiritual direction. They encompass his directing her reading of Browning to reflections on some of the great themes that Williams had shared with her over the years, and that had developed through the Celian lucidity.

Dante provided numerous parallels. In particular, the vision had thrust itself on Williams much as it had on Dante:

> The general maxim of the whole way in Dante is attention; "look," "look well." At the beginning he is compelled to look by the shock of the vision;

later his attention is enforced by command and he obeys by choice. At the beginning, two of the three images—poetry and the city—are habitual to him though still fresh and young they do not astonish him. But Beatrice does. *Incipit Vita Nova.* It was, with Dante as with Wordsworth, "the bodily eye . . .

> Which spake perpetual logic to my soul,
> And by the unrelenting agency
> Did bind my feelings even as in a chain.[57]

The perpetual logic expressed itself with an unrelenting pace in his letters. On August 17, 1938, Williams wrote a long letter from Amen House shortly before the move to Oxford. The letter contains a reminder of the integrity of the original vision, but contains one or two other elements that were present in the poems. The blurring of the distinction between not just Phyllis but Celia and the godhead remains. At one point he invokes a Celian Hail Mary: "Hail, full of grace, The Lord is with thee, and so believe it or not, he is. It is now, for it was."[58] After a conventional opening, he reopens the letter with his idiosyncratic, mannered formula: "Exalted and most precious, now and forever, by the unpretended beauty that held us, and you in whom it was so fresh." The context becomes a conversation that Williams had had with others about her, and he compares their impressions with his vision.

> "You all of you," said I once, "talk of this and that in her, and you admire or you dislike, and you love, and so on, but none of you all believes in her as I have done, do, and shall do." But the details of our acquaintanceship I did not give; only I went on: "and if she chooses (within herself) this or the other way, why, that is her affair, but I believe in her as I saw, and I will believe in her till I die and after" and so, whatever she does, whatever she is, I most assuredly do." And something like that I really, did say, and I really did mean. I don't blame them, of course; they hadn't the same advantages. But I must be allowed my own knowledge. And when you cannot believe . . . whatever, why, you will know that I believe in you, and you will—I dare not say "rest" in that. . . .
>
> I have written myself into what may sound like encouragement or what not; it was not meant that way so much as the mere fact. Overlook it, and let us return to other things.[59]

His reference to the clarity of his sight of her is intended to offer her some support in the face of both her difficulties and also what appears to be her plunging self-esteem. On a number of occasions he offered her what amounted to spiritual direction that derived from what he had seen.

> Is it quite impossible to explain to anyone that the fact that God has chosen to reveal the Celian glory of Celia through Celia leaves Celia as mortal, as sinful, as disgusting as—oneself? I forgive B.,[60] because the language is akin to him, but I should like to disillude [*sic*] him. I will bet a good deal that even he has no lower opinion of you than I have, and as for the higher—that is no "opinion" but a revelation, and not any where or at anytime can that alter, as you—
>
> Your Commander has just arrived in the Library and rung me up: I'll resume later.

Williams refers on at least two occasions to luncheon appointments with Lieutenant Commander McDougall, the man she will marry after her divorce. When he does resume it is to offer some guidance about her experience of isolation and hellishness. He points out the practical necessity of interdependence, the co-inherence of all our lives as we depend on one another and God, and the reality of despair felt by both Messias and St. Paul. His fountain pen has dried and is faint as he begins to write again:

> My pen has abandoned me; excuse. But, having said all that, it is true that you are not to believe, in any sort of kind of way, final.[61] It is one of the Dark Lights—"things spoken seem unfamiliar when they happen." You are precisely not in hell; hell is final loss. You are not cut off, though it may seem, smell, and taste like it. You are not cut off—you are much more like in union with Love and Dante and St Paul. You can't save yourself—but you can believe (if only in the most usual way) that others will.
>
> "Others he saved; himself he cannot save." Consider, most dear lady, that if Messias knew that state, it was probably because of something mildly serious. "O wretched man that I am, who shall deliver me from *the body of this death?*" If St Paul meant that, he probably meant something almost tangibly corrupt.
>
> *Tanto è amora, che poco è piu morte*—probably Dante meant *precisely* that he re-discovered himself in the midst of a dark and savage wood—just like that—and the voice of Virgil was faint as of a ghost.

> We do not begin to know ourselves until we are left to ourselves—it is like the Particular Judgement—there we are, and there is Abraham's bosom or Beatrice or whatnot, and we have taken the wrong turning—quite deliberately, quite unconsciously, quite certainly. We knew it at the time, though we may have forgotten it now. Why this? "my dear fellow—my dear girl—you *would* have this?" you would—so whatever. You would have *you:* this *is* you. Have it—
>
> "In the midst of this confusion and amazement, where no thought could be formed or any idea retained, save grim, eternal death possessing my whole man, a voice was formed and uttered in me, as from the centre of boundless darkness: 'thy will, O God, be done: if this be thy act alone, and not my own, I yield my soul to thee.'"
>
> So Mr Thomas Storey's[62] on the first of February, 1689; you will remark his method is not to try to move it—the grim eternal death—but to push into it. "Press inward; it is there the thing yields."[63]

As Phyllis moves out of her marriage to Billie Somervaille and toward an attachment to Lieutenant Commander McDougall, Williams attempts to offer some personal consolation. In particular he refers both to his vision of her and the sense of her potential that it incorporates, and also a mythic scheme of development of maturation (which incorporates part of what he was offering Lang-Sims, and places it in a broader context). It appears to be less the fixations of sadomasochistic abuse—however mild—and more a mythic journey, the final aspect of which is described as "Galahad state." These elements suggest the task was understood in terms of the reconciliation of the balanced duality of affirmation and negation celebrated in the Taliessin cycle. David Llewellyn Dodds describes the state of Galahad as that of turning from God's images to God himself.[64] In the "Departure of Dindrane," Dindrane hears Galahad's voice—exclaiming his last words according to Malory (XVll, 22), and giving them the new synthesis of the two ways:

> "Fair Lord, salute me to my Lord Sir Lancelot my father,
> and bid him remember this unstable world"
> The grand Rejection sang to the grand Affirmation.[65]

Williams combines this with the distinctive imaginative leap of relating the menstrual periods to the crucifixion, and therefore the menopause to the making of the Wounded King at Carbonek:

That was before lunch; I resume, having spent a long and conversational lunch with your Commander. We have looked at the situation from every point of view, and parted at the bottom of Ludgate Hill. But nothing recurs to me as of high urgency to mention that he could not do much better himself. We do not always see absolutely eye to eye, but we have at least in common the tendency to treat you as actuality—my romantic view leading us at once to a lower and higher aspect of you than his, but that's of no value.

I imagine that, at present, there can be very little light or joy in Middleton:[66] that sounds heavy; 'tis not meant so. But as far as these family situations go I have them (you will let me say) taped. I cannot think of any worse situation than yours (except possibly Billy's)—and if I say it is universal you will not think I reckon it the less trying. But you will not think you are necessarily less inclined towards sanctity (if—) because the surroundings and you seem like hell. I'm not sure how much you meant the word to cover. . . .

This is all very badly put. I revert, on the chance of answering you, to myself. It has occurred to me lately that my next group of poems may deal with two points in which, you know, I have always half believed (i) the relation of woman's periods to the Crucifixion (ii) the debatable problem of whether women are more admirable, after, say, 45 or 50 than before. I was struck the other day by the notion that the "change of life" in women is not so unlike the healing of the Wounded King at Carbonek by the High Prince. Both involve the cessation of bloodshed, and both involve the showing of a clearer pattern than previously. It seems to me that one might reasonably consider life—especially feminine life—in three stages:(a) the slave-state (b) the Blanchefleur state (c)—after the change—the Galahad state. (my Galahad—not Lord Tennyson's or whoever). In fact that, wherever the first two have been adequately followed, the ensuing third might make the vision even more effectual than before. I have never, as you know much believed in this failing of the beauty of women after 45 or so, and if the Healing of Pelles is, in some sense, the change of life, then it's mere nonsense. Undoubtedly the myth bears this understanding. I know it is not popular, but what is popular that is great?

You will say this is not very clear; perhaps not. But anyhow I propose to throw it out as a suggestion to any young woman I know; if they can expect the change as (mythically) the coming of the High Prince in the

> blood into achievement, so much the better. As for you, I have said so too often for you to doubt my principles on the matter, and (if all goes as we hope) I recommend it to you as the method of your expectation.
>
> I leave it at that.[67]

In a passage of unusual lucidity he offers a "quadruple explanation" to Phyllis of the significance that the body, and in particular her arms, has for him. His poetry depends heavily on the symbolism of physical imagery, and always attracts comment, so that it is of considerable interest when he links her arms both to the notion of sensual energy but also to what he describes as the "universal imagination." It is, he claims, also a way of describing his essential notion of the "feeling intellect." In the letter he underlines "feeling" as though the sensuality and physicality of the body is the means to accessing an affective element to balance the cerebralness of the notion of intellect. In case, despite the erotic overtones of his letter to her, she thinks this applies only to her, he explains "that I am aware that this quadruple sense of the arms applies everywhere—to everybody, I mean, and one moves often in a light sensuous and imaginative cloud of it." This explanation of his understanding of sexual energy goes some way to explain his ritualistic behavior with Lang-Sims[68] and one or two other women.[69] The statement does at least set his approach within his aesthetic as well as intellectual response to surrounding reality and his understanding of the metaphysical. The revelation also demonstrates an integration of the aesthetic, intellectual, physical, and sexual in his own experience. The question as to whether or not this was a result of his immersion in hermetic culture, or whether the latter was an expression of his own preferences, is left open.

> Arms? did you ask or did I dream? but If I were answering, what should I say? I should say:
>
> 1. The sight of your arms rouses in me both sensation and imagination. I feel them within me, thrust into my physical centre, probing, exciting, and uniting round them all the bodily functions; so that to touch or kiss them is an achievement and a great need.
> 2. At the same time there is an intense visual sense—an imagination, a vision—of seeing the very centre of all living measurements. They are everything I mean by "the hazel." "The hazel" has many categories, but your arms are, at the time, the central "identity" of what they all mean. That is why, as I said yesterday, when you pick up a ruler,

the ruler is their unliving prolongation (the cut hazel, but they are both the cut and the servant.)

3. They are Will. Thus, for them to be given or held is an act of will. Now the union of wills is in fact sweeter even than (1), though more rarely felt; and is an example of (2) the greatest example. So that to feel and see your will in them, knowing and assenting to (1) and (2) is the crown of a mutual activity. Whether that activity was writing poetry or writing Browning or doing other things I am not sure that the frustration of any discovery of this mutual will is not the most serious defeat.
4. But the arms are only part of the body. and what is true of them is true of the whole body, in many complex ways—sensual and intellectual. They are a whole country and yet a frontier. And this double sense in them is another, as it were, initiation.
5. I am aware that this quadruple sense of the arms applies everywhere—to everybody, I mean. and one moves often in a light sensuous and imaginative cloud of it. but there are very few indeed of whom one begins to feel (1) and fewer from whom one wishes (3). so that, by and large (and allowing for momentary diversions), the effect of the cloud is to send one back to the primary examples of the cloud. I allow (being more sexual than ever before) that this is sexual energy: but also (being more imaginative than ever before!) I think the sexual is part of the universal imagination. It is, in its way precisely the "*feeling* intellect"![70]

In an undated poem entitled "A Letter," which would appear to have been written later than 1941 (since it follows on from a letter of that date referring to Mother Julian below), Williams summarizes his reflections on the arms and associates himself with Julian theology:

finding, after so long,
the august Authority, holy Imagination,
living in body and soul, the great single
revealed Union (short of the final union)—
that is all I was saying in *Taliessin;*
you should now feel your new faculties,
the perfect recognition, one with it:
(though I admit the greater might destroy the lesser
and the mirror of the highest reaches be broken in the reaches)

we always need another arm to thrust
the ship on: as in Virgil's poem—O marvel!—
"the fine fair arm of pine-changed Cymodocea"
thrust Aeneas to Rome. O arms, arms!
everything sensual and metaphysical there
rides together: the central neural spasm
blurs it, too much considered: the arms are space,
the arms are hazel—I saw it so once;
everything is in the body—source and measurement:
I am the most material poet that lived
since Lucretius: almost as sensual indeed
as the Lady Julian of Norwich, that recluse of sanctity,
who said where the soul and flesh met God
built his City. It is the City we explore—
the hazel, Blanchefleur, Galahad; modes of the City:
you? all; all three;
    Pass: good-bye.[71]

What we do know from the internal evidence of the poem is that it was written in the middle of the night, during which Williams was being kept awake by physical pain; and in the letter he begs for sleep as the aeroplanes are noisy still, "and I want to sleep before the last lecture / on the Incantation of Wordsworth's glory." In another letter, which is dated July 1941, he amplifies what he means by his sense of theological kinship with Mother Julian:

> [W]as it not the lady Julian who said: "where Circassia and Celia meet, there God builds his city," and she did, you know; she did say *precisely* that, substituting "sensualitie" and "self-soul," but they mean that: and I will give you the maxim again as a first truth—"where Circassia and Celia meet there God builds his city." Is not the Blessed Sacrament itself *eaten?*"[72]

Commentators and critics have noted Williams's preoccupation with the idea of power,[73] but in his letters to Phyllis he provides some insight as to how the myth of Celia and the presence of Phyllis provide power or energy. He compares Wordsworth and Yeats, and then comments on how this power needs to be evoked:

> I think you had and have power—"the feeling intellect" upon which I have dilated to the University. I think certainly that probably all power

> has to be evoked—in me by the vision of structure, in you by the images of love. You have power, but it works better under evocation and in . . . order,[74] say; just as mine works better for, as it were, a signal flashed along the line of creation. Do I talk nonsense? or too obscurely? I do not think so. "we live by others"; you and I know that—though very unexpected others we may find ourselves living by. Be blessed always so.[75]

Later in the letter he refers to Celia as the original "hazel" and is attempting to encourage her to enter into a correspondence about Browning (which she does). He makes the suggestion, albeit obscurely, that if she applies herself to verse—in this case Browning—a power is evoked: "and is not the measurement of the power of verse part of the business of the hazel? What else did Virgil give it to Taliessin for? And are not you always free to impose yourself on any verse as you chose."

He insists that he will not have her "unfair to her spirit; no human being could be as full of celerity as you seem; nor you?" This evocation of poetic power provides part of the expression of the reality of the myth of Celia. In another passage on Wordsworth, he writes about the association between Wordsworth and Celia in his mind, again connecting them both with the notion of power: "there is no power in the Prelude unless one draws it out," he writes, and the myth of Celia the means of evoking that power. The occult overtones arise from his suggesting to her that there are "ways" of dealing with sleeplessness, measures that he will not use, and "a magical method for banishing an image." But her image has kept him awake:

> You go on in my head exactly like a trumpet—yes; a kind of sight instantaneously transmuted into sound—a silent sound, I suppose . . . no, of course, I have it wrong; it is sound transmuted into sight, I now realise that you are a kind of sound, and one way that becomes you to the rights and another way it sets you up a kind of exact echo in the actions of others about you, as in my poetry or whatever and all the rest answers to that in me. Well, but I did not mean to go all metaphysical or whatever you call it. It is three o'clock in the morning; you have kept me awake for hours. . . . It must, I think be Wordsworth; one can never quite separate Wordsworth from you—at least when one thinks of what he means by Power. You are to-night the very image of that Power; you are it living and tangible. O I know, I know; a score of other Images, feminine and other, move on the edge—as if on the edge of the circle, the magical circle of the central height where you are—I will dissolve and free you (which, I allow, is a gift of

> freedom to one at the moment unconscious of the circle), but the power, I expect, is like a trumpet call made visible. Wordsworth and Celia, Celia and Wordsworth—is the double name sweeter than either single? perhaps not? why compare? "say but again" "Celia and Wordsworth, Wordsworth and Celia" (which I did aloud as I wrote, and you have no idea how well it sounded), unless it be unique.
>
> Power—you will reject the word, rashly perhaps. But I agree it might be a dream like use of the words; no, nonsense; we do not dream, not dream. After all, there is no power in the Prelude unless one draws it out, yet the verbal shape is there.[76]

In that same letter, he continues by reflecting upon the inadequacies of the pentagram as a symbolic representation of reality when compared to his sense of her at the Eucharist. As in "A Century," he continues to combine in her both a romantic and aesthetic potency along with attributions of religious devotion that are almost Marian in tone. He writes of how at the midnight celebration three weeks before, "I almost saw you over the altar among the incense smoke."

A letter dated the following year, Maundy Thursday 1941, is a rambling and increasingly incoherent piece of writing. Cavaliero describes the growing incoherence of this period as observed in the letters to Lalage. "Some of them are so elliptical and allusive as to be well nigh unintelligible . . . reading more like the words of a man in colloquy with himself than those engaged in a dialogue with another."[77]

The context here is also one of rambling associations, for which he anticipates being rebuked by Celia—"but you will say 'this is old stuff; I know it all by heart; change or cease the song.'" But in the middle of the deluge of associations, Williams turns to Yeats, and the question of the attributes that women who are loved by the poets assume:

> The women whom the poets loved—did they put on any of the poets' genius, or remain their earthly selves?—based on the question asked by Mr. William Butler Yeats—"did she put on his knowledge with his power?" but I think the answer ought to be that her power was her own, and his powers his own, and that she put on only his knowledge (or perhaps that strange quality which we call "faith"), so their powers intermingled and became a new power—perhaps of a lowlier hierarchy.[78]

This comes as close as he ever does to describing the symbiosis between poet and myth that produces the energy or power to create; the cultural overtones are hermetic. Hierarchies played an important part in the Sephirotic and Q'abalistic cultures, and it is to that language that he turns in order to describe the noncorporeal intermingling of his art and its muse.

This was a period of transition. Although at this stage of his life he began his letters to Lois Lang-Sims, the evidence of the letters to Michal[79] suggests that at this time, around about 1942, he found a new energy and level of romanticized engagement with his wife.

One might interpret it as either born of emotional need (since there is little doubt that his state of mind was becoming increasingly fragile) or that it was the response of the disappearance of the second myth personified in Celia/Phyllis McDougall. This myth that may have proved artistically fruitful was personally destructive.[80]

One of his unpublished poems to Phyllis (which did not appear in "A Century") expresses something of the profound frustration; viz., the Celian vision imposed on him and his increasing sense of isolation and discomfort:

> O by thy presence and thine absence thou,
> I cannot love but thee, I cannot need
> but thee, I cannot falter or succeed
> but by the desperation of that brow
> which throws back what it gathers up; then how
> may I endure society? My greed
> lies hungry at my heart, grown sick to feed
> on what illusions the whole world endow.
> I hate them, and that gathered hatred swells
> into the greed in nourishes; the sneer
> mocks its own source, and every movement tells
> itself in me it moves out of thy sphere.
> A madness bites my throat; strike these, and call
> that hatred thine, and strive with me in all.[81]

The last letters to Celia are dated in 1942, and they show a growing and disturbing incoherence. Phyllis McDougall commented: "The Oxford period was the period when our relations were at their lowest. That was the period when I had married again. After Roddy was born (1942), I don't suppose I saw him except at a distance for the last years of his life."[82]

The letters to Michal begin after Sept. 7, 1939, when Williams moved with his colleagues from the press at Amen House to Oxford. He was billeted with the Spaldings at 9 South Parks Road. From there he wrote to his wife regularly throughout the Second World War, until his final letter on May 8, a week before his unexpected death on May 15, 1945.

He associated a more subtle form of myth with his wife than many of the others. It may have been in part because her reputed force of character acted as a constraint on her mythologization. Certainly her being named Michal, for King Saul's daughter who mocked David when he danced, is evidence of her robust character: "I have observed before that it is generally recognised in the England of today that the one practically certain way of getting me to do anything is to pray to God to move you to suggest it. I may do things you do not suggest, . . . [b]ut that I should not accept your High Lordliness's suggestions or dicta is unheard of."[83]

The early letters share this tone, and the romantic affirmations of the letters written after 1943 are, on the whole, missing. There is a banter in the letters that paints in some of the colors of the marriage at this stage and reflects Michal's robust character. She contributed to two additional mythical literary figures, the Bors-Elayne figures in the Taliessin cycle and also Beatrice. Neither of these myths contained her whole personality; but they both were to some extent inspired or evoked by her.

Williams's letters to his wife fall between a mundane realism that one might expect in a marriage that was twenty-two years old and had weathered the crisis of the disruption of an all-too-long "Celian moment" and, toward the end, heightened romantic awareness. This revivified romanticism appears to gather pace in 1942, the year he ceased writing to Celia.

Unlike the letters to Lalage or Celia, there is no soliloquizing.[84] The writing is sharp, open, and honest. At first sight the romanticism of the previous three years seems rather strained. This may partly be that Williams at his lesser moments, as C. S. Lewis criticized him, was capable of combining the style of Dante with that of P. G. Wodehouse.[85] This barb may be more realistically descriptive of his novels, but something of the style crept into his letters when he was at his most lyrical. The cause may also be due in part to his trying too hard, as compensation for the years when his romantic vision had been fixed on another compass bearing. As his death approaches and he experiences a creeping mental and physical deterioration, it becomes clearer that both his dependence and sincerity become authentic.

The early letters contain a cooler tone and slimmer emotional investment. He remains wedded to an intellectual commitment to Michal, even if his emotional and aesthetic-erotic instincts have been redirected. As always, he depends on the notion of vision for his perception of her significance. He writes of a medieval cerebralism that rationalizes the split between head and heart, or rather, between his unconsciously galvanized life of instinct and the more consciously controlled commitment that grew out of his alert sense of metaphysical propriety:

> There was in the Middle ages a phrase "Amor Intellectualis," intellectual love, and for that matter there still is; the philosophers use it; but that is the way in which I look at you. For as I have always said and shall always say, the speed of your motion is a thing to be studied carefully. In the period between my early verse and—all that I have not yet been able to do—I ought to be doing more—I have continuously brooded on that movement and that speed: indeed I think any speed in the present verse is due to your physicality. "Amor Intellectualis," I love you with vision, but though the vision is mine, the spectacle is yours: that is you provide it.[86]

Given that Elayne is portrayed with hair the color of Celia's—"It was said once that your hair was the colour of corn"[87]—it is safer to say that Williams related to Bors as the husband of Michal, rather than making a direct connection between Michal and Elayne. But it is also clear that if Williams identified with Bors, he did so under the influence of Michal and marriage.

"Your letters are so sweet and kind and loving that they almost made me cry; at least they did this morning . . . [a]nd I must content myself and I hope God (How strange it is that I always feel my late verse so responsible to God and you. . . . Though as far as Taliessin goes, neither God nor you are directly mentioned, but you both brood over it.)"[88]

When he had written the poem on Bors to Elayne, "On the King's Coins," he showed no great sense of passionate involvement. His attention was focused more on aesthetic vision, such as the "doctrine" in her hands. Bors "saw you stand, in your hand the bread of love, in your head the lightness of law."[89] In a letter written on November 29, 1944 (below), he shows that a movement of identification that has taken place from Taliessin to Bors. This may reflect the reorientation of his priorities from that of flourishing as an established poet to simply surviving with Michal. His later letters put a high premium on survival. A month from his death he wrote: "Now I know better. I would rather have a comfortable home for the rest of our lives than write the Aeneid."[90] But in November 1944 he contemplated the addition of verses that reflect his renewed devotion. The beginning and end of his adult life are reconciled in an experience that fuses his fractured domestic vision in the integrity of co-inherence:

> I am thinking of inserting a passage in one of the Bors-Elayne poems beginning
>
> Shall I fall in love with you all over again?
> Twice—with you then as with you now,
> either co-inherent in either, that brow
> in this and this in that, but both now
> known in the one, and a double glory so . . . .
>
> All this through looking at your photograph in the small room. Bors in the poems is a sound fellow, and I hope I am not too unlike him; the divine Taliessin himself is too great for me, and is indeed not so much a man at all as the very Nature of Poetry. Now there is something for you to tell the later enquirers when they come. But I am still very cross at not being able to send more poems at once—or to write them at least.
>
> I'm very glad about 31, and it's sweet for you to be pleased. You'll observe that in old age I'm getting far more quick at what you might call "taking notice." Like Bors again, who (I feel) would be absolutely efficient; which was why he was let in on the Grail. Taliessin would have written a long metaphysical poem about it! no—don't let's be unfair; but he was hardly of human birth (see the Stars) and could hardly enter into domesticity; anyhow, he never did.[91]

However the image of Beatrice first impinged on Williams, with him as with Dante, "it remained there and was deliberately renewed."[92] The book is dedicated, "For Michal in redemption of a promise," and he is explicit in attributing to his marital experience the galvanizing of his vision of Dantean interpretation. Michal's presence made a difference to his writing. He wants to come home and begin *The Figure of Arthur:* "I should like to begin it at home during this next weekend—like the Missionary Play;[93] I believe or like to believe, but in fact I do—things go better then. After all Beatrice was written with You about and it's been the only good book I've done since '39."[94]

But his appreciation is for more than just her presence. Michal was central to the whole exposition: "It's not been an easy business—for me or for you—and yet, O sweet, to what a labour you committed us both when you first admired the Silver Stair. You might . . . [y]ou have always been the first and great Influence; Dante was but because of you."[95]

When *The Figure of Beatrice* was published, Williams took great care to send his wife a copy of T. S. Eliot's review in the *Times Literary Supplement:*

> I send you herewith the T. L. S. review of Beatrice. I searched Oxford for a copy of this; not only because it's quite a good & certainly a long review, but also because it is the best short statement, by anyone but me. If you substitute Michal for Beatrice, then you get the whole thing, so far as I can see it, that I have been saying since I met you on that January day in 1907.
>
> How astonishing it seems to me that your Sublime Serenity should ever have doubted that unceasing cry! What is the intellect (admirable as yours and mine is!), what is this or that, what is happiness itself, compared to that intuitive knowledge? That—which is never clouded by disputes over the years; that which is apt to gleam as brightly from your smile or your wit, your head or your hand, as ever it did; that, to which I have never, never been false—not though the whole of creation had, and has, to be, its balance and compare; that—to which you and (one must certainly add) Beatrice are the only public witnesses in 600 years. O I could add "that" to "that" & never stop. Why, to send you money (poor as it is) is not, and never has been, merely to send money to one's wife; it is to maintain in action that translucent thing, it is to serve a demi-goddess ("she seemed to him the daughter of a god"), to bear witness to a Fact as fixed as breath itself. Live up to it? can you? can I?—but lose it ever? never you, never I. And infinite charity is demanded by it; this is its seal in heaven; its certificate on earth. Still wear that royalty darling! I am often a fool, but never the kind that is blind to that. You need not fear—it is not only unnecessary, it is impossible, for that Virtue to fail. My ink runs out. Believe. Serge.

Although Williams appeared pleased with the review, it is not uncritical of what Eliot believed to be unnecessary obscurity.[96] But Eliot did suggest that when Williams wrote about "the poem" in a passage he quoted: "If the name of Beatrice be substituted for 'the poem' throughout this admirable passage, the result will accurately express the way in which, according to Mr Williams's view, the whole of Dantean thought is summed up in her person."[97]

"Beatrice" embodies the poem for Eliot, and "Michal" embodies Beatrice for "Serge." But when Williams goes further to reassure her, in the face of her doubt, that she and Beatrice are the only public witnesses to the intuitive knowledge of this insight, there is some possibility that "public" may covertly refer to the intrusion of Celia. Whatever the subtext, it becomes clear as the correspondence develops that Michal was responsible for an ongoing validity of the vision that enlightened Williams's poetic metaphysic. There was a very practical side to the love she represented. Williams was, in fact, considerably dependent on her.

> As for pride, I was very much struck by your distinction between it and the assumption of it; let us discuss it. But not at all noblest of women, by your other distinction. Your great gifts which are rare and beautiful, are as much given as mine and mine as yours. Yours are Beauty, Intelligence, Speed, Charity, and Delight. (I include Wit under Intelligence). Mine are Speech, Doctrine, Poetry and a certain Lucidity. And we have Labour in Common. Yours are of value to things done; mine to things known. We are the world's infinite complements; we are necessary to each other. I study in you the Thing happening. You observe in me the Thing declared . . . O I babble, but we do but grow to one Thing in two modes. And indeed three—you, I and we. The we being now much more the root of you and I than the other way round. Which is why we carry ourselves with a high courtesy towards each other . . . or as high as our fallen natures allow.[98]

The relationship was fueled by more than the welcome generative complementarity that flourished between them. Williams credits his wife for bolstering him against a good deal of mental and spiritual distress: "I ought always to be grateful to you for saving me from persecution manias, false fancies and all the rest. Consider dearest that any obstinate accuracy of mine is very largely due to you; who never allowed me to get into the grip of grim shadows. It is no doubt your eyes which (as I had the honour to say) are as bright as ever, and which illuminate the mind and soul as well as the flesh."[99]

In February 1945, he had come to feel with conviction and clarity that "all I want in this world is you, a bearable place to live, some money and enough distant publicity to bring in money and be amusing." But he had been experiencing a distressing distancing of himself from his surroundings.

> I feel more and more as if a kind of shell of me went on operating in the world, and being as adequate as possible and even (let us hope!) agreeable, but without any communion with me. It's a very odd sensation, but I suppose inevitable when one has lived for years, most of the time, in a town where no-one touches one's heart, or makes the slightest difference to one's feelings. . . . [B]ut where is the real "I"? In your heart (the rest is missing . . .).[100]

As the untimely end approached he noticed that this detachment in him had grown. He wrote of it in a letter dated February 17, 1945. This depersonalization was only modified and moderated in his intimacy with Lewis, Eliot, and particularly at home; but nowhere else:

> As for the rest—I'm a little conscious myself of a certain new detachment. What you might call my "field of operations" has widened, but it's more markedly remote. I mean that I'm even more of a . . . prophet? priest? something—more of a Voice and less of a man everywhere except at home. At least, that's what I feel. I always was pretty much of a slightly non-personal figure, and all my "interests" in figures rather than in people. Perhaps the people in my novels grew more real as my consciousness of actual people decreases. I've never been able to express this very well; but somehow, except at home . . . and perhaps at Magdalen or with Eliot. . . . I am always aware of a gulf. My voice or my style goes across it, but my heart doesn't.[101]

In much the same way as he had always been inspired by the body of the beloved he expressed his love for Michal in the acceptable hermetic, enculturated, spirit-infused physicality. He missed her. "The turn of the wrist, the gleam of the brow, the glance, the agreement, the togetherness . . . where are these? In London."[102] But more categorically, "your face fixed the Universe," he claimed, following Yeats and the language of hermetic culture: "The civilised centre of my own time and space lies in London; your face fixed the Universe, and it is of that hint that we speak. 'A beautiful woman's body' said Yeats, 'is a passion of the intellect'; when I am old I shall find you proper praise. Be content with this the while."[103]

The image of her physicality was matched by her way of loving, what Williams referred to as a "diagram of charity." Not content with his own vision, he attributes it to St. Paul and his ecclesiology:

> It is fresh fire as well as fresh springs which leap in you. Your excellency is to consider that few women retain their fresh-fire of nature and supernature so long. Charity is justified in you; say, love; the N. T. and you make the word believable. You are a "form" of love, a diagram of charity; you "suffer long and are kind" O exquisite definition! Yet St. Paul did not know you when he wrote it.
>
> I will suppose he foresaw you on a vision—in his prison at Rome. Why not? It is on such beauty of sanctity as yours that the whole Church depends. I do but write truth. My eyes are coldishly [*sic*] watering; or is it tears of admiration? Call it so; they could never be sufficient.[104]

He mused once on the prospect of becoming a parish priest, and although he saw himself as a poor priest capable of teaching doctrine only, all the babies and old ladies in England would have moved into the parish to be taught love by her.[105]

Two letters from the last six months of his life contain small endearments that are deeply poignant in the light of his approaching death. He wrote at the end of a dull and dreadful day: "Why are you not meeting me? and why are we not having a beautiful and drunken dinner—like what we both had once in a Corner House, after going up Westminster Cathedral Tower in a lift, do you remember?"[106]

In his last letter, dated two days before he collapsed on May 10, he wrote words heavy with pathos, carrying a double meaning. He meant them to refer to the ending of the hostilities on V-E Day, May 8, 1945, but they were also personally prophetic:

> I have missed you a great deal today. I should have liked to knock about with you—but there it is!
>
> And it's done. I've a dim sense of relief. . . . [T]he awful days when I thought the enemy might forever be between me and you didn't come to the worst. The mournings and the buryings are done. And presently. . . . There couldn't have been a better Peace Sunday than last. I wish we were here together, but that was very good. And now it's nice to be done.[107]

Forty-eight hours later he was taken ill. He was admitted to the Radcliffe hospital, and on the fifteenth of May he died. His struggle with the "impossibility" was over. Faced with the irreconcilable dual vision of romantic adoration, Williams struggled to retain what integrity he could and endure to the end. It is not possible to enter into anything more than a superficial judgment. To what extent had he reconciled both visions in Michal in the later years? We know too little of the complexities of his mind and heart to exercise an accurate judgment. But he appears to have done so. Equally important, he maintained a consistency with his own analysis of what was required by those who had begun a journey that held fidelity to the image and the principle within and beyond the image. If his hermetic reflexes enabled him to identify the vision and the image beyond it, something more than that gave him the courage to pursue the development of the state to its proper end. As he wrote in *The Figure of Beatrice:*

> Where this romantic adoration exists, there this proper intellectual investigation of it ought to exist. The clearest possibility of this Way, and perhaps the most difficult, may be in marriage. . . . [H]ero-worship, and

even more sentimental states, are only vaguer and less convincing images of the quality which this love is. They are often foolish, but they are apt also to have that kind of sincerity which may, one way or another, become fidelity to the image or to the principle within and beyond the image. One way or another this state is normal; what is not yet normal is the development of that state to its proper end.[108]

Conclusion

In death Williams remains as he was in life, not widely known, yet captivating to those who have learned to recognize and appreciate the distinctive contribution of his art. His fellow Inklings, J. R. R. Tolkien and C. S. Lewis, both also engaged the tools of myth and enchantment and became and remain highly popular. Williams's lack of widespread popularity can be partly attributed to the style of his writing, which is characterized, as Brian Horne suggested, "by a peculiar quality of density."[1]

The abstruseness of his hermetic language and culture plays its part. The influence of the hermetic culture is felt in two respects. First, and constructive, it does so by providing his novels with the ingredients of excitement and drama of the preternatural world. Despite the barb that his technique combines Wodehouse and Dante, many readers find both his style and the contents of his novels show him to be an engaging and highly distinctive novelist. But second, his later poetry is wreathed in a world so steeped in hermetic allusion and reference that it limits its immediate accessibility for many.

Williams's neo-Rosicrucian culture was not incompatible with the essentials of Christian theology, rather it provided the antidote to a prevailing tendency toward dualism. Williams's journey of maturation allowed him to escape the paraphernalia of the esoteric and draw from it a means of recalibrating the theology of mainstream Christianity. By the end of his life Williams had performed his own journey of intellectual integration, and he achieved much at the level of personal resolution. He had drawn from hermeticism a mechanism for perceiving and describing a more universal potential integration, recapturing the notion with the patristic term "co-inherence." The highly specific and exclusive esoteric language had, to some extent, the effect of unhappily masking the remedial vision that was intended to facilitate integration. That quest for the integration of polarized opposites, which he found in the hermetically inspired vision of co-inherence, enables Williams's ideas to remain influential and prophetic in the new millennium.

The central gift underlying his vision is the confrontation of dualism. The habitual tendency in Christian theology to separate spirit and matter has diverted religious and visionary energy from the practicalities of much of everyday life. The secular has been stripped of the sacred and the energy for renewal and transformation that the sacred carried with it. Secular aspirations for transformation have been expressed in either political or psychotherapeutic terms. The secular has lacked a metaphysical language capable of enabling a change that was more than ephemeral or cosmetic reorganization. The sacred was left to languish in a preoccupation with the metaphysical that lacked the oxygen of pragmatic application. Williams's philosophical and theological healing of the division with his capacity for integration yields two consequences. Each of them has the capacity for transformation; both of the way in which romantic experience is interpreted and of the reconfiguring of humanity's independence from our environment to interdependence with it.

The first consequence is a theology that claims romantic experience as part of the Christian theophany. The consequences of allowing romantic love to remain outside the religious language of Christian theology have allowed one of the most perennial and dramatic experiences of our culture to remain immune from any possibility of religious interpretation. In consequence it has remained essentially secular. It has taken with it the music, poetry, and art that mirrored it and that might have acted as a bridge between religious and romantic culture. Williams's great achievement was to reinterpret medieval Dantean vision and make the theological task of integration of two disparate cultures at least possible. He saw the common experience of romantic vision as the threshold for many to a journey of religious exploration that added an ontological dimension: "The present point about the work of [Dante] is that it refers us not to a rare experience but to a common; or rather it begins with one that is common and continues on a way which might be more common than it is."[2]

That the wider church has yet to help make the connection between the original experience and the religious development of a way of mutual transformation is as much a theological and philosophical failure of imagination as it is a consequence of Williams's occasional opaqueness.

The second consequence provides a theological vision for the integration of matter and spirit. A number of areas have been damaged by the abdication of a theological involvement or critique, ecology being one. It represents both a crisis in itself and a symbol of complex interrelatedness that creates serious challenges. Williams's vision of co-inherence provides the justification for linking the progress of the human condition perceived in classical theological terms with the need for social and political transformation. He offers a revived ethical and metaphysical critique. Recent "green" theologies of ecology have been largely pragmatic. The connections between human beings and their environment were restricted to a reading of the theology of Genesis that concentrated on the domination of creation by humanity. Williams is a visionary who, far from being secluded in a hermetic subculture, becomes a prophet of potent social and political significance. He gave us early warning of the postmodern appreciation of our interdependence and in particular a pattern for ecological ways of thinking about the world and the way it connects with human perceptions and activity.[3]

"Ecological ways of thinking" may have become fashionable and pressing but insofar as they offer a model for thinking, their success lies in avoiding the crude mechanistic polarizations that shaped our recent culture. Williams's genius was to offer a renewed vision of integration that carries the reader past Renaissance mechanism into a worldview that has rediscovered the hermetic principle of interrelatedness.

Angelika Schneider rightly claims:

> Because it affirms the reality of both the separateness and the givenness of the material world we experience and the validity of our search for unity and meaning, Williams's world view still seems prophetic in a period of growing polarization between, on the one hand, economic well-being as the only value in a coincidental cosmos void of meaning and, on the other, religious fundamentalism as the attempt to deny reasons in order to force a pattern on chaos. Between the two, visionary scientists, theologians, and the more important "new age" philosophers are saying just what Charles Williams's works . . . [e]xpressed in a different and highly individual idiom fifty years ago.[4]

Paradoxically, by adopting and evolving hermetic metaphysics, Williams created a mythic worldview that removed him from the natural language of his contemporary culture, only to provide and foreshadow a theological, philosophical, and artistic language that could be appreciated and adopted by the postmodern.

Williams fused together opposing polarities. He was, like his poet Taliessin, "Druid born and Byzantium trained."[5] The Druidic implies the hermetic; the Byzantine, the conventional and the established. By combining them as he did, Williams establishes a pattern and a potential for a more comprehensive integration that addressed the fractured nature of all that he believed could be, and would be, reconciled.

Notes

Introduction

1. T. S. Eliot, *The Times Literary Supplement,* July 24, 1943.

2. *To Michal from Serge: Letters of Charles Williams to His Wife, Florence, 1939–1945,* ed. Roma A. King Jr. (Kent, Ohio: Kent State Univ. Press, 2002).

3. Some correspondence to Celia up until 1938 has been lodged in the Bodleian Library. Letters from 1938 onward were not expected since A. M. Hadfield, Williams's biographer, had wrongly assumed that the relationship had come to a close. The letters were given to me by Phyllis McDougall in 1992.

1. The Encounter between Poet and Magus

1. R. A. Gilbert, *Magician of Many Parts: A Biography of A. E. Waite* (Wellingborough: Crucible, 1987), 148. Gilbert will be relied on heavily during this chapter. He is the single source for material on Waite apart from the works themselves.

2. A. M. Hadfield, *Charles Williams: An Exploration of His Life and Work* (Oxford: Oxford Univ. Press, 1983), 30.

3. James Charles Wall, *Shrines of British Saints* (London: Methuen, 1905).

4. Ibid., ix, x.

5. Anne Ridler, "*The Image of the City*" (Oxford: Oxford Univ. Press, 1958), xiv.

6. Hadfield, *Charles Williams,* 29.

7. Ibid.

8. Glen Cavaliero, *Charles Williams: Poet of Theology* (Grand Rapids, Mich.: Eerdmans, 1983), 4.

9. Roma A. King Jr., *The Pattern in the Web: The Mythical Poetry of Charles Williams* (Kent, Ohio: Kent State Univ. Press, 1990), 12.

10. Dennis L. Weeks, *Steps toward Salvation,* American Univ. Studies, Ser. IV, English language and literature (N.Y.: Peter Lang, 1991).

11. Andrea Freud Loewenstein, *Loathsome Jews and Engulfing Women: Metaphors of Projection in the Works of Wyndham Lewis, Charles Williams, and Graham Greene* (New York: New York Univ. Press, 1993).

12. Brian Horne, ed., *Charles Williams: A Celebration* (Leominster: Gracewing, 1995).

13. Marie Mulvey Roberts and Hugh Ormsby-Lennon, *Secret Texts: The Literature of Secret Societies* (New York: A. M. S. Press, 1995).

14. These factual disparities are also followed by Humphrey Carpenter in his book *The Inklings.* Carpenter not only repeats Hadfield's errors but compounds them by the

assumption of elements of occultism that a better informed understanding of A. E. Waite and the Fellowship of the Rosy Cross would dispel. Carpenter writes: "The line between religion and magic is sometimes hard to draw and since its foundation thirty years earlier this Order (the 'Order of the Golden Dawn') had wavered rather uncertainly between the two." Humphrey Carpenter, *The Inklings* (London: George Allen and Unwin, 1978), 81.

In this reference to the Order of the Golden Dawn he is correct. What he has failed to uncover is the rationale for Waite's critique of the Order of the Golden Dawn, his analysis of occultism, and the basis for his new order. Carpenter goes no further than quoting an initiatory vow from the Order of the Golden Dawn and claiming that Waite simply formed "his own temple" after a schism (Carpenter, *Inklings,* 81). This is misleading factually and fails to take into account the distinctiveness of Waite's views, or the quality of his influence on Williams. This error is perpetuated in one of the most recent studies of co-inherence published in 1991 by Weeks, *Steps toward Salvation.* He continues writing of the Order of the Golden Dawn vows.

Probably they were harmless enough, based as they seem to have been on Waite's enthusiasm for Freemasonry, vaguely Christian mysticism, and Rosicrucianism, a system of occult beliefs that combines the symbolism of Christianity with the terminology of alchemy, and has the Rosy Cross as its central feature. Carpenter, *Inklings,* 81. R. A. Gilbert takes a more pragmatic line over Waite's relationship with Masonry: "The most probable reason for Waite's seeking admission to Freemasonry . . . [w]as his growing awareness that only by passing through the Craft degrees and the Holy Royal Arch would he be able to enter those Higher Degrees whose rites he so eagerly desired; initiation into Craft Masonry brought no spiritual enlightenment to Waite; after his initiation, he commented 'It was patent throughout that I could have told the Worshipful Master all that he was communicating to me.'" Gilbert, *Magician,* 128.

This distinction between mysticism and magic is of considerable importance. Williams's reputation has been tarnished by assumptions and bolstered by commentators, such as Carpenter, that his preoccupations were with magic rooted in the occult. His novels contain a great deal of symbolism and material drawn from esoteric culture; they also demonstrate an evolving worldview that became increasingly, overtly Christian and orthodox. In order to demonstrate this progression, I will contrast the two earliest novels, which demonstrate a fascination with and an admiration for the role of the alchemical or occult adept, with his last two novels, where the magus who deals in the arena of the conventionally occult assumes an antipathetic role. Williams creates a revised and evolved form of adeptship. It takes the form of adeptship as artist, both poet and (in the plot of *All Hallows' Eve*) painter, and acts to express a developed metaphysics of co-inherence and exchange.

15. Mme. Horos and her husband had tricked Mathers out of Order of the Golden Dawn rituals and set up a temple of their own in London that was a cover for sexual debauchery. In 1901 Mr. Horos was charged with rape, and during the trial, the Order of the Golden Dawn was held up to severe ridicule and scandal by association. See Gilbert, *Magician,* 113.

16. Charles Williams, *Divorce* (Oxford: Oxford Univ. Press, 1920). This book was dedicated "To my father and my other teachers."

17. Ridler, *"Image,"* xxiii.

18. A. E. Waite, *Shadows of Life and Thought* (London: Selwyn and Blount, 1938), 229.

19. Ridler, *"Image,"* xxiv.

20. Hadfield, *Exploration,* 29.

21. A. E. Waite, *The Hidden Church of the Holy Graal* (London: Rebman, 1909).

22. Gilbert, *Magician,* 148.

23. The influence of Daniel H. S. Nicholson may be in part gauged by the fact that Williams dedicated his seminal work on the Holy Spirit and Christian history, *Descent of the Dove: A Short History of the Holy Spirit in the Church* (London: Longmans, 1939), to

"D.H.S.N., who nobly and happily disputed the Nature of Love." Preface to the first edition, Religious Book Club, London. He was also to dedicate *Outlines of Romantic Theology* (Grand Rapids, Mich.: Eerdmans, 1990) to both D. H. S. Nicholson and A. H. E. Lee, and also to Fred Page.

24. The Independent and Rectified Rite was the name given to Waite's breakaway group from the "O.G.D.," formed on Oct. 7, 1903.

25. Gilbert, *Magician,* 149.

26. The minutes, which are in the possession of R. A. Gilbert, give the details of Williams's relationship with the Fellowship of the Rosy Cross.

27. "The brother who thirsts, let him come" (or arrive).

28. Hadfield, *Exploration,* 29, quoting from a letter in the Marion E. Wade Center, Wheaton College, Ill. Hadfield repeats again the error that his membership lasted "probably no more than four or five years."

29. This reference is to the robe makers used by Waite and others for clothing initiates and members.

30. A. E. Waite to Charles Williams, unpublished letters, Wade Center, Wheaton College, Ill.

31. The division of the fellowship grades:

0=0	Grade of Neophyte,
1=10	Grade of Zelator (corresponding to Sephirah of Malkuth on the Tree of Life) located in the world of action (Assiah) and comprised the First Order.
2=9	Theoreticus
3=8	Practicus
4=7	Philosophus corresponding to Yesod, Hod, and Netzach were in the Second Order and were held to be the World of Formation (Yetzirah).

The Third Order in the World of Creation (Briah), comprised the Portal of the Third Order, and the Grades of

5=6	Adeptus Minor
6=5	Adeptus Major
7=4	Adeptus Exemptus corresponding to the Sephiroth, Tiphereth, Geburah, and Chesed.

There was a Portal of the Fourth Order, in the World of Supernals (Atziluth), but no rituals for the grades corresponding to the first three Sephiroth were ever worked, although Waite began to construct them toward the end of his life.

32. He retained his robes with him in Oxford until his death. Joan Wallis carried out his wishes by burying his regalia in the garden after his death, as she disclosed in an interview with me on July 30, 1992.

33. Ridler, "*Image,*" xxv.

34. "Charles later used the Order's image of the Sephirotic tree with its branches of opposed or balancing qualities leading through created beings and the frame of man up to Ain Soph, the unknowable God, Limitless Light. He uses 'O emanation of Ain Soph!' in a letter to Phyllis Jones" (held in the Bodleian Library, no. 269 reserved). Hadfield, *Exploration,* 29.

35. Gilbert fails to mention that Waite's mystical works are written in an interminably abstruse and convoluted style that, when wrapped as they are in elongated pomposity, make it a considerable achievement to read any of his material at length. His larger occult audience may be a function of their having been convinced that his obscurity is designed to hide a secret wisdom, or simply reflect the perennial interest in the occult, rather than reflect on the irrationality of our age.

36. Gilbert, *Magician,* 13.

37. W. B. Yeats identified him as the foremost expositor of Louis Claude de Saint-Martin, a mystical philosopher deemed unusually problematic, and John Masefield is chronicled as being numbered among those who valued his writing on the spirituality and the history of alchemy. Gilbert, *Magician*, 12, 13.

38. R. A. Gilbert notes that if some of his work is particularly abstruse, nonetheless he clearly had a potent influence on a number of other authors, Robert Browning, Arthur Machen, and Charles Williams among them. It was as mystic rather than occultist that Waite impinged. Aiden and Reynolds describe the first meeting between Waite and Machen in 1887. "They immediately became friends, and very quickly close friends. With similar interests but totally dissimilar opinions on nearly every question of importance, they were still fifty years later assailing each other's theories with huge enjoyment and unabated vigour." Aidan Reynolds and William Charlton, *Arthur Machen* (London: John Baker for the Richards Press, 1963), 28.

39. Gilbert, *Magician*, 14.

40. Ibid., 52.

41. Ibid., 87.

42. Ibid., 96.

43. Here lay also the embryonic ideological form of the Fellowship of the Rosy Cross, which in its turn was to influence the concept and purpose of the Companions of the Co-inherence, which was established in Sept. 1939. See Hadfield, *Exploration*, 173–74.

44. Christopher McIntosh, *The Rosicrucians: The History, Mythology, and Rituals of an Occult Order* (Wellingborough: Crucible, 1980, revised, 1987), 19.

45. It was this emphasis on *fin-de-siècle* renewal, being on the cusp of a new age, that made hermeticism so attractive to both Yeats and, in the form of Rosicrucianism, also to Williams. It provided the philosophical and metaphysical material for a language in which myth proved to offer an aesthetic and creative elasticity.

46. Despite the apparent anonymity of the publication, commentators appear to be reasonably confident that the real author (or coauthor) of the *Fama* was likely to have been a Tübingen Protestant theologian named Johann Valentin Andreae. McIntosh, *Rosicrucians*, 19.

47. As Waite, and following him Williams, will describe it, "arch-natural."

48. Frances A. Yates, *The Rosicrucian Enlightenment* (St. Albans: Paladin, 1975), 14.

49. Each of the different celestial objects exercised specific influences that a magus had to learn to control. Saturn influenced abstract study and controlled melancholia and depression. Venus influenced love. There were associations with stones, gems, plants, animals—a web of co-inherent relationships. A whole range of aims might be achieved with this intellectual magic: success in business, escape from prison, overcoming enemies, success in love, curing disease, and promoting health.

50. Pico della Mirandola (1463–94). The nephew of Marsilio Ficino, he was born at Mirandola near Modena. He studied law at Bologna but developed a wider intellectual appetite. At the age of eighteen he traveled extensively in France and Italy, accumulating a large library and acquiring a wide range of knowledge sacred and profane, which his prodigious memory made readily accessible. In 1486 he arrived in Rome and proposed 900 theses or propositions, dealing, as he said, "*de omni re scibili*" (with everything knowable), inviting all comers to debate them with him and offering to pay their traveling expenses if poverty prevented their taking up the challenge. However, Pope Innocent VIII intervened by a bull in 1487 to prevent the discussion. Thirteen theses were singled out and condemned as heretical. Pico withdrew to Florence and defended himself in an *Apology* (1489), but the attacks continued until Alexander VI absolved him of the taint of heresy and protected him from further persecution. Under the influence of Savonarola Pico he withdrew to a life of austere piety and died of fever at thirty-one. Like so many Renaissance philosophers, Pico sought to reconcile theology and philosophy. He approached the problem through a variety of avenues, notably the study of the Q'abalah, in which he believed

he had found the quintessential truth that would harmonize the scriptures and secular philosophy. A graphic description of the impact of Pico's personality on contemporaries comes from Politian, who described him as "the Phoenix of the wits." Pico's biography was written by his nephew Giovanni and translated into English (1510?) by Sir Thomas More.

51. When the Inquisition was to apply the *Malleus Maleficarum* of James Sprenger and Henry Kramer written in 1490, the criteria used for rooting out witchcraft and heresy were based on an understanding that there was a grand conspiracy between the devil and his followers to discover or create an organic relationship other than the organic relationship that exists in the divine principles of the universe. See Williams, *Witchcraft* (London: Faber and Faber, 1941), 127. The precise origin of the powers or forces that were being invoked became critical.

52. Margaret Wertheim, *Pythagoras' Trousers* (London: Fourth Estate, 1997), 87.

53. Yates, *Rosicrucian,* 15.

54. There is considerable variety in the spelling of Q'abalah. "Q'abalah" will be used in this book, unless quoting from another author whose spelling differs; there the original will be preserved.

55. Quoted by Kathleen Raine in *Yeats the Initiate: Essays on Certain Themes in the Work of W. B. Yeats* (Portlaoise: Dolmen Press; London: George Allen and Unwin, 1986), 186.

56. Luis Alvarado, *Psychology, Astrology and Western Magic: Image and Myth in Self-Discovery* (St. Paul, Minn.: Llewellyn Publications, 1991), 15.

57. Blake was familiar with these principles, which he calls the "Four Zoas," that were taken to relate to reason, feeling, prophetic imagination, and sensory life; they have been made more commonly available in the writings of C. G. Jung, where they are seen as the four functions of the psyche.

58. Williams will use exactly this concept in both his later novels, *Descent into Hell* and *All Hallows' Eve.*

59. Charles Poncé, *Kabbalah: An Introduction and Illumination for the World Today,* 2d ed. (Wheaton, Ill.: Quest Books, 1980), 53; quoted by Alvarado in *Psychology, Astrology and Western Magic,* 5.

60. This principle underlies Williams's use of the idea in two of his novels: *All Hallows' Eve,* where Simon the Clerk will exercise hermetic power by the perfect pronouncement of the tetragrammaton, and *Many Dimensions.*

61. McIntosh, *Rosicrucians,* quoting Heinrich Cornelius Agrippa von Nettesheim, *De Occulta Philosophia* (London, 1651), 35.

62. Williams, *Witchcraft,* 30–31. A similar theme, the conquest by Christ of magic, can be found in G. K. Chesterton's *The Everlasting Man.*

63. Yates, *Rosicrucian.*

64. Ibid., 264.

65. "The second half of Dee's career is still more important in relation to the Rosicrucian movement, if, as I believe, the Dee movement was used by Anhalt for building up the Elector Palatine as King of Bohemia." Ibid., 266.

66. A hermetic link between Williams and Shakespeare may be suggested. The close association of author and character is not without difficulty. But Williams clearly sees Stanhope in *Descent into Hell* as a figure he identifies with. Stanhope at one dramatic moment identified *himself* with Prospero as he quotes, "'I'll deliver all; and promise you calm seas. . . . ' His voice became an incantation; his hand stretched upward in the air, as if he invoked the motion of the influences, and the hand was magical in her sight." Williams, *Descent into Hell* (London: Faber and Faber, 1937) 178.

67. Yates, *Rosicrucian,* 276.

68. Quoted in McIntosh, *Rosicrucians,* 62.

2. *Modern Hermeticism*

1. However one defines "magic," mystically or pragmatically, theurgists also followed the hermetic Doctrine of Correspondence, "as above, so below," and as a consequence were of the view that man-made objects could be imbued with a life and intelligence of their own through the use of symbols, or tokens. Twelve short stanzas supposedly deriving from Hermes Trismegistus comprise "The Emerald Tablet." The two that have a bearing on this point are:

> 1 In truth certainly and without doubt, whatever is below is like that which is above, and whatever is above is like that which is below, to accomplish the miracles of one things.
>
> 7 It rises from earth to heaven and comes down again from heaven to earth, and this acquires the power of the realities above and the realities below. In this way you will acquire the glory of the whole world, and all darkness will leave you.

Quoted in Alvarado, *Psychology, Astrology and Western Magic,* 197n1.

2. Gilbert, *Magician,* 105.

3. In an interview with me in Bristol, on Sept. 3, 1994.

4. Gilbert, *Magician,* 106, quoting from *The Rosicrucian Society of England* (1915), 3.

5. The wise sister will be ruled by the stars.

6. Waite makes the cryptic comment in his autobiography: "It transpired presently that Macgregor Mathers—who assumed the additional patronymic presumably to sustain the cause—was something to do with the darkly glittering business. The name of Wynn Westcott also loomed remotely. Mathers was like a comic Blackstone of occult lore and Westcott like a dull owl, hooting dolefully among cypresses over tombs of false adepts." Waite, *Shadows of Life and Thought* (his autobiography), 124; written fifty years later. Quoted in Gilbert, *Magician,* 109.

7. The definitive history of the Order of the Golden Dawn is Ellic Howe's *The Magicians of the Golden Dawn: A Documentary History of a Magical Order, 1887–1923* (York Beach, Maine: Samuel Weiser, Inc., 1984).

8. Gilbert, *Magician,* 107.

9. Ibid., 113.

10. Gilbert does not document who they were.

11. George Mills Harper, *Yeats's Golden Dawn: The Influence of the Hermetic Order of the Golden Dawn on the Life and Art of W. B. Yeats* (London: Macmillan, 1974), 119.

12. Peter Washington, *Madame Blavatsky's Baboon: Theosophy and the Emergence of the Western Guru* (London: Secker and Warburg, 1993), 92.

13. Yeats arguably spans at least three poetic generations: late Victorian, Edwardian, and Modernist.

14. Richard Ellmann, *Yeats: The Man and the Masks* (Oxford: Oxford Univ. Press, 1979).

15. W. B. Yeats, *Essays and Introductions* (New York: Macmillan, 1961), 28.

16. Yeats, *Essays,* 43. See also Ellmann, *Yeats,* 90.

17. Ellmann, *Yeats,* 56.

18. Williams writes out of his preoccupation with this possibility in the plot of his novel *Shadows of Ecstasy.* See chapter 8.

19. Yeats's own experience of this took place in 1893, when he attained the inner Order of the Golden Dawn, and in the initiation of the Path of the Portal lay down in the tomb, died a symbolic death, and "rose" reborn in spirit, "Christified."

20. Not least for Yeats in the ambitions of Irish nationalism.

21. Williams also turned to the imagination for inspiration. But he can be found advocating social reform equally strongly as a consequence of his attention to the significance of the material in his essay "Sensuality and Substance." Ridler, "*Image,*" 74.

22. Harper, *Yeats's Golden Dawn,* quoted on 51.

23. Ellmann, *Yeats,* 193.

24. Gilbert, *Magician,* 109.

25. Ibid.

26. Ibid., 110, quoting from Waite's autobiography, *Shadows of Life and Thought.*

27. Harper, *Yeats's Golden Dawn,* 124.

28. Gilbert, *Magician,* 120.

29. Armstrong was the biographer of Evelyn Underhill; Underhill was also a member of the Order of the Golden Dawn. She joined Waite's breakaway group in 1905. Christopher J. R. Armstrong, *Evelyn Underhill* (London: Mowbrays, 1975), 42.

30. Williams, 1937. See chapter 11.

31. Harper, *Yeats's Golden Dawn,* 265–66, appendix K; W. B. Yeats, "Is the Order of R. R. & A. C. to Remain a Magical Order?" Written in Mar. 1901 and given to the Adepti of the Order of R. R. & A. C. in Apr. 1901.

32. Gilbert, *Magician,* 116, 196.

33. Gilbert reminds us of the ideological fracture that ran alongside the political one: "For all that Waite urged mysticism upon them, the members of the Rite would not willingly give up astral travelling, visions and phenomena; faced with the demand to reject the cipher manuscripts, they could not bring themselves to accept the inevitable consequence: the rejection of the glamour of magic. Instead they rejected Waite." Gilbert, *Magician,* 139.

34. The text continues, "which find their strict correlation in the external heresies of doctrine, wherein also there is no light, as we shall see immediately. If the resolution has not been made already, and that definitely, it is time—and it is high time that the whole domain of phenomenal occultism should be transferred to the care of psychological science." A. E. Waite, *The Hidden Church of the Holy Graal* (London: Rebman Ltd., 1909), 523. These strands of exploration were re-woven to great effect later in the century by C. G. Jung.

35. Quoted by Raine in her book *Yeats the Initiate,* chapter 7, "Yeats, the Tarot and the Golden Dawn," 185.

36. Gilbert, *Magician,* 123.

37. This has strong gnostic overtones with a theology of the "return" of the soul.

38. For Williams's own definition, see his comments on the occult in "The Index of the Body," in Ridler, *"Image."*

39. McIntosh, *Rosicrucians,* 117.

40. This ms. was kindly provided by R. A. Gilbert during an interview in Bristol on Sept. 3, 1994.

41. Waite, "The Ceremony of Consecration on the Threshold of Sacred Mystery," 7.

42. Ibid., 12.

43. Romans 12:2. Revised Standard Version (R.S.V.).

44. See below, chapter 6.

45. Waite, "Ceremony," 12.

46. Ibid., 14.

47. Ibid., 26, 27.

48. See *Purgatorio,* 185.

49. The imagery of the mountain is of course common in many other places, including St. John of the Cross, both Testaments, and Dante. On linking Beatrice with the mountain in *Purgatorio,* Williams comments, "Most lovers have called the adored 'the cause and occasion of all joy,' and meant it. In that sense Beatrice and the Mountain are one." Williams, *Figure of Beatrice,* 145; and "Beatrice is herself the mountain. She is, as so many of her sisters have been to their lovers, the means by which purification takes place." Williams, *The Figure of Beatrice* (London: Faber and Faber, 1943), 147.

50. Waite, "Ceremony," 26.

51. Ibid., 43. These last words are drawn from Bonaventura (as cited by Williams, *He*

Came Down from Heaven [London: Heinemann, 1938], 105) and also Meister Eckhart's description of the nature of God.

52. Waite, "Ceremony," 53.

3. *The Q'abalah,* The Secret Doctrine in Israel, *and the Influence of A. E. Waite*

1. Elements of eroticism as part of mystical or religious experience were not at all uncommon in the lives of the mystics; St. Teresa of Avila and St. John of the Cross are examples. But they were uncommon in general lay experience.

2. Williams links Yeats with Donne in his essay on Yeats: "Is this the voice of the dreamer, the faery student, the occultist, the lover of beauty? Well, it might very well (*mutatis mutandis*) be the voice of Landor or of Donne." And, "The young Marlowe as well as Donne seems to be recalled by this poet whose 'aspiring mind' is also concerned with 'the wondrous architecture of the world.' Nor is it only in their magniloquence that he is like them, but in their worldliness; his feet are planted as firmly on the earth as theirs are." Williams, *Poetry at Present* (Oxford: Clarendon Press, 1930), 58, 59, 60.

3. W. B. Yeats, *The Shadowy Waters,* quoted by Charles Williams, *The Silver Stair* (London: Herbert and Daniel, 1912), iii.

4. Ridler, "*Image,*" xxv.

5. A. E. Waite, *The Secret Doctrine in Israel* (London: William Rider and Son, 1913), 14, 15.

6. Z., Pt.1, fol. 236b; De Pauly, II, 533; ibid., 24.

7. Waite, *Secret Doctrine,* 190.

8. Waite's views, like those of the author of the Zohar, were clearly developed without reference to Graf-Wellhausen's "Documentary Hypothesis on the Pentateuch," involving J. D. E and P. See John Bright, *History of Israel* (London: Student Christian Movement, 1960), chapter 2.

9. Z., Pt.11, fol. 161b, 162a; De Pauly, IV, 101, 102; Waite, *Secret Doctrine,* 191.

10. Waite, *Secret Doctrine,* 193.

11. Ibid., 213.

12. Ibid.

13. Ibid., 215.

14. Ibid., 216.

15. Ibid., 227.

16. Footnote 1 reads: Z., Pt.111, fol. 66b; De Pauly, V, 182. The hour of entrance is when the sacred King is united to Matrona. For a description of the term "Matrona," Waite writes, describing the Shekinah, "In respect of the manifest universe, she is the architect of worlds, acting in virtue of the Word uttered by God in creation. In respect of the myth of paradise, the Shekinah is the Eden which is above, whence the river of life flows forth that waters the garden below, and this is also Shekinah as she is conceived in external things—or Bride, Daughter, and Sister in the world below. Considered in her divine womanhood, in the world of transcendence, She is the beloved who ascends towards the heavenly Spouse, and she is Matrona who unites with the King, for the perfection of the Divine Male is in the Divine Female," p. 192. Waite, *Secret Doctrine,* 228.

17. Descriptions vary, but this would be a commonly accepted table of the Sephiroth, which are numbered 1–10 and are placed in fixed positions on the Tree of Life. Each number is given a place regarding the order of its creation and properties are associated with the number, regarding its conception order and its placement on the pillars of the Tree:

1 is named KThR, Kether, The Crown, and Eheieh, I Am.

2 is named ChKMH, Chokmah, which is Wisdom. Wisdom comes into being as the reflection of the One being added to the original One, thus creating two. 1+1=2

3 is named BINH, Binah, Understanding. She is co-equal to Chokma because Chokma

was powerless without the existence of the third point. She comes into being through the union of one and two. She is the point defined by two others.

4 is named ChSD, Chesed is defined as mercy and love. Chesed is conceived from the union of 3 (Binah) and 1 (Kether).

5 is named GBVRH, Geburah, which is defined as strength or fortitude. The 5th emanation is also called DIN, which is defined as justice.

6 is named ThPARTh, Tiphereth, Beauty and Mildness. She is the centre, unifying, sephira.

7 is named NTzCh, Netzach, firmness, endurance, and victory.

8 is named HVD, Hod, splendour and majesty.

9 is named ISVD, Yesod, the foundation and basis.

Netzach, Hod, and Yesod form the third triad, representing the material world.

10 is the negative existence of 0 combined with the positive existence of 1 The Father, Kether.

10 is named MLVTh, Malkuth, the inferior kingdom, and ShKINH, Shekinah.

Shekinah is the Talmudic concept, representing God's dwelling and immanence in the created world. It is equated with the people of Israel.

18. Z., Pt.1, fol. 228b; De Pauly, II, 501; Waite, *Secret Doctrine,* 229.

19. Waite, *Secret Doctrine,* 230.

20. Ibid., 232.

21. It may be no more than simple coincidence that the pattern of Williams's own life involved his wife on earth, Michal, and a helpmate who for much of his life was, if not unseen, then partially covert. Phyllis was either clothed in the myth of Celia or physically not there. However, excursions into psychopathology *ex post facto* are notoriously fallible.

22. Waite, *Secret Doctrine,* 233.

23. Ibid., 234.

24. Z., Pt.1, fol. 101b; De Pauly, II, 11; ibid., 235.

25. Waite, *Secret Doctrine,* 236.

26. There is an interesting parallel here with the author of the first letter to Timothy in the New Testament Canon, where in 1 Timothy 2:15, the claim is made that women are saved "through bearing children." There has always been a considerable debate over what understanding of sex lies behind what is otherwise a disjointed piece of esoteric theology.

27. Waite, *Secret Doctrine,* 238; Z., Pt.1., fol. 186b; De Pauly, II, 338.

28. Waite, *Secret Doctrine,* 238, 239.

29. Coventry Patmore's influence on Williams was considerable. The overlap of their interest was precise. Frederick Page in *Patmore: A Study in Poetry* quotes Alice Meynell, who made an anthology of Patmore's poetry as she links Dante, Wordsworth, and Patmore: "And when it is Alice Meynell who says 'Essentially Patmore had one subject—human love as a mystery' the scrupulous reader will substitute 'life' for her world 'love.' Patmore's subject was that of Wordsworth and Dante, and Wordsworth's subject was not landscape; nor Dante's Beatrice; nor Patmore's marriage. Patmore's one essential subject was the soul, with whatever is necessary to it—that is society. . . . [T]he great society of men, of Angels, and of God." Frederick Page, *Patmore: A Study in Poetry* (London: Oxford Univ. Press, 1933), 15, 16.

30. Waite, *Secret Doctrine,* 239.

31. Ibid., 239, 240.

32. A similar interchange of gender attribution is found in *The Egyptian Gospel* (circa 350 A.D.), one of the mss. in *The Gnostic Scriptures,* where praise is offered to the "masculine, female, virgin. Iouel." *The Gnostic Scriptures,* ed. Bentley Layton (New York: Doubleday, 1987), 108.

33. Waite, *Secret Doctrine,* 241n.

34. Ibid., 66.
35. Ibid., 242, 243.
36. Ibid., 243.
37. The Matthean Exception is a reference to the Gospels in the New Testament that has Jesus prohibiting divorce outright, except in St. Matthew, where adultery provides the exception. A good deal of commentary flows from this exploring the legitimacy of divorce in both the Old and New Testaments.
38. Williams, *Outlines of Romantic Theology* (Grand Rapids, Mich.: Eerdmans, 1990), 47.
39. Ibid.
40. Alice Mary Hadfield suggests in her introduction to *Outlines* that as he wrote it he did so out of the experience that "his love for, and marriage to Florence was not widening and deepening as it should. He was quite right. Maybe he was, to use his own phrase, keeping back 'something of the price'; maybe Florence was over-concentrating on their one child and under-participating in Charles' quickly opening life at the Press. Be that as it may, turmoil lay close ahead." Williams, *Outlines,* xi.
41. Williams carries his theology of the body to some lengths. He will suggest in a later essay, "The Index of the Body," that women share in the role of sacrificial victim by virtue of their menstruation. See Ridler, "*Image.*" In chapter 10, below, he identifies the menopause with the healing of King Pelles in a letter to Phyllis McDougall.
42. Williams, *Outlines,* 24.
43. Ibid., 25.
44. Williams will borrow this idea from both Waite and Patmore when he writes in his poem, "Vexilla regis prodeunt, / The double banners move, / Before one altar to confront,— / Twice manifested love." Williams, *Divorce,* 73.
45. Williams, *Outlines,* 36.
46. In an unpublished letter to Phyllis Jones in 1940, he connects her with the Eucharist, but in a different manner. "Do you think, when I think of you, I forget for more than five instants your own burden of fear? Never. We have not so learned our Celia; any more than I am at ever at a Eucharist without thinking of you—no banishing pentagrams there. At Christmas, at the midnight celebration I almost saw you over the altar among the incense smoke." Jan. 26, 1940.
47. Williams, *Outlines,* 44, text and footnote.
48. Coventry Patmore, "Winter," in *The New English Book of English Verse* (London: Victor Gollancz, 1935), 750.

4. The "Two Ways" and the "Theology of Romantic Love"

1. Williams, *Beatrice,* 188.
2. Williams, *Descent of the Dove,* 55.
3. Ridler, "*Image,*" xxxix.
4. A private letter quoted in Ridler, "*Image,*" xl.
5. Williams, *Descent of the Dove,* 7.
6. Mathematically, a line that continually approaches a given curve but does not meet it within a finite distance.
7. A letter dated 1933 presumably to Anne Ridler, quoted in Ridler, "*Image,*" xl.
8. Williams, *Descent of the Dove,* 31.
9. Ibid., 181.
10. Anne Ridler, "Williams Affirmation," in *Charles Williams: Selected Writings,* ed. Anne Ridler (Oxford: Oxford Univ. Press, 1961), 134.
11. Elaine Pagels, *Adam, Eve and the Serpent* (New York: Random House, 1988).
12. Ibid., 95.

13. "Death came upon all humanity because of Adam 'in whom' all sinned" (instead of because all sinned)."

14. Professor Pagels offers two suggestions for the infectiousness of Augustine's theology, one political and the other psychological:

> i—the political;—the needs of a more authoritarian state which was quite prepared to adopt a theology that required its citizens to allow themselves governed; but also ii—the psychological—the fact that it is a condition of our escapist humanity when trying to find an explanation for the sufferings of the innocent, that we would rather feel guilt than utter impotence,—we would rather know ourselves to be shamed than helpless.

Ibid., 119.

15. There may be a number of different views on this conundrum, and the reasons why the Reformers and Puritans came to accept marriage, but still maintain a blanket distrust of sexuality. It may be that Manichaeanism or its modern dualistic equivalent is a permanent feature of psychological projection flowing from the splitness of the wounded human psyche. If so, the orthodox view of the Incarnation, and the unitive worldview it implies, has a therapeutic as well as doctrinal relevance.

16. Williams, *Descent of the Dove,* 64.

17. *The Confessions of St. Augustine,* ed. and trans. Henry Chadwick (Oxford: Oxford Univ. Press, 1991).

18. Williams, *Descent of the Dove,* 64.

19. Ibid., 69, 70.

20. Ibid., 57.

21. Ibid.

22. John Heath-Stubbs, *Charles Williams,* Writers and Their Work, No. 63 (London: Longmans, Green, 1955), 18.

23. Williams, "Index of the Body," in Ridler, "*Image,*" 86.

24. Williams, *Beatrice,* 13, 14.

25. Wordsworth, *Prelude,* book 8, 279–81, quoted in Williams, *Beatrice,* 64.

26. In a footnote in *Beatrice,* Williams identifies the origin of this connection: "In the notes to his translation of the *Commedia* Mr. J. D. Sinclair has drawn attention to the Eucharistic relevance of the procession and appearance of Beatrice. This relevance would require another book than this to discuss, if it were possible to discuss it at all; one in which the life of our Lord as enacted in the love-relationship could be touched on—which is the heart of Romantic Theology. It is sufficient here to render Patmore's maxim in *The Rod, The Root and the Flower;* ' . . . The Holy Eucharist, in the beginning, is desired because it resembles the lower but still "great" sacrament of human affection; afterwards the lower sacrament is explained and glorified by its resemblance to the higher.'" Williams, *Beatrice,* 188n.

27. "The banners of the King move forward." Williams, *Divorce,* 73. The double banners may also represent an aspect of "asymptotic" nonconvergence. Both represent lines of thought that appear at some point to come together but only as an aspect of perspective.

28. Williams, *Divorce,* 26.

29. Charles Williams, *He Came Down from Heaven,* chapter 5, "The Theology of Romantic Love" (London: William Heinemann Ltd., 1938), 87.

30. Williams, *He Came Down,* 96, 97.

31. C. S. Lewis, *Arthurian Torso* (Oxford: Oxford Univ. Press, 1963; Grand Rapids, Mich.: Eerdmans, 1974), 116.

32. Williams, *He Came Down,* 107.

33. Ridler, "*Image,*" Williams, "Sensuality and Substance," 75.

34. Ibid., xliii.

35. Chesterton's belief that we all share an almost prenatal leap of astonishment at the world itself may provide evidence for a connection between Williams and Chesterton at this point.

36. Williams, *Beatrice,* 7.
37. Ibid., 7, 8.
38. Ibid., 29.
39. Dorothy L. Sayers, *The Poetry of Search and the Poetry of Statement* (London: Gollancz, 1963), 45–68.
40. Cavaliero, *Poet,* 153.
41. Betraying the prurience of our times, I asked her.
42. Williams, *The English Poetic Mind* (Oxford: Clarendon Press, 1932), 59.
43. Ibid., 49.
44. See chapter 10, below, for an analysis of their early relationship.
45. Williams, *Beatrice,* 122.
46. Ibid., 124.
47. Ibid., 128.
48. Ibid., 147.
49. Ibid., 227.
50. Ibid., 161.
51. Ibid., 196.
52. Ibid., 231.
53. Ibid., 232.

5. Alchemy as Metanarrative

1. Stephen Medcalf, "The Athanasian Principle in Williams's Use of Images," in *Rhetoric of Vision,* ed. Charles A. Huttar and Peter J. Schakel (London: Bucknell Univ. Press, 1996), 42.

2. Shideler describes Williams's concept of redemption as "precisely a conversion of energy." Mary McDermott Shideler, *The Theology of Romantic Love: A Study in the Writings of Charles Williams* (Grand Rapids, Mich.: Eerdmans, 1962), 62.

3. Johannes Fabricius in his *Medieval Alchemists and Their Royal Art* provides a historical overview (Copenhagen: Rosenkilde and Bagger, 1976), 6.

4. Keith Thomas, *Religion and the Decline of Magic: Studies in Popular Beliefs in Sixteenth and Seventeenth Century England* (London: Weidenfeld and Nicolson, 1971; Penguin, 1991), 265.

5. William Vaughan, *The Golden Grove,* 1600, sig.Y8^{V}; quoted by Thomas, *Religion and the Decline,* 268.

6. Thomas, *Religion and the Decline,* 320–21.

7. Waite, *Hidden Church,* 486.

8. The Familists—Family of love—were perfectionists, closely linked to the Behmenists, who followed the writings of the German mystic Jacob Böhme. The Familists held that Christ was "a type and but a type" and believed that it was possible for a person to be totally inhabited by Christ. They were perfectionists who believed that complete sanctification could be achieved in this present life. They had a strong influence on the Quakers. Böhme's mysticism was founded upon the old doctrines of microcosm and macrocosm and preserved important elements in the hermetic tradition. See Thomas, *Religion and the Decline,* 146–47.

9. The backwash of this debate still continues. In his latest book *After God* (New York: Basic Books, 1997), the Anglican theologian Don Cupitt pursues a rationalistic and pragmatic deconstructionalism the is based on his, some might say passé, dependence on his belief in the objective truth of empirical science.

10. Fabricius, *Medieval Alchemists,* 8. Fabricius goes on to suggest that their greatest achievement lay in the exploration of the darkness of the blind alley they had journeyed down, which would lead to the exploration of the unconscious. See C. G. Jung, *Psychology and Alchemy,* Collected Works, vol. 12 (London: Pantheon, 1953).

11. Waite, *Hidden Church,* 537. He continues, "Expositors of the subject have gone astray over the generic purpose of the art, because some have believed it to be (a) the transmutation of metals, and that only, while others have interpreted it as (b) a veiled method of delineating the secrets of the soul on its way through the world within, and besides this nothing. We have on our part to realise that (a) there were two schools making use of the same language in a distinct sense, the one branch seeking the transmutation of metals and the art of prolonging life; the other branch investigating the mysteries of the arch-natural life; and that (b) more than one text book of physical alchemy would seem to have been re-edited in this more recent exotic interest. . . . We can leave to the physical alchemists those things of Caesar which belong to them, retaining the things which concern the mysteries of divine symbolism."

12. After reading *Hidden Church,* Williams sent Waite a copy of his *Silver Stair.* Gilbert, *Magician,* 148.

13. First published in London by Kegan Paul, Trench Trubner and Co. Ltd., 1926. The edition used here is Stuart and Watkins, London, 1969.

14. Waite refers here in a footnote to the work of Johann Gottfried Jugel, *Physica Mystica et Physica Sacra Sacratissima* (Berlin and Leipzig, 1782).

15. Waite, *Secret Tradition of Alchemy,* 360, 361.

16. Ibid., 540.

17. Ibid., 489.

18. Ibid., 534.

19. Ibid., 478.

20. St. Paul's letter to the Romans, 12:2. (R.S.V.)

21. Williams, *A Myth of Shakespeare* (Oxford: Oxford Univ. Press, 1928), 97.

22. Williams, *The Chaste Wanton,* 79, in *The Three Plays,* ed. Sir Humphrey Milford (London: Oxford Univ. Press, 1931).

23. Williams, *Chaste Wanton,* 86.

24. The reference is to St. John 14:23, "Those who love me, will keep my words, and the Father will love them and we will come to them and make our home in them"; as well as the sacramental imagery from both Johannine and Synoptic Gospels. The Eastern Church made much more of this process of "divinization" than the Western Church; but at such points there is close overlap with the notion of sharing in the life of the divine that esotericism so valued.

25. Williams, *Chaste Wanton,* 125.

26. Ibid., 131, 132.

27. Williams, "The Last Voyage," in *Taliessin through Logres* (London: Oxford Univ. Press, 1938), 85.

28. Williams, *Taliessin,* 87.

29. Anne Ridler, "John Milton: An Introduction to the World's Classics Edition of his Poems," 1940, in "*Image.*"

30. Anne Ridler, "The Dublin Review," 1940, in "*Image,*" 101.

31. Williams, *Beatrice,* 112.

32. Ibid., 135.

33. Ibid., 187.

34. David Llewellyn Dodds suggests that the difference between the earlier and the later Arthurian poetry involves his adoption of a more refined unifying, integrating, and comprehensive image in the later poetry. He suggests that this is paralleled in the writing of the novels. David Llewellyn Dodds, "Continuity and Change in the Development of Charles Williams's Poetic Style," in Huttar and Schakel, *Rhetoric,* 201.

35. Charles Williams, *Shadows of Ecstasy* (London: Gollancz, 1933), 9.

36. See below in this chapter.

37. Williams, *Shadows,* 213, 214.

38. Ibid., 216.
39. Ibid., 224.
40. Ibid., 146.
41. Ibid., 152.
42. Another indicator of Williams's development during this period can be found mirrored in his changing attitude toward Milton over this period, documented by Charles Huttar.
43. Williams, *Shadows,* 11.
44. Ibid., 86.
45. The relationship between words and objects is commented on by Thomas in *Religion and the Decline,* 266, who writes: "Neoplatonic theory also emphasised the influence of the imagination upon the body, of the mind upon matter and of words, incantations on physical objects. By the exercise of his imagination, and the use of magic, symbols and incantations, the operator could transform either himself or the victim."
46. Williams, *Shadows,* 41.
47. In his letters to his wife written from Oxford in the last years of his life, he is only too aware of his own need for a rejuvenated imagination: "Now more than at most times, I must compel my imagination, which is slow and dull. Wordsworth—as I have proclaimed to all Oxford—said that it was power. But mine has gone into a rock cell and will not come out." Dated June 21, 1943. Marion E. Wade Center, Wheaton, Ill.

See also Williams's introduction to *The Figure of Beatrice* where he explains his reliance on Wordsworth for his recognition of the role of the imagination: "Wordsworth rather reminded us of the Way than defined it for us. But he did remind us of the business of the Imagination which is the faculty by which images, actual or poetic, are understood."

Imagination—here the power so-called
Through sad incompetence of human speech,
That awful Power, rose from the mind's abyss.
and again
This spiritual love acts not nor can exist
Without Imagination; which, in truth,
Is but another name for absolute power,
And keenest insight, amplitude of mind,
And Reason in her most exalted mood
and
Imagination having been our theme,
So also hath this spiritual love,
For they are each in each, and cannot stand
Dividually. Here must thou be, O man,
Power to thyself; no helper hast thou here;
Here keepest thou in singleness thy state.
No other can divide with thee this work.
No secondary hand can intervene
To fashion this ability; 'tis thine,
The prime and vital principle is thine,
In the recesses of thy nature, far
From any reach of outward fellowship,
Else is not thine at all. But joy to him

The last lines of the stanza fashion a link with the growth toward perfection of our humanity and the notion of transformation:

For all that friendship, all that love can do,
All that a darling countenance can look,
Or dear voice can utter, to complete the man,

Perfect him, made imperfect in himself,
All shall be his; and he whose soul hath risen
Up to the height of feeling intellect
Shall want no humbler tenderness.

Williams, *Beatrice,* 12.

48. Williams, *Shadows,* 95.

49. Ibid., 103.

50. Ibid., 71, 72.

51. Another example of the injunction Williams was to set later in a more orthodox voice, that of Dante: "look well." Williams, *Beatrice,* 16.

52. Williams, *Shadows,* 72.

53. *The Hermetic Papers of A. E. Waite: The Unknown Writings of a Modern Mystic,* ed. R. A. Gilbert (Wellingborough: Aquarian Press, 1987), 18, 19.

54. Williams, *Shadows,* 73.

55. Ibid., 85.

56. It would be fruitless to attempt to analyze the extent to which Williams identified personally with Considine or his views. Two things are clear: Williams's presentation of the antihero in his novels will clarify as the novels develop; and in chapter 10, below, his letters to his wife and poetry to "Celia" will show evidence of his capacity for despair and an awareness of the ambiguity of his own motives. See particularly the poem no. 72.

57. Williams, *Shadows,* 83.

58. Ibid., 53.

59. Ibid., 111.

60. Ibid., 112.

61. George L. Scheper in his chapter "*All Hallow's Eve*: The Cessation of Rhetoric" in Huttar and Schakel, *Rhetoric,* comments, "It is very misleading if we are to follow Williams own metaphysics to speak of opposites of dichotomies at all; concerning 'spirit' and 'matter,' the saintly Lester, we are told, 'did not dichotomize,'" 171.

In the essay "Anthropotokos," Williams, who is writing an article in a review of *True Humanism* in *Time and Tide,* explains, "There is but one dichotomy: that between those who acknowledge that they live from the life of others, including their 'enemies,' and those who do not. It is in this sense, indeed, that we must 'forgive' our enemies. And the moment the dichotomy is admitted, it immediately becomes a temptation. Whoever does not admit it is regarded as an 'enemy,' and we deny that we can possibly live and be nourished by him. He at least is alien? No. Terrible humility! we derive from those we denounce; 'though they slay me, yet will I trust in them.'" Ridler, "*Image,*" 113.

There is another article from *Time and Tide* where in a review called *John Calvin* by A. Dakin, he suggests, "There is nearly always in such men a central energy which our lesser minds dichotomize. What in them is a union, becomes in us a variation and even a contradiction. Thus Dante, in whose vision flesh and spirit were so greatly one, has been turned into a spiritual teacher and even into something like a refined preacher of spirituality as separate from the body. Thus Kierkegaard has turned agnostics into Catholics and Catholics into agnostics. Thus St. Paul himself has been turned into a mystic or an institutionalist. Thus Calvin has been made a predestinarian." Ridler, "*Image,*" 142.

62. Williams, *Shadows,* 115.

63. Ibid., 121.

64. Ibid., 185.

65. Quoted by Scheper, "Cessation of Rhetoric," in Huttar and Schakel, *Rhetoric,* 147, referring to Charles Huttar, *Charles Williams, Novelist and Prophet,* 63, 60. In a footnote (32) he refers us to another article by Huttar, who refined his views on Considinian ambiguity by relating them to a period when Williams's views of Milton's Satan were undergoing radical transformation.

66. Charles Huttar, "Williams's Changing Views of Milton and the Problem of *Shadows of Ecstasy*" (*Inklings-Jahrbuch* 5, 1987), 224.

67. Huttar, "Changing Views," 229, quoting "The Hero in English Verse," *Contemporary Review* 118 (1920): 831–32.

68. He was to write of the post-Montanist early church, "Ecstasy was no longer to specially be desired, for the ordinary daylight was as much He as the extraordinary night. The Church leaned strongly to the idea that dullness was more reliable than drama." Williams, *Descent of the Dove,* 76. This criticism is clearly not confined to that era.

69. Something of the culture of London at the turn of the twentieth century is captured by the comments of William Seabrook in *Witchcraft: Its Power in the World Today* (New York: Harcourt, Brace, 1940), 82. "Wonder was in the air—whether it was expressed by a minor poet's languishing eroticism or by Sherlock Holmes in the cataloguing of endless varieties of cigar ash. Something was stirring and it stirred most vigorously in London. Behind the facade of London lurked who knew what marvels or horrors? Behind the faces of Londoners lurked who knew what good and evil." London was filled with groups and clubs in search of the unusual. There were suicide clubs, freak clubs, cults of the horrible, hellfire clubs, and many others.

70. Williams, *Shadows,* 203.

71. Williams writes of the dangers of perverting the natural religious instinct into the self-sufficiency and egotism of the one who becomes adept in an alternative wisdom that places the self in a position of gnostic and artificial esteem: "Most children and most youths take pleasure in fancies; the secrecy of those fantasies is sometimes a part of them. That one's parents may be but foster parents, that one's blood is particular, that one is predestined, that a hidden greatness looms in one's heart—such things are common imaginations. The revolt in our own natures must have its way there, even if those natures are, in fact, subdued to what they work in. Religion is its opportunity often; to be a child of God and an inheritor of the kingdom of heaven credits the mind with an infinite sense of importance—no less dangerous, even if true. But if a religious heart and mind were for some reason, oppressed and antagonised by the order of religion in the world, or if greed or curiosity sprang high, there might be every kind of opportunity to welcome and enjoy some other fancy, however preposterous,—what fancies are not?—of a powerful, satisfying and secret justification of oneself." Williams, *Witchcraft,* 155.

72. Considine explains that jilted love first drove him to attempt domination by magic. "A girl jilted a boy, and the boy said, 'why do I suffer helplessly? This also is I—all this unutterable pain is I and I grow everywhere through it into myself.'" Williams, *Shadows,* 202. This seems to combine Williams's own duality—renunciation as the theme of his first love poems—with the transcending egoism represented at this stage of the novel.

73. Williams, *Shadows,* 181.

74. Ibid., 182.

75. Ibid., 219.

76. Ibid., 218.

77. Ibid., 222.

78. Charles Williams, *War in Heaven* (London: Gollancz, 1931), 37.

79. Ibid., 89.

80. Ibid., 42, 43.

81. Ibid., 135.

82. Revelation 1:17–18.

83. Williams, *War in Heaven,* 204.

84. Glen Cavaliero, *The Supernatural and English Fiction* (Oxford: Oxford Univ. Press, 1995), 109.

85. Amos 3:6.

86. Williams, *War in Heaven,* 180, 181.

87. *Theology* (May 1939), reprinted in Ridler, *"Image,"* 68–75.

88. Ridler, *"Image,"* 72. In the same essay Williams writes of the sheer thrill that the first reading of *Lady Chatterly* gave him and links it coincidentally with the stimulus provided by his reading of alchemical texts: "The first reading of the full version of *Lady Chatterly's Lover,* its moving beauty, its increasing repetitions; in the half jest, the half assent with which one heard of the 'dark gods'—dimly recollecting at the same time the fiery darkness of Boehme or the monstrous fables of alchemical design." Ridler, *"Image,"* 70.

89. Quoted in Ridler, *"Image,"* 68.

90. Ibid.

91. Williams, *War in Heaven,* 239.

92. Julian of Norwich, *Showings,* 13th revelation, 27th chapter, trans. E. Colledge and J. Walsh (London: SPCK, 1978), 224, 225, long text.

93. Julian, *Showings,* 233.

94. Ibid., 243.

95. In his review in *Theology* of C. S. Lewis's book *The Problem of Pain,* he was to commend Lewis on his tackling one of the critical issues at stake here—that of divine omnipotence: "Mr Lewis's . . . [s]tyle is what style always is—goodness working on goodness, a lucid and sincere intellect at work on the facts of life or the great statements of other minds. . . . [T]he chapter on Hell is especially terrifying and that on Divine Omnipotence especially lucid." *Theology* 52 (Jan. 1941).

In his criticism of Origen he wrote, "The imaginations of the Alexandrian Fathers were courteous; their visions were humane. Origen extended that vision so far as to teach the final restitution of all things, including the devils themselves. It is impossible that some such dream should not linger in any courteous mind, but to teach it as a doctrine almost always ends in the denial of free will. If God has a character, if man has a choice, an everlasting rejection of God by man must be admitted as a possibility; that is, hell must remain." Williams, *Descent of the Dove,* 40.

96. Williams makes the necessary distinction in "Sensuality and Substance" when he writes of the godhead, "God, it has been said, loves Himself as the Good, and not as Himself." Ridler, *"Image,"* 71. One might carry forward an argument here about the nature of self and suggest that Williams and the Christian tradition work from an impoverished sense of the nature of self. While there was something alluringly Jungian about Considine's concern for unity with self, nonetheless Jung made helpful distinctions between the Freudian executive ego and the emerging self, which in terms of the individuative process he saw as coterminous with the soul.

97. Williams, *War in Heaven,* 244.

98. Ibid., 245.

99. In a later work Williams clarifies the dynamics that lie behind our deepest choices. In *Judgement at Chelmsford* (London: Oxford Univ. Press, 1939), Williams sets out to expose society's false concepts of "love, power and grace" (p. 5). He uses the figure of the "Accuser" to clarify the relationship between the individual and their desires. The Accuser acts rather like the "Graal," in that he becomes whatever people invoke. The difference is that by 1939 Williams will make the distinction between the kind of power desired and the real nature of God. The theological assumption in the play is that humanity's profoundest desire is for the reality of God, but that some other prevenient appetite masks it. When asked to justify the practice of witchcraft in Essex, the Accuser answers,

> I have done no worse
> than to exhibit to men their own desires,
> their love, their hunger their hold on hell. If
> they strongly deceive their bodies with their hope
> they see me in the image of false belief,
> as these perhaps this night. You Christians,
> you are not responsible for hell, but only

for how you help high heaven to deal with hell
whether in a hellish way or in a heavenly . . .
[G]od has made me to be the image of each man's desire—
a king or a poet or a devil—and rarely Christ.
Most men when at last they see their desire,
fall to repentance—all have that chance.

Williams, *Judgement,* 31, 32.

100. Williams, *War in Heaven,* 118.

101. Victor Gollancz, Williams's publisher, comments on *War in Heaven* in a BBC broadcast on the Third Programme on Sept. 13, 1961 (produced by Terence Tiller in a documented compilation by Ruth Spalding).

Ruth Spalding asked, "Would you like to say something about his characterisation? And also particularly whether or not you have a liking for his good people?"

Gollancz replied, "It's a little difficult to answer that question. I used to have an enormous liking for his good people, I mean the Archdeacon in *War in Heaven,* I used to adore the Archdeacon, and I suppose I did until quite recently, because I've often re-read Charles—I read one or another of Charles' books about once every three or four months. I'd hate to introduce a note of criticism, because I'm immensely fond of him, perhaps I find the good characters now a trifle sentimental."

102. While T. S. Eliot when writing on Baudelaire, and in *The Hollow Men* and *Waste Land,* posits an ethical hierarchy in which it is better to have chosen evil than not to have made any choice at all, this celebration of Persimmons suggests a choice of evil that is in part motivated by its duplication of some of the values of virtue; "the rush of ardent faith, full dependence, sacraments living realities, adoration, supernatural union," and so on.

103. My emphasis.

104. Williams, *War in Heaven,* 174.

105. "'I don't want any cold sausages,' Adrian said hurriedly. 'No my angel, but it's the 27th of the month and there's never any money then,' Barbara said." It is very likely that this scene to some extent reflects Williams's own domesticity.

106. Williams, *War in Heaven,* 167.

107. Ibid., 237.

108. Ibid., 241. A sentiment of sympathy is also constructed enigmatically for Gregory when, in response to being offered the verse "He shall give his angels charge over you," he responds, "perhaps He managed it in time. They've usually been rather late. My wife, Stephen and even poor old Pattinson. But is doesn't matter." Ibid., 187.

109. *All Hallows' Eve* was written after his essay "The Cross," in which his theology of substitution was expressed further.

110. Williams, *War in Heaven,* 76.

111. Ibid., 217.

112. Ibid., 242. It is in this context that Williams understands his own desire for annihilation as he has Lionel Rackstraw ask it of Prester John. Ibid., 251.

113. Ibid., 236.

114. Ibid., 212.

115. Ibid., 136.

116. Ibid., 137.

117. Williams was acutely aware of the difficulties of Eucharistic definition: "From the days of St. Paul the holy celebrations had continued, and the presence of the Messias had been acknowledged. . . . [T]he nature of the change had not been defined, nor had the means or moment of change been settled. Only the most subtle theologians can adequately discuss the nature of that Presence."

118. Williams, *Descent of the Dove,* 113. Williams will write passages similar to this describing the movement of creation, but independent of the devise of the Grail, most notably the one that focuses on the river Thames in the city in *All Hallows' Eve,* where the river

is the devise through which we see all things brought together into co-inherence, see pages 223 and 224.

119. Williams, *War in Heaven*, 137.

120. Ibid., 246.

121. The perennial concern in Jewish theology to avoid any form of idolatry would require in spoken Hebrew the use of Adonai—"the Lord"—in its presentation of God in the Old Testament text instead of Yahweh, "I am that I am."

122. See Shideler, *Theology*, 62.

6. The Goetic, Theurgic, and Wisdom Traditions

1. Williams, *Witchcraft*.

2. "No one will derive any knowledge of initiation from this book. . . . [I] have not wished to titillate or thrill; so far as I can manage it, this is history." Williams, *Witchcraft*, 9 (from the preface).

3. "Perversion," as shall be noted later, is the model for the goetic he uses in his last novel, *All Hallows' Eve*, written during the same period as *Witchcraft*.

4. Williams, *Witchcraft*, 20, 21.

5. Ibid., 31.

6. Ibid.

7. Ibid., 32.

8. Ibid., 34–35.

9. Gilbert, *Hermetic Papers*, chapter 4, "Thomas Vaughan and his *Lumen de Lumine*," 69.

10. Gilbert, *Hermetic Papers*, 73.

11. Williams uses the word to describe the process of change taking place in Simon the Clerk's followers in *All Hallows' Eve*, p. 45 (see chapter 11). It characterizes the hermetic tradition's preoccupation with the evolution of the soul. Marlowe has Faust use it in his final speech: "Ah, Pythagoras' *metempsychosis*, were that true this soul should fly from me and I be chang'd into some brutish beast: all beasts are happy." Christopher Marlowe, *Dr. Faustus* (London: Methuen, 1956), 146. Pythagoras was regarded as the author of the Doctrine of the Transmigration of Souls from one body to another.

12. The phrase is dependent on the biblical phrase of 1 Peter 2:4, but amended to include the realm of philosophy in keeping with the gnostic overtones of Rosicrucianism. See following note. Waite comments further on this in his work *The Hidden Church of the Holy Graal*: "That which the text books have agreed from time immemorial to term a Stone, is that also which we find in the greater Gospel books, where it is described as a stone not made with hands, and the transmutation performed thereby is the work of inward conversion, resulting in the condition which one of the adepts recommends to his disciples when he exclaims: Transmutemini, etc." (545).

13. See pages 76–80 of *Hermetic Papers*, where we find Waite's contention that he disagrees with the conclusion that the Q'abalistic Doctrine of our Descent from the Divine cannot be reconciled with Christianity.

14. Waite, *Hidden Church*, 77.

15. Ibid., 79, 84. "That his school was that of the Hermetic Tradition with important derivations from other and especially Kabalistic sources. But *per accidentia* he was a Hermetic Philosopher of the school of metallic transmutation and he worked upon a fantastic adaptation of the Divine promise continued in the Divine Counsel: 'Seek first the Kingdom of God and His justice, and all other things shall be added unto you.'"

16. Williams, *Witchcraft*, 156.

17. Quoted in ibid., 222.

18. Ibid.

19. Ibid., 223.

20. Ibid.
21. Williams, "Index of the Body," Ridler, *"Image,"* 83.
22. Ridler, *"Image,"* 84.
23. Williams, "The Doctrine of Largesse," Ridler, *"Image,"* 140.
24. Williams, *Beatrice,* 10.
25. Williams, *Witchcraft,* 224.
26. Ibid.
27. Williams, *Descent of the Dove,* 55.
28. Gilbert, ed., *Hermetic Papers*: "Add further in this connection, that a work said to have been written by Dee in the year 1564, though it was not published until 1581, albeit in no sense Rosicrucian itself, became of Rosicrucian importance." (63).
29. "Out of this vale of misery, and out of the misery of this vale and out of this kingdom of darkness and out of the shadows of that kingdom, to the holy mountain and the celestial tabernacle." Williams, *Witchcraft,* 225, 226.
30. Ibid., 227.
31. One recent work that has provided a sympathetic treatment of Doctor Dee can be found in the novel by Peter Ackroyd, *The House of Doctor Dee* (London: Hamish Hamilton, 1993).
32. Williams, *Witchcraft,* 228.
33. Ibid., 229.
34. Ibid., 230.
35. Ibid., 230, 231.
36. Ibid., 231.
37. Ridler, *"Image,"* xxxii.
38. Ibid., 74. See also chapter 9 of this work.
39. Williams, *Witchcraft,* 232.
40. Ibid., 233.
41. Ibid., 232. See Helen Waddell's treatment of this in *The Wandering Scholars* (London: Constable and Co. Ltd., 1907).
42. From the perspective of the history of the early twentieth century, there was a movement throughout European society to found orders in various forms. One extreme political variant lay within fascism.
43. Williams, *Witchcraft,* 239. The footnote reads: "*Book of Ceremonial Magic,* A. E. Waite: from which the quotations are taken."
44. Ibid., 311.
45. Ibid., 246.

7. The Integration of the Natural and Supernatural in Charles Williams

1. Cavaliero, *Supernatural,* 113.
2. Charles Williams, *Region of the Summer Stars* (London: Oxford Univ. Press, 1944), 26.
3. Weeks, *Steps toward Salvation.*
4. Michal Williams reminisced: "We would take Charles's book and boon companions along with us; Shakespeare and Wordsworth and Milton, Donne and Crashaw, St. Athanasius, or rather his Creed, St. Aug.ine and the Lady Julian of Norwich. Also came Swinburne and George Meredith and Coventry Patmore, Francis Thompson and Alice Meynell." "As I Remember," unpublished manuscript, Apr. 18, 1955, 3.
5. Williams, *Descent of the Dove,* 59.
6. The diminution of the status of matter is a problem with an ancient heritage. A good deal of scholarship has been dedicated to analyzing the extent to which John's Gospel is dependent on gnostic categories of thought, particularly the distinctions between light and darkness and the kingdom and the world. See, for example, Raymond Brown's

article on his comparison of John's Gospel with alternative gnostic gospels discovered at Chenoboskion in Egypt, 1947; and in particular his treatment of Bultmann's approach to the problem in "John and reconstructed Christian Gnosticism," in his article "Proposed Influences in the Religious Thought of the Fourth Gospel," in the first volume of his commentaries (*The Gospel of John* [London: Geoffrey Chapman, 1966]), 53.

7. J. R. R. Tolkien deals with the distinction in a different way by inverting the categories: "Supernatural is a dangerous and difficult word in any of its senses. But to fairies it can hardly be applied unless super is taken merely as a superlative prefix. For it is man who, in contrast to the Fairies is supernatural; whereas they are natural; far more natural than he." *On Fairy Stories: Essays Presented to Charles Williams* (Oxford: Oxford Univ. Press, 1947), 39.

8. Waite, *Hidden Church,* 534, 535. This might appear to be a misprint for "arch-natural," but is not. The context reads, "To ascertain whether the concurrent or succeeding schools of secret thought, which appeared in Europe before or after the canon of the Graal was closed, offered any analogies to the notion of an arch-national Eucharist, or—in other words—to the existence, prosecution and success of the Great Experiment."

9. Ibid., 484.

10. Ibid., 537.

11. Williams, "Sensuality and Substance," *Theology* (May 1939), reprinted in Ridler, "*Image*," 68.

12. Williams, "Sensuality," in Ridler, "*Image*," 69.

13. Ibid.

14. When writing about the historical experiment in the third century with the *Subintroductae,* he suggests that the use of sex in this experiment might have been "to pass below itself and release the dark gods of D. H. Lawrence directly into the kingdom of Messias." The consequence of failing led to the loss of any theology of marriage and the teaching of monogamy and meekness. Williams, *Descent of the Dove,* 14. Williams is commenting on a recent biography of Lawrence, *D. H. Lawrence,* by Hugh Kingsmill.

15. Williams, "Sensuality," in Ridler, "*Image*."

16. Ibid., 72.

17. The word "docetic" comes from the Greek meaning "to appear," and usually attaches itself to ideas that suggest that Jesus only "appeared" to be human, but ultimately did not experience full human vulnerability, but was only God in a form of human disguise. It has the effect of devaluing the body and the material since the Christ slipped them on as a form of disguise to achieve incarnation, rather than entering completely into the somatic and material. The issue of to what extent he entered into the "sexual" is usually sidestepped; and when not avoided is restricted to arguments made from silence; never a good platform to work from.

18. *Theology* (May 1939), reprinted in Ridler, "*Image*," 74.

19. Williams, "Natural Goodness." It is presumed that when Williams uses the term "substance" here, he does not mean to locate it within the resonance that *ousia* carried in the Greek creeds that explore the term in the context of *homoousios.* There "substance" means almost the opposite linguistically from his present argument.

20. Williams, *Beatrice,* 64, 65.

21. Ibid., 48.

22. Ibid., 63.

23. Ibid., 77.

24. Ibid., 95.

25. Ibid., 97.

26. Ibid., 101, 102.

27. Ibid., 104.

28. Glen Cavaliero, "Metaphysical Epiphany? Charles Williams and the Art of the Ghost Story," in Huttar and Schakel, *Rhetoric,* 91, 92. Cavaliero suggests there are three literary traditions: one that treats the supernatural not as being abnormal but as paranor-

mal, lying beyond the range of human knowledge, not in kind but in degree; preternatural signifies any kind of physical manifestation not attributable to known laws of cause and effect; and hermetic, in which material and spiritual realities are treated as aspects or dimensions of each other and as subject to the transcendence of the "mysterium."

Ellmann also adopts "preternatural" in his biography of Yeats, *Yeats: The Man and the Masks,* xviii, xvix.

29. Cavaliero, *Supernatural,* 58, 59.

30. Hadfield, *Exploration,* 173–74, quoted in Weeks, *Steps toward Salvation,* 8, 9. He is a little careless in the details of his reproduction.

31. Weeks also perpetuates the mistake of the Order of the Golden Dawn connection and claims Williams wrote occult studies and dabbled in magic. He appears to be unnecessarily defensive and he is at pains to prove that a Christian reading of Williams is more important than a magical one. It is hoped that this book will contribute to a change in the tenor of these misreadings of both fact and interpretation.

32. Weeks, *Steps toward Salvation,* 17.

33. Charles Williams to Florence Williams. Unpublished letters, held in the Wade Center, Wheaton College, Ill. Dated Dec. 3, 1944.

34. Michal Williams, "As I Remember," 1. See also footnote 59 in chapter 11.

35. See both biographies by A. M. Hadfield; also Mary McDermott Shideler, *Charles Williams: A Critical Essay,* part of the Contemporary Writers in Christian Perspective Ser.; A Continuing Ser., edited by R. Jellema (Grand Rapids, Mich.: Eerdmans, 1966); also Thomas Howard, *The Novels of Charles Williams* (New York: Oxford Univ. Press, 1983; San Francisco: Ignatius Press, 1991).

8. The Second Phase of Maturation

1. Williams, *The House of the Octopus* (London: Edinburgh House Press, 1945), 97.

2. Williams, *Beatrice,* 138.

3. Cavaliero, commenting on *Et in Sempiternum Pereant,* suggests that both that work and *Descent into Hell* mark the passage of Williams's imagination from the occult understanding of the supernatural to the visionary. Cavaliero, *Poet,* 78–79.

4. Williams, *Descent into Hell,* 209.

5. Ibid., 174.

6. Ibid., 15.

7. Ibid., 31.

8. Ibid., 111.

9. Ibid.

10. Williams, *Descent of the Dove,* 28.

11. Williams, *Descent into Hell,* 171.

12. Ibid., 207.

13. Medcalf suggests that Williams describes Pauline's transfiguration in language recalling Aquinas on Christ's transfiguration when "clarity overflowed from His Godhead and from His soul into His body, not as an immanent quality affecting His very body, but rather after the manner of a transient passion, as when the air is lit up by the sun." St. Thomas Aquinas, *Summa Theologiae* (3a, 45.2), trans. S. Parsons and A. Pinheiro (London and New York: Eyre and Spottiswoode, 1971). In Huttar and Schakel, *Rhetoric,* 40.

14. Williams, *Descent into Hell,* 174.

15. Zohar, Pt.III, fol. 7a; De Pauly, V, 18; Waite, *Secret Doctrine,* 237.

16. Williams, *Descent into Hell,* 190.

17. The passage is reminiscent of Francis Thompson's "Hound of Heaven": "And she fled after it on feet that were much swifter than her own and yet in those infinite halls and corridors could never overtake it while it fled." Williams, *Descent into Hell,* 191.

Thompson writes: "I fled Him down the nights and down the days; I fled Him down the arches of the years; I fled Him down the labyrinthine ways of my own mind . . . from those strong Feet that followed, followed after." Francis Thompson, *Poetical Works* (Oxford: Oxford Univ. Press, 1913), 89.

18. Williams, *Descent into Hell,* 209.

19. Ibid., 66.

20. Ibid., 67.

21. Ibid.

22. Ibid., 68.

23. Waite's Rosicrucian liturgy reads: "The Guide is that which is said in an old traditional story to lead the seeker of the Rosy Cross up a mountain in the midst of the earth, otherwise at the middle place of the world. I say unto you that this mountain is within and that it is found at our own centre. It is a place of many treasures which the world does not value, because they do not bear its marks, or come out of its mint, as current coins accepted in its Houses of Exchange. It is said to be encompassed by cruel beasts and ravening birds, which are the evil passions within us—all the false desires They are the lawless parts of our nature in all the ways of life, the spirit of the word within us that strives with the SPIRIT OF GOD. . . . The lion and dragon, the eager birds of prey shall fly before that which is our Guard, as well as Guide in Paths. I say unto you: Believe and find. On a wind of the Spirit you shall all go up the Hidden Mountain. All that is of dead stone in your nature shall be rent like rocks. . . . there shall follow a great calm. The day and the day star shall rise on the Mount of GOD, and the place of treasure shall unveil." Waite, "Ceremony," 47.

24. Williams, *Descent into Hell,* 71–72.

25. Ibid., 72.

26. The same description will be applied to Mary the Theotokos, in *All Hallows' Eve.* "Redeemed from all division in herself, whole and identical in body, she uttered the Word, and the Word became flesh in her" (62).

27. Williams, *Descent into Hell,* 118.

28. Ibid., 124.

29. Williams, *He Came Down,* 80.

30. Williams, *Descent into Hell,* 80.

31. In a piece of writing that is clinically astute, Williams suggests that this penchant of Wentworth's is a danger universal among the pious:

> Every pious man—and of course, woman—
> has one, just one—surface where religion and he
> are so delicately mixed in his soul as to be
> indistinguishable; he is never quite sure—
> and does not (believe me!) ever want to be sure—
> whether his religion or he is being soothed
> into a lascivious spiritual delight.
> All of them, Prefect, are at bottom religious lechers,
> fornicating with their fancies.

Williams, *House of the Octopus,* 39.

32. Williams, *Descent into Hell,* 90.

33. Ibid., 88.

34. Ibid., 181.

35. Ibid., 142.

36. Ibid.

37. J. J. Kollmann, "Complex Rhetoric for a Simple Universe," in Huttar and Schakel, *Rhetoric,* 113.

38. Williams, *Religion and Love in Dante,* 40, quoted in Shideler, *Theology,* 204.

39. The beginnings of this development in the notion of self are found in Isabel in *Shadows,* but there the focus of attention is on Considine.

40. Williams, *Descent into Hell,* 132.

41. If the suggested diagram of the two axes is followed at this point, one might propose a connection between what Martin Buber described as the "I-Thou" relationship between humankind and God standing for the vertical aspect of the Doctrine of Correspondence; while the lateral aspect makes the same identification, in the light of the first, with other people, or the "neighbour."

42. Williams, *Descent into Hell,* 188.

43. Ibid., 127.

44. Ibid., 64.

45. Ibid., 206.

46. Ibid., 148.

47. Ibid.

48. Ibid., 150–51.

49. Ibid., 77.

50. Ibid., 132.

51. Ibid., 10.

52. Hadfield in *Exploration* writes of a letter from R. W. Chapman, secretary to the delegates of the press, writing to Humphrey Milford on Jan. 9, 1929, "How CAN we put C.W. over 'Shall we try announcing him as the most unsaleable of all Oxford authors?'" (79n).

53. "The text was then ascribed to Peter Stanhope, a name which I have used elsewhere as that of a writer of verse, in order that no question of approval or disapproval of my other work might interfere with the special occasion and purpose of this." Williams, *Judgement,* prefatory note.

54. Hadfield, *Exploration,* 142.

55. Williams, *Descent into Hell,* 102.

56. Ibid., 179–80.

57. Ibid., 107.

58. Williams, "Anthropotokos." In this review Williams is comparing the way in which the church is dependent upon Mary for the bearing of salvation, and the manner in which other dependencies, often unacknowledged, are the universal norm. Ridler, "*Image,*" 113.

59. Williams, *Beatrice,* 147.

60. Charles Moorman, *Arthurian Triptych* (Berkeley: Univ. of California Press, 1960), 2.

61. Ibid., 88, 89.

62. He did express a similar sentiment at the end of his life on one of his last visits home to his wife, who recalled him saying, "And I shall write one more novel which my faithful public will not like I think. This time it will be a straightforward one. There will be no black magic, no dancing figures, and no supernatural beings wandering though its pages." Michal Williams, "As I Remember," 1.

63. Moorman, *Triptych,* 153–55.

64. Scheper, "Cessation of Rhetoric," in Huttar and Schakel, *Rhetoric,* 146.

65. Ibid., 147.

66. Ibid. For further reference on this theme in *War in Heaven,* see 203n508.

67. Williams, *Descent into Hell,* 138.

68. Williams, *All Hallows' Eve* (London: Faber and Faber, 1945). Quotations will be taken from the later edition by Eerdmans (Grand Rapids, Mich., 1981), 58.

69. Ibid., 263.

70. Ibid., 32.

71. Ibid., 33.

72. Ibid., 27.

73. Ibid.

74. Ibid., 147.
75. Williams, *English Poetic Mind,* 123, 124.
76. Williams, *Beatrice,* 97.
77. Williams, *All Hallows' Eve,* 62.
78. Ibid., 64.
79. Ibid., 109.
80. Ibid., 119.
81. Ibid., 150.
82. Ibid., 199.
83. Ibid., 210.
84. This is reminiscent of the same imagery used in *War in Heaven,* where the "Graal" is described in terms of "through that gate, upon those tides of retirement, creation moved." There is the same apprehension of the flow on spirit-infused matter (137).
85. Williams, *All Hallows' Eve,* 222–24.

9. *Vocabulary and Imagery*

1. Williams, "The Coming of Palomides," in *Taliessin through Logres* (London: Oxford Univ. Press, 1938) p. 33, lines 1–4.
2. Williams, "Index of the Body," from the *Dublin Review,* 1942, in Ridler, *"Image,"* 82.
3. Waite, *Secret Tradition in Alchemy,* 276.
4. Ibid., 279.
5. Ibid., 59.
6. Williams, "Index of the Body," Ridler, *"Image,"* 86.
7. Ibid., 87.
8. Ibid., 82, 83.
9. "Astrology then was a high and learned science; it was forbidden for good reasons, but it was not fatalistic. It did not say 'this will certainly happen'; it said: 'Given these stellar and individual relations, this result is likely.' But the will of God and the wills of men were allowed much freedom to interfere with the result. *Sapiens Dominabitur Astris.* The paragraphs in our papers today bear as much resemblance to the science as texts lifted up on boards outside churches do to the whole dogmas of the Church. The paragraphs are, I allow, more likely to harm; the texts, on the whole, are innocuous." Ibid., 83.
10. Ibid., 86.
11. Ibid., 87.
12. Brain Horne, "The Systematic Theology of Charles Williams," unpublished doctoral thesis submitted to the University of London, 1970, p. 258.
13. Williams, *He Came Down from Heaven,* chapter 4, "The Precursor and Incarnation and Incarnation of the Kingdom" (London: Heinemann, 1938).
14. Ibid., 58–59.
15. Charles Huttar provides a scholarly treatment of some of these issues in chapter 6 of *Charles Williams: A Celebration* (ed. Brian Horne) in his "Arms and the Man: The Place of Beatrice in Charles Williams's Romantic Theology" (Leominster: Gracewing, 1995).
16. Williams, *Shadows,* 56.
17. Ibid., 99.
18. The full quotation is from Dante Gabriel Rossetti, *Love Lily,* 21–24.

> Ah! let not hope be still distraught,
> But find in her its gracious goal,
> Whose speech Truth knows not from her thought
> Nor Love her body from her soul.

19. Williams, *All Hallows' Eve,* 213.

20. Williams, *The Forgiveness of Sins* (London: Geoffrey Blises, Centenary Press, 1942), 108.

21. Williams, *Thomas Cranmer of Canterbury* (Oxford: Oxford Univ. Press, 1936), 36.

22. Williams, *Forgiveness of Sins,* 90.

23. Williams, *Arthurian Torso* (London: Oxford Univ. Press, 1948), 239.

24. Ibid., 242.

25. Thierry of Chartres was a scholastic theologian and philosopher who became a major figure on the Platonist and humanist traditions. He was archdeacon of Dreux and later taught at Paris. He is particularly known for his *Heptateuchon,* a manual of the seven liberal arts that provides a comprehensive collection of available knowledge of the period. His scientific interests were reflected in his commentary on creation, *De Sex Dierum Operibus.*

26. Quoted in Wertheim, *Pythagoras' Trousers,* 48.

27. Ibid., 48.

28. Hadfield, *Explorations,* 155.

29. Williams, *Taliessin,* p. 35, lines 55–70.

30. Ibid., 36.

31. William Wordsworth, *Prelude,* ed. De Selincourt, corrected by Stephen Gill (New York: Oxford Univ. Press, 1970), book 5, lines 103–5, pp. 69–70. See also Hadfield, *Exploration,* 155.

32. Williams, *Forgiveness of Sins,* 64.

33. Williams, *All Hallows' Eve,* 213.

34. Williams, "Notes on the Way," *Time and Tide* (London), Feb. 28, 1942, in Ridler, *"Image,"* 170–71.

35. Williams, *Taliessin,* 9.

36. Shideler, *Theology,* 18.

37. Williams, *Bacon,* quoted in Shideler, *Theology,* 19. This is a slight reworking of Bacon's description of *Philosophica Prima,* in the *Advancement of Learning.*

38. Williams, *Thomas Cranmer,* 39.

39. Ibid., 69.

40. Ibid., 46.

41. Williams, *Taliessin,* 1.

42. Moorman, *Triptych,* 88, 89.

43. Shideler, *Charles Williams,* 33.

44. Williams, "The Sister of Percivale," in *Taliessin,* p. 51, line 19.

45. Hadfield describes how this was drawn by Lynton Lamb at Williams's request and direction.

46. Williams, "Notes on the Way," in Ridler, *"Image,"* 170–71.

47. Williams, *Taliessin,* "The Vision of the Empire," p. 9, lines 3–7.

48. Williams, *Taliessin,* pp. 12, 13, lines 5–12.

49. Ibid., 36.

50. Ibid., 149.

51. Ibid., 140, 145.

52. Dodds, "Development of Williams's Style," in Huttar and Schakel, *Rhetoric,* 206.

53. Angelika Schneider, "Co-inherent Rhetoric in *Taliessin,*" in Huttar and Schakel, *Rhetoric;* Waite, *Secret Doctrine,* 147.

54. Waite, "Secret Doctrine," 213.

55. Schneider, "Co-inherent Rhetoric in *Taliessin,*" in Huttar and Schakel, *Rhetoric,* 182.

56. Williams, *Taliessin,* 24–25. A better interpretation of this would appear to be a special vision of the transfigured unity of body and soul that Bors's love enables him to perceive. It is also a revelation of the Incarnation, with Christ represented as he is traditionally, by the fish.

57. Ibid., 17.

58. Ibid., 46.

59. Ibid., 49.
60. Ibid., 51.
61. Schneider, "Co-inherent Rhetoric in *Taliessin*," in Huttar and Schakel, *Rhetoric*, 182.
62. Ibid., 185.
63. Williams, *Region of the Summer Stars*, 52.
64. See Williams, "Notes on the Arthurian Myth," in Ridler, *"Image,"* 177.
65. John Heath-Stubbs, *Time and Tide* (May 1, 1948).
66. Brian Horne, *Charles Williams Society Newsletter*, No. 64, 1991, p. 13.
67. Shideler, *Theology*, 181.
68. Williams, in Ridler, *"Image,"* 83.
69. Quoted by Williams, *Beatrice*, 52.
70. This description is drawn from King who takes it from A. E. Waite, *The Holy Kabbalah* (New Hyde Park, N. Y.: Macmillan Company, 1929), 191–213.
71. Williams, in *Region*, "Taliessin in the Rose Garden," lines 180–88.
72. Ibid., line 197.
73. R. A. King Jr., "The Occult as Rhetoric in the Poetry of Charles Williams," in Huttar and Schakel, *Rhetoric*, 171.
74. Williams, "The Coming of Galahad," in *Taliessin*, lines 97–99.
75. Ibid., line 162.
76. R. A. King Jr., *Pattern in the Web*, 15, 16; and also in Huttar and Schakel, *Rhetoric*, 175.
77. Williams, *Taliessin*, 79.
78. Waite, *Secret Doctrine*, 54, 55.
79. The nature of love in kenotic incarnation is implicit in the nature of a loving God who searches out in person his lost creation. Williams, *Taliessin*, 80.
80. Williams, "Taliessin in the Rose Garden," in *Taliessin*, 25.
81. Williams, "The Calling of Taliessin," in *Taliessin*, 12.

10. The Quest for Integration

1. Hadfield, *Exploration*, 129. Referring to correspondence in the Bodleian (Somervaille) no. 0355., n.d.
2. Hadfield, *Exploration*, 164.
3. Williams, *English Poetic Mind*, v.
4. *The Letters of Evelyn Underhill*, ed. and intro. Charles Williams (London: Longmans, Green and Co., 1943), 15.
5. In a private letter from Michal Williams to Glen Cavaliero, dated Oct. 22, 1956, she wrote commenting on a draft ms. he had written, "Only one thing is wrong. However much Charles' seven year itch with that virgin tart masqueraded as love in excelsis it was as sordid and unhealthy as all such affairs."
6. Williams, Letter to Raymond Hunt, dated Mar. 1, 1940. Wade Center.
7. Hadfield, *Exploration*, 72, 73.
8. The archivist at the Oxford University Press has no records to help clarify the details.
9. Williams, "A Century of Poems 1926–1927." Unpublished poems, the Bodleian, no 88.
10. In an interview with Phyllis McDougall, she recalled the experience of what today would be described as being stalked by Williams after her rejection of him in what she thought was 1927, but we redate as 1929: "He would follow me through the streets. When I was living in Upper Bedford place, I would be walking down one side of the street and I would be conscious of him walking down the other side of the street, just sort of talking to himself." Feb. 21, 1992.
11. No. 72, "Daydreams." See below in this chapter.
12. Charles Williams, *The New Book of English Verse* (London: Gollancz, 1935).
13. Hadfield, 122, quoting from letter no. 360, the Bodleian, 1935.

14. Williams, *New Book,* 13.

15. In his note on Marvell (328) he writes: "Against such fantastic explorations of Celia as it is made in *The Match* or the precise statement of the first stanza of *The Definition,* such lesser but pleasant verses as William Whitehead (1715–85) take on an additional charm. They abandon the effort."

> Her voice, her touch, might give the alarm,
> 'Twas both perhaps or neither;
> In short, 'twas that provoking charm
> Of Celia altogether.

Williams, *New Book,* 800.

16. Presumably because they give so much credit to his wife, his more historic muse.

17. Charles Williams to Phyllis Somervaille, unpublished letter lent by the recipient.

18. Williams, *New Book,* 13.

19. Ibid., 15.

20. Ibid.

21. Ibid., 17.

22. Those who are familiar with Williams's early poetry cannot avoid some comparison with the material in *The Silver Stair* (1912), *Poems of Conformity* (1917), *Divorce* (1920), and *Windows of Night* (1924). These volumes of poems were inspired by his wife and dedicated to her. For a description and analysis, see Glen Cavaliero, *Poet of Theology,* who devotes a chapter to them (9–21); and also Charles Huttar's "Arms and the Man: The Place of Beatrice in Charles Williams's Romantic Theology," which constitutes chapter 6 of Horne, *A Celebration,* where Huttar explores the role of Michal as a source of religious inspiration.

23. Williams, "A Century of Poems for Celia," unpublished, original mss., Bodleian. "On a thwarted invitation to lunch: also, on a question about the Rosicrucians," no. 2.

24. Williams, "Century," no. 24.

25. Ibid., no. 33.

26. Ibid., no. 34.

27. Ibid., no. 36.

28. Ibid., no. 38.

29. Ibid., no. 48.

30. Ibid., no. 49.

31. Ibid., no. 50; Lois Lang-Sims, *Letters to Lalage: The Letters of Charles Williams to Lois Lang-Sims,* ed. Glen Cavaliero (Kent, Ohio: Kent State Univ. Press, 1989).

32. Williams, "Century," no. 52.

33. Ibid., no. 53.

34. Cavaliero was exploring the issues raised by Lois Lang-Sims in her collection of letters, *Letters to Lalage,* in the form of accusations that Williams was merely using Lang-Sims manipulatively within the confines of the myth of the slave girl Lalage. Cavaliero suggested that an element of spiritual direction was being exercised that Lang-Sims had misjudged: "But in view of Williams' own fascination with images and the practise of power, one can see a personal compulsion fulfilling itself as well. Theologically, the slave girl embodies a necessary stage of growth, for in the mind of God Lois is identical with Lalage and her successive fulfillments; but in the life of time and fallen humanity, the roles fail to coincide. Williams' spiritual direction of souls was designed to clarify their various functions." (10).

35. Williams, "Century," no. 54.

36. Ibid., no. 70.

37. Ibid., no. 72.

38. Ibid., no. 78.

39. Ibid., no. 83.

40. This may well be a contrast between loving Michal and loving Celia.

41. Williams, "Century," no. 89.

42. Ibid., no. 50.

43. Ibid., no. 82.

44. Ibid., no. 19. "*The fringéd curtains*" is a quotation of Prospero to Miranda. Williams will associate himself with Prospero again through Stanhope in *Descent into Hell.*

45. Williams, "Century," prologue.

46. Ibid., no. 44.

47. Ibid., no. 57.

48. Ibid., "On the Proposal that in a Second Masque, She Should Present the Soul Ecstasy, and on Her Objections," no. 58.

49. Ibid., no. 68.

50. In correspondence with the author, Charles Huttar made the observation that "the opposite interpretation may be possible: that the spiritualising of the erotic is in fact a helpful mechanism in his (so far as we know successful, at least on the physical level) resistance to adultery. In *Arms and the Man* I argue that the mythologizing (in part, at least) and the spiritualising were a well-chosen means of sublimation; I also connect it with the Dantean image of the Second Love. . . . So in my view what you call confusion is deliberate, purposeful, in harmony with his antidualistic stance." Private letter, dated Oct. 4, 1999.

51. Williams, "Century," no. 82.

52. Ibid., no. 89.

53. Ibid., epilogue.

54. Quoted by Hadfield in *Exploration* as a "letter of the time" (1929–31), 81.

55. Williams, unpublished, undated poem addressed to Phyllis entitled, "A Letter," circa 1942.

56. Author's interview with Phyllis McDougall, Feb. 21, 1992, at her home in Henley on Thames.

57. Williams, *Beatrice,* 16.

58. Williams to Phyllis Jones, unpublished letter, Aug. 17, 1938. The private collection of Mrs. Phyllis McDougall.

59. Williams, unpublished letter to Phyllis Somervaille, Aug. 17, 1938.

60. Quite probably her separating husband, Billie. The private collection of Mrs. Phyllis McDougall.

61. Although ungrammatical, he appears to be adopting a colloquial tone for emphasis. The private collection of Mrs. Phyllis McDougall.

62. *The Dictionary of National Biography* suggests that Storey might be Mr. Thomas Story (1670?–1742), an Anglican who read law and entered a Chambers in Carlisle. He underwent a conversion to Quakerism in 1689 and became a close associate of William Penn. Charles Williams excerpted Story's "A Song of Praise for the Saints in Zion" in *The Passion of Christ* (Oxford: Oxford Univ. Press, 1939), 4.

63. Williams, unpublished, undated. Probably circa 1938/39.

64. Charles Williams, *Arthurian Poets* (Rochester, N.Y.: Boydell Press, 1991), 12.

65. Williams, *Region of the Summer Stars; Arthurian Poets,* 123.

66. Phyllis was staying in Middleton-on-Sea, West Sussex.

67. Williams, unpublished, undated. Probably circa 1938/39.

68. Documented by Lois Lang-Sims in *Letters to Lalage.*

69. In an interview at her home in 1993 with the author, Joan Wallis discussed the phenomenon of Williams asking for some help in the form of submitting to a form of ritual that was intended to release artistic creative energy for writing. In response to being asked why she allowed herself to be put through the experiences he faced her with: "Because if I refused he would ring down the curtain as he did with Lois, and in return he gave her so much else. And it was so unlike him to want his own way without offering an explanation.

He delighted in always offering explanations, in every other sphere. It must have caused him a great deal of pain and bewilderment.

"He remains the most remarkable and good man I've ever met. I've never met anyone who honoured goodness more than Charles. Charles had prepared me for recognising strains of goodness in people, and the strains in Charles were pure gold."

70. Williams, unpublished letter to Phyllis Somervaille, Mar. 1940.

71. Williams, unpublished letter to Phyllis Somervaille, circa 1941. Hadfield quoted from this on pages 200 and 201 of *Exploration,* but omits to note that the poem is in fact a letter in the form of a poem to Phyllis. It begins, "then / suddenly a little daemon sitting in my ear / whispered: 'it is a long time since by night / alone, and dreaming of myth, you wrote to Celia.'"

72. Williams, unpublished letter to Phyllis McDougall, July 1, 1941.

73. Cavaliero, *Poet,* 60, 165. Shideler prefers to deal with it under the label "energy." *Theology,* 240; and of course Lois Lang-Sims interprets the practice of power as lying behind her the events her correspondence reflects in *Letters to Lalage.*

74. Williams's ellipsis.

75. Williams, unpublished letter to Phyllis McDougall, Feb. 11, 1940.

76. Williams, unpublished letter to Phyllis McDougall, Jan. 26, 1940.

77. Cavaliero, introduction, *Letters to Lalage,* 7, 8.

78. Williams, unpublished letter to Phyllis McDougall. Maundy Thursday 1941.

79. Letters from Charles Williams to his wife, Michal Williams, held at the Wade Center.

80. Many tensions accumulated and may have affected him: the pressures of the war, anxiety about London, where he had left Michal and Michael, and his lecturing at Oxford, nominally on Comus, but actually on chastity. For his forthcoming biography of Williams, Professor Grevel Lindop has uncovered lecture notes taken during this period by his former students.

81. Williams, unpublished and undated poem among the papers of Phyllis McDougall.

82. Interview with Mrs. Phyllis McDougall, Feb. 21, 1992.

83. Letters to Michal, July 29, 1940.

84. He is aware of his capacity for it: "It's perhaps as well, though tiresome, that I shouldn't send you another cheque today. But I wish I did a few things, not even lecturing to a large and clamorous audience, which is hardly how I should describe my present—give me as much joy. This is as beautiful as it is proper; and I cannot be sufficiently grateful. It is one of the more exquisite results of love. You will say I talk too much of it; no, indeed; I do but soliloquise to you, and to whom but one's wife should one soliloquise." Nov. 21, 1944.

85. C. S. Lewis, commenting on Williams's style in the novels: "The L.C.M. between Dante and P. G. Wodehouse is a difficult thing to hit, and I'm not sure it's a good thing to aim at." Unpublished letter, Wade Center, Sept. 23, 1937.

86. Williams, letter to Michal, unpublished letter, Wade Center, Aug. 11, 1941.

87. The color of her hair is dictated primarily by the poem's theme of corn and bread, and "lady" is related to "hlafdige," which means "loaf-kneader." *Taliessin,* in D. L. Dodds, "Bors to Elayne: On the King's Coins" in *Arthurian Poets: Charles Williams,* p. 53, line 9.

88. Letters from Charles Williams to his wife Michal Williams, Oct. 28, 1944.

89. Dodds, "Bors to Elayne," in *Arthurian Poets,* p. 53, line 9.

90. Letters from Charles Williams to his wife, Michal Williams, Apr. 11, 1945.

91. Ibid., Nov. 29, 1944.

92. Williams, *Beatrice,* 7.

93. Williams, *House of the Octopus.*

94. Letters from Charles Williams to his wife, Michal Williams, Dec. 5, 1944.

95. Ibid., Feb. 17, 1945.

96. T. S. Eliot makes a link in the review between Williams's Rosicrucian expertise and the lure and obscurity of Dante's allegorical and anagogical style: "Mr Williams, is a catholic student of the occult. It was almost inevitable that he should sooner or later turn to the interpretations of Dante, who above all the great poets chooses to bury hidden meanings, layer beneath layer, under the surface of his verse. These occult meanings, consistent with themselves through the whole of Dante's life work, from the Vita Nuovo to the Paradiso, Mr Williams finds focused in the single figure of Beatrice." *Times Literary Supplement,* July 24, 1943.

97. Ibid.

98. Letters from Charles Williams to his wife Michal Williams, Nov. 16, 1944.

99. Ibid., Oct. 19, 1944.

100. Ibid., June 9, 1943.

101. Ibid., Feb. 17, 1945.

102. Ibid., Nov. 27, 1944.

103. Ibid., May 6, 1943.

104. Ibid., Nov. 11, 1943.

105. Ibid., Oct. 15, 1943.

106. Ibid., Nov. 7, 1944.

107. Ibid., May 8, 1945.

108. Williams, *Beatrice,* 15, 16.

Conclusion

1. Horne, "The Systematic Theology of Charles Williams," in Huttar and Schakel, *Rhetoric,* 279.

2. Williams, *Beatrice,* 11.

3. See Charles Huttar's précis of Schneider's argument in Huttar and Schakel, *Rhetoric,* 22.

4. Schneider, "Co-inherent Rhetoric in Taliessin," in Huttar and Schakel, *Rhetoric,* 180.

5. Williams, "Taliessin in the Rose Garden," in *Region,* 25.

Bibliography

Unpublished Works

Correspondence

Letters from Charles Williams to Phyllis Jones (Celia). 1938–1943. Mss. Originals are the property of Phyllis McDougall (née Jones).

Letters from Charles Williams to Florence Williams (Michal). 1940–1945. Mss. Marion E. Wade Center, Wheaton College, Illinois.

Letters from Florence (Michal) Williams to The Rev. Dr. Glen Cavaliero. 1955–1957. Mss. Originals are the property of Glen Cavaliero.

Poetry

"A Century of Poems for Celia." Typescript. Mss. in Bodleian. 1926–1927.

Miscellaneous

Williams, Florence (Michal). "As I Remember." Apr. 18, 1955. Unpublished Mss.

Transcript of BBC broadcast on the Third Programme on Sept. 13, 1961, produced by Terence Tiller in a documented compilation by Ruth Spalding. Typescript.

Theses

Chandler, John Herrick. "Charles Williams: The Poet of Co-inherence." Doctoral Thesis, Univ. of Chicago, 1963.

Enright, N. H. "Charles Williams and His Theology of Romantic Love: The Novels, the Poetry." Doctoral Thesis, Drew Univ., Madison, New Jersey, 1986.

Frazer, J. H. "An Introduction to the Hermetic Novels of Charles Williams." Doctoral Thesis, Graduate College of Texas A&M Univ., 1975.

Fullman, C. E. "The Mind and Art of Charles Williams." Doctoral Thesis, Univ. of Wisconsin, 1954.

Horne, Brian. "The Systematic Theology of Charles Williams." Doctoral Thesis, Univ. of London, 1970.

Locke, C. A. "The Negative Way in Christian Mystical Tradition and the Affirmative Way in Charles Williams' Novels: A Comparison and Contrast." Doctoral Thesis, Univ. of Indiana, 1979.

Mordecai, T. H. "Charles Williams' Understanding of Evil and Salvation with Particular Reference to his Novels." M.A. Thesis, Univ. of London, 1992.

Interviews

With Phyllis McDougall (née Jones), Feb. 21, 1992.
With Joan Wallis, July 30, 1992.
With Anne Ridler, Sept. 3, 1992.
With Lois Lang-Sims, July 8, 1993.
With the Rev. Dr. Glen Cavaliero, Jan. 6, 1994.
With R. A. Gilbert, Sept. 3, 1994.
With John Heath-Stubbs, Sept. 15, 1995.

Published Works

Ackroyd, Peter. *The House of Doctor Dee.* London: Hamish Hamilton, 1993.
Alvarado, Luis. *Psychology, Astrology and Western Magic: Image and Myth in Self-Discovery.* St. Paul, Minn.: Llewellyn Publications, 1991.
Armstrong, Christopher J. R. *Evelyn Underhill (1875–1941): An Introduction to Her Life and Writings.* London: Mowbrays, 1975.
Arnold, Paul. *La Rose-Croix et ses Rapports avec La Franc-Maçonnerie: Essai de Synthèse Historique.* Paris: Editions G. P. Maisonneuve & Larose, 1970.
Baigent, Micheal, Richard Liegh, and Henry Lincoln. *The Holy Blood and the Holy Grail.* London: Corgi, 1982.
Brennan, J. H. *Ancient Spirit: An Exploration of Magic.* London: Warner, 1993.
Bright, John. *History of Israel.* London: Student Christian Movement, 1960.
Brown, Raymond. *The Gospel of John.* London: Geoffrey Chapman, 1966.
Carpenter, Humphrey. *The Inklings.* London: George Allen and Unwin, 1978.
Cavaliero, Glen. *Charles Williams: Poet of Theology.* Grand Rapids, Mich: Eerdmans, 1983.
———. "Metaphysical Epiphany? Charles Williams and the Art of the Ghost Story." In *Rhetoric of Vision.* Ed. Charles A. Huttar and Peter J. Schakel. London: Bucknell Univ. Press, 1996.
———. *The Supernatural and English Fiction.* Oxford: Oxford Univ. Press, 1995.
Chadwick, Henry, ed. and trans. *The Confessions of St. Augustine.* Oxford: Oxford Univ. Press, 1991.
Churton, Tobias. *The Hermetic Philosophy.* Sabiot Trucohn Books, 1998.
———. *The True Story of the Rosicrucians.* Sabiot Trucohn Books, 1998.
Cohn, Norman. *Europe's Inner Demons: An Enquiry Inspired by the Great Witch-Hunt.* London: Chatto and Heinemann, 1975.
Cupitt, Don. *After God: The Future of Religion.* New York: Basic Books, 1997.
Dante, Alighieri. *The Divine Comedy.* Trans. D. L. Sayers. Penguin (*Inferno,* 1949; *Purgatorio,* 1955; *Paradiso,* 1962).
Dodds, David L., ed. *Charles Williams.* Athurian Poets Series. Rochester, N.Y.: Boydell Press, 1991.
———. "Continuity and Change in the Development of Charles Williams's Poetic Style." In *Rhetoric of Vision.* Ed. Charles A. Huttar and Peter J. Schakel. London: Bucknell Univ. Press, 1996.
Eliot, T. S. *Times Literary Supplement,* July 24, 1943.
Ellmann, Richard. *Yeats: The Man and the Masks.* Oxford: Oxford Univ. Press, 1979.
Fabricius, Johannes. *The Medieval Alchemists and Their Royal Art.* Copenhagen: Rosenkilde and Bagger, 1976.
Gilbert, R. A. *The Elements of Mysticism.* Shaftesbury: Element, 1991.
———, ed. *The Hermetic Papers of A. E. Waite: The Unknown Writings of a Modern Mystic.* Wellingborough: Aquarian Press, 1987.
———. *Magician of Many Parts: A Biography of A. E. Waite.* Wellingborough: Crucible, 1987.

Gorceix, B. *La Bible des Rose-Croix: Traductions et Commentaire des Trois Premiers Écrits Rosicruciens* (1614, 1615, 1615). Paris: Presses Universitaires de France, 1970.

Hadfield, Alice Mary. *Charles Williams: An Exploration of His Life and Work.* New York: Oxford Univ. Press, 1983.

———. *Introduction to Charles Williams.* London: Robert Hale Ltd., 1959.

Harper, George Mills. *Yeats's Golden Dawn.* London: Macmillan, 1974.

Heath-Stubbs, John. *Charles Williams.* Writers and Their Work, No. 63. London: Longmans, Green, 1955.

———. *Time and Tide.* May 1, 1948.

Holmyard, Eric John. *Alchemy.* New York: Pelican, 1957.

Horne, Brian, ed. *Charles Williams: A Celebration.* Leominster: Gracewing, 1995.

———. *Imagining Evil.* London: Darton, Longman, and Todd, 1996.

———. "Notes on the Taliessin Cycle." *Charles Williams Society Newsletter* 64 (Winter 1991).

Howard, Thomas. *The Novels of Charles Williams.* 1983. San Francisco: Ignatius Press, 1991.

Howe, Ellic. *The Magicians of the Golden Dawn: A Documentary History of a Magical Order, 1887–1923.* York Beach, Maine: Samuel Weiser, 1984.

Huttar, Charles A. "Arms and the Man: The Place of Beatrice in Charles Williams's Romantic Theology." In *Charles Williams: A Celebration.* Ed. Brian Horne. Leominster: Gracewing, 1995.

———. "Williams's Changing Views of Milton and the Problem of Shadows of Ecstasy." *Inklings-Jahrbuch* 5 (1987): 224, 229.

———, and Peter J. Schakel, ed. *The Rhetoric of Vision.* London: Bucknell Univ. Press, 1996.

Julian of Norwich. *Showings.* Trans. E. Colledge and J. Walsh. London: SPCK, 1978.

Jung, Carl Gustav. *Psychology and Alchemy.* Collected Works, Volume 12. New York: Pantheon, 1953.

King, Roma Alva, Jr. "The Occult as Rhetoric in the Poetry of Charles Williams." In *Rhetoric of Vision.* Ed. Charles A. Huttar and Peter J. Schakel. London: Bucknell Univ. Press, 1996.

———. *The Pattern in the Web: The Mythical Poetry of Charles Williams.* Kent, Ohio: Kent State Univ. Press, 1990.

Kollmann, J. J. "Charles Williams: The Place of the Lion and Neoplatonic Fantasy." *Kansas Quarterly* 16.3 (Summer 1984): 35–42.

———. "Complex Rhetoric for a Simple Universe: *Descent into Hell.*" In *Rhetoric of Vision.* Ed. Charles A. Huttar and Peter J. Schakel. London: Bucknell Univ. Press, 1996.

Lang-Sims, Lois. *Letters to Lalage: The Letters of Charles Williams to Lois Lang-Sims.* Ed. Glen Cavaliero. Kent, Ohio: Kent State Univ. Press, 1989.

Layton, Bentley, ed. *The Gnostic Scriptures.* New York: Doubleday, 1987.

Lewis, C. S. *Arthurian Torso.* Oxford: Oxford Univ. Press, 1948. This edition, Grand Rapids, Mich: Eerdmans, 1974.

———. *Essays Presented to Charles Williams.* Ed. C. S. Lewis. London: Oxford Univ. Press, 1947.

———. *They Asked for a Paper.* London: Geoffrey Bles, 1962.

Loewenstein, Andrea Freud. *Loathsome Jews and Engulfing Women: Metaphors of Projection in the Works of Wyndham Lewis, Charles Williams, and Graham Greene.* New York: New York Univ. Press, 1993.

Malory, Sir Thomas. *Le Morte D'Arthur* (1485). Everyman, 1906.

Marlowe, Christopher. *Dr. Faustus.* London: Methuen, 1956.

McIntosh, Christopher. *The Rosicrucians: The History, Mythology, and Rituals of an Occult Order.* Wellingborough: Crucible, 1980; 2d ed., 1987.

Medcalf, Stephen. "The Athanasian Principle in Williams's Use of Images." In *Rhetoric of Vision.* Ed. Charles A. Huttar and Peter J. Schakel. London: Bucknell Univ. Press, 1996.

Moorman, Charles. *Arthurian Triptych: Mythic Materials in Charles Williams, C. S. Lewis, and T. S. Elliot.* Berkeley: Univ. of California Press, 1960.

Page, Frederick. *Patmore: A Study in Poetry.* London: Oxford Univ. Press, 1933.

Pagels, Elaine. *Adam, Eve and the Serpent.* New York: Random House, 1988.

———. *The Origin of Satan.* New York: Random House, 1995.

Parker, John. *At the Heart of Darkness: Witchcraft, Black Magic, and Satanism Today.* London: Sedgewick and Jackson, 1993.

Poncé, Charles. *Kabbalah: An Introduction and Illumination for the World Today.* 2d ed. Wheaton, Ill.: Quest Books, 1980.

Prestige, George Leonard. *God in Patristic Thought.* London: Heinemann, 1936.

Radice, Betty, ed. and trans. *The Letters of Abelard and Heloise.* Harmondsworth: Penguin, 1974.

Raine, Kathleen. *Yeats the Initiate.* Ireland: Dolmen Press; London: George Allen and Unwin, 1986.

Reynolds, Aidan, and William Charlton. *Arthur Machen: A Short Account of His Life and Work.* London: John Baker for the Richards Press, 1963.

Reynolds, Barbara. *The Passionate Intellect: Dorothy L. Sayers' Encounter with Dante.* Kent, Ohio: Kent State Univ. Press. 1989.

Ridler, Anne, ed. *Charles Williams: Selected Writings.* Oxford: Oxford Univ. Press, 1961.

———. *"The Image of the City" and Other Essays.* Selected by Anne Ridler with a Critical Introduction. London: Oxford Univ. Press, 1958.

Roberts, Marie Mulvey, and Hugh Ormsby-Lennon. *Secret Texts: The Literature of Secret Societies.* New York: A. M. S. Press, 1995.

Sayers, Dorothy L. *The Poetry of Search and the Poetry of Statement.* London: Gollancz, 1963.

Scheper, George L. "*All Hallows' Eve*: The Cessation of Rhetoric." In *Rhetoric of Vision.* Ed. Charles A. Huttar and Peter J. Schakel. London: Bucknell Univ. Press, 1996.

Schneider, Angelika. "Co-inherent Rhetoric in *Taliessin through Logres.*" In *Rhetoric of Vision.* Ed. Charles A. Huttar and Peter J. Schakel. London: Bucknell Univ. Press, 1996.

Seabrook, William. *Witchcraft: Its Power in the World Today.* New York: Harcourt, Brace, 1940.

Sherwood-Taylor, F. *The Alchemists: The Founders of Modern Chemistry.* New York: Schuman, 1949.

Shideler, Mary McDermott. *Charles Williams: A Critical Essay.* Grand Rapids, Mich.: Eerdmans, 1966.

———.*The Theology of Romantic Love: A Study in the Writings of Charles Williams.* Grand Rapids, Mich.: Eerdmans, 1962.

Thomas, Keith. *Religion and the Decline of Magic, Studies in Popular Beliefs in Sixteenth and Seventeenth Century England.* London: Weidenfeld and Nicholson, 1971.

Thompson, Francis. *Poetical Works.* Oxford: Oxford Univ. Press, 1913.

Underhill, Evelyn. *The Life of the Spirit Today.* London: Methuen and Co., 1923.

Waddell, Helen. *The Wandering Scholars.* London: Constable and Co. Ltd., 1907.

Waite, Arthur Edward. *The Brotherhood of the Rosy Cross.* New York: University Books, 1910.

———. *The Hidden Church of the Holy Graal: Its Legends and Symbolism Considered in Their Affinity with Certain Mysteries of Initiation and Other Traces of a Secret Tradition in Christian Times.* London: Rebman, 1909.

———. "The Hidden Life of the Rosy Cross." Privately Printed. N.d.

———. *The Holy Kabbalah: A Study of the Secret Tradition in Israel as Unfolded by Sons of the Doctrine for the Benefit and Consolation of the Elect Dispersed Through the Lands and Ages of the Greater Exile.* New Hyde Park, N.Y.: Macmillan, 1929.

———. *The Real History of the Rosicrucians.* 1887. Blauvelt, N.Y.: Steinerbooks, 1977.

———. *The Secret Doctrine in Israel.* London: William Rider and Son, 1913.

———. *The Secret Tradition of Alchemy.* London: Kegan Paul, Trench Trubner and Co. Ltd., 1926.

———. *Shadows of Life and Thought: A Retrospective Review in the Form of Memoirs.* London: Selwyn and Blount, 1938.
Wall, James Charles. *Shrines of British Saints.* London: Methuen, 1905.
Washington, Peter. *Madame Blavatsky's Baboon: Theosophy and the Emergence of the Western Guru.* London: Secker and Warburg, 1993.
Weeks, Dennis L. *Steps toward Salvation: An Examination of Co inherence and Substitution in the Seven Novels of Charles Williams.* American University Studies, Ser. IV, English language and literature. New York: Peter Lang, 1991.
Wertheim, Margaret. *Pythagoras' Trousers: God, Physics, and the Gender Wars.* London: Fourth Estate, 1997.
Willard, Thomas. "Alchemy and the Bible." In *Centre and Labyrinth: Essays in Honour of Northrop Frye.* Ed. Eleanor Cook et al. Toronto: Univ. of Toronto Press, 1993.
Williams, Charles. *Arthurian Poets.* Ed. David Llewellyn Dodds. Rochester, N.Y.: Boydell Press, 1991.
———. *Arthurian Torso.* Commentary by C. S. Lewis. London: Oxford Univ. Press, 1948.
———. *All Hallows' Eve.* London: Faber and Faber, 1945.
———. *Bacon.* London: Arthur Barker, 1933.
———. *The Carol of Amen House.* Privately printed. Music by Hubert Foss, 1927.
———. *Century of Poems for Celia.* Unpublished mss., 1926–28, London.
———. *Descent of the Dove: A Short History of the Holy Spirit in the Church.* London: Longmans, 1939.
———. *Descent into Hell.* London: Faber and Faber, 1937.
———. *Divorce.* Oxford: Oxford Univ. Press. 1920.
———. *The English Poetic Mind.* Oxford: Clarendon Press, 1932.
———. *The Figure of Beatrice: A Study in Dante.* London: Faber and Faber, 1943.
———. *The Forgiveness of Sins.* London: Geoffrey Blises, 1942.
———. *The Greater Trumps.* London: Victor Gollancz, 1932.
———. *He Came Down from Heaven.* London: Heinemann, 1938.
———. *Henry VII.* London: Arthur Barker, 1937.
———. *The House of the Octopus.* London: Edinburgh House Press, 1945.
———. *"The Image of the City": and Other Essays.* Selected by Anne Ridler (editor) with a Critical Introduction. London: Oxford Univ. Press, 1958.
———. *James I.* London: Arthur Barker, 1934.
———. *Judgement at Chelmsford: A Pageant Play.* London: Oxford Univ. Press, 1939.
———, ed. *The Letters of Evelyn Underhill.* London: Longmans, Green and Co., 1943.
———. *Many Dimensions.* London: Victor Gollancz, 1931.
———. *The Masque of the Manuscript.* Privately Printed. 1927.
———. *A Masque of Perusal.* Privately Printed. 1929.
———. "The Masque of the Termination of Copyright." Unpublished. 1930.
———. *A Myth of Francis Bacon.* Privately Printed. 1932.
———. *A Myth of Shakespeare.* Oxford: Oxford Univ. Press, 1928.
———. *The New Book of English Verse.* London: Victor Gollancz, 1935.
———. *Outlines of Romantic Theology; With which is Reprinted, Religion and Love in Dante: the Theology of Romantic Love.* Grand Rapids, Mich.: Eerdmans, 1990.
———. *The Passion of Christ.* Oxford: Oxford Univ. Press, 1939.
———. *The Place of the Lion.* Mundanus. London: Victor Gollancz, 1931.
———. *Poems of Conformity.* London: Oxford Univ. Press, 1917.
———. *Poetry at Present.* Oxford: Clarendon Press, 1930.
———. *Reason and Beauty in the Poetic Mind.* Oxford: Clarendon Press, 1933.
———. *Region of the Summer Stars.* London: Oxford Univ. Press, 1944.
———. *Religion and Love in Dante: The Theology of Romantic Love.* Westminster: Dacre Press, 1941.

———. *Rochester.* London: Arthur Barker, 1935.
———. *Seed of Adam and Other Plays.* Ed. Anne Ridler. New York: Oxford Univ. Press, 1948.
———. *Selected Writings.* Ed. Anne Ridler. London: Oxford Univ. Press, 1961.
———. *Shadows of Ecstasy.* London: Victor Gollancz, 1933.
———. *The Silver Stair.* London: Herbert and Daniel, 1912.
———. *Taliessin through Logres.* London: Oxford Univ. Press, 1938.
———. *Three Plays* (*The Witch, The Rite of the Passion, The Chaste Wanton*). Ed. Humphrey Milford. London: Oxford Univ. Press, 1931.
———. *Thomas Cranmer of Canterbury.* London: Oxford Univ. Press, 1936.
———. *To Michal from Serge: Letters of Charles Williams to His Wife, Florence, 1939–1945.* Ed. Roma A. King Jr. Kent, Ohio: Kent State Univ. Press, 2002.
———. *War in Heaven.* London: Victor Gollancz, 1931.
———. *Windows of Night.* London: Oxford Univ. Press, 1924.
———. *Witchcraft.* London: Faber and Faber, 1941.
Wordsworth, William. *Prelude.* Ed. De Selincourt, corrected by Stephen Gill. New York: Oxford Univ. Press, 1970.
Yates, Frances A. *The Rosicrucian Enlightenment.* St. Albans: Paladin, 1975.
Yeats, W. B. *Essays and Introductions.* New York: Macmillan and Co. Ltd., 1961.

Index